METAPHORS OF INTERRELATEDNESS

SUNY SERIES, ALTERNATIVES IN PSYCHOLOGY
MICHAEL A. WALLACH, EDITOR

METAPHORS OF INTERRELATEDNESS

Toward a Systems Theory of Psychology

Linda E. Olds

STATE UNIVERSITY OF NEW YORK PRESS

Published by
State University of New York Press, Albany

Printed in the United States of America

For information, address State University of New York
Press, State University Plaza, Albany, N.Y., 12246

Production by Diane Ganeles
Marketing by Dana E. Yanulavich

Library of Congress Cataloging-in-Publication Data

Olds, Linda E.
Metaphors of interrelatedness : toward a systems theory of psychology / Linda E. Olds.
p. cm. — (SUNY series, alternatives in psychology)
Includes bibliographical references and index.
ISBN 0-7914-1011-0 (alk. paper). — ISBN 0-7914-1012-9 (pk. : alk. paper)
1. Psychology—Philosophy. 2. Systems theory. 3. Metaphor.
I. Title. II. Series.
BF38.048 1992
150'.1'1—dc20 91-18490
CIP

10 9 8 7 6 5 4 3 2 1

To Gene

CONTENTS

PREFACE

This book is a highly textured lattice, woven from the strands of thought and influence that have characterized a lifetime of questioning and efforts at integration. Mirroring the diversity of its content, which seeks to explore the potentially unifying role of systems metaphors in psychology, science, and religion, the web bears witness to a fabric of indebtedness. As a web that is never finished, the book in fact sets a lifelong project in which there is always another strand to integrate.

I am deeply grateful to those in my immediate personal life whose conversation and encouragement have nurtured the questions and energy from which this book is born. To my husband Gene R. Thursby, whose judicious support and dialogue, editorial consultation, and generous patience have accompanied this process, I give my special thanks. To my mother Eva B. Olds and father Glenn A. Olds, I extend deep appreciation not only for their careful readings of my manuscript as it has evolved, but for their inspiration and passion for wholeness that has informed my life. I also wish to thank Lucile and Jack Housley, Robin Lawton, Shirley Kishiyama, and the many friends who have inspirited and nurtured this project, through sharing not only in its ideas but in the conviction of the importance of the search.

Special thanks go also to Huston Smith and my colleagues in the National Endowment for the Humanities Summer Seminar in Berkeley in 1987, for the stimulating dialogue which helped to sharpen many of the concerns of this book. I also wish to thank the National Endowment for the Humanities for this support, Martin E. Marty and the Institute for the Advanced Study of Religion at the University of Chicago Divinity School for the opportunity to enrich my work on metaphor in religion during a period as a Research Fellow there in spring 1981, as well as Linfield College for the sabbatical leaves that have bracketed and helped to frame this work over the years of its research and preparation. I am also grateful for the invitation to present the 1985 Palmer Lectures at Alaska Pacific University, an opportunity which allowed an early exploration of material relating to the systems emphases of this book.

Many thanks go also to my students in psychology and interdisciplinary courses (ranging from Theories of Personality, Senior Seminar in Psychology, Psychology of Religion and Consciousness, Psychology East and West, to the College Honors Orientation Seminar), to participants in seminars at Ghost Ranch in New Mexico, and to those who have heard me speak on numerous occasions relating to these topics, all of whom have added questions, comments, and helpful insights into this fabric. I feel much appreciation for my department colleagues who have supported my theoretical and interdisciplinary work and extend special thanks to James A. Duke, who generously read sections of an earlier version of my manuscript. Likewise, I am very appreciative of my other colleagues at Linfield with whom I have shared a vital interest in interdisciplinary issues, systems thinking, and paradigm change. I also thank Susan Charland Burke who helped in typing a preliminary version of some parts of the book.

I feel much gratitude to the late Clyde A. Holbrook for introducing me, through a course on Modern Religious Thought at Oberlin College, to an in-depth study of Alfred North Whitehead's thought, an interest which prefigured in many ways the direction and concerns of this book regarding interrelatedness. Also while at Oberlin as an undergraduate religion major, I had the good fortune of studying with Edward L. Long, whose commitment to social ethics supported and informed a major direction of my thinking regarding implications of interconnectedness for action in the world. Special appreciation goes to David L. Hall for his careful reading of my manuscript and to the readers for the State University of New York Press whose comments were greatly helpful for revisions. I am grateful to Joanna Macy, who generously shared with me her manuscript on *Mutual Causality in Buddhism and General Systems Theory* shortly before its publication. Great respect and appreciation also go to the State University of New York Press, and its director William D. Eastman, for an ongoing commitment to innovative, interdisciplinary work, and support for making these kinds of projects more widely accessible. In addition, my thanks go to Diane Ganeles, editors, and staff at the State University of New York Press for facilitating work on the production of this book.

INTRODUCTION: MINDSCAPES AND METAPHOR

There is something immensely affirming about a Gothic cathedral, rising as it does above its city and landscape, dwarfing its surroundings by comparison. It is a constant reminder of a transcendent reality against which all else pales and through which all has access to meaning. For centuries the Gothic cathedral stood as a profound outer expression of a living faith that the world made ultimate sense and possessed a wholeness accessible to everyone as part of creation. The Gothic cathedral spoke a language of image and metaphor, and stood as living symbol of a unified sense of reality for its age.

Yet the cathedral was a vertical image, an aspiring testimony to a vertically conceived God, to a spirituality of transcendence in which the soul sought refuge above and beyond the realities of this world. The soul's eye and reach were directed upwards past the flying buttresses and arches and vaulted ceilings, past the towers and spires, to meet the embrace of a God beyond the tangible. If there was unity, it was a unity imposed from above by virtue of precedence, hierarchy, levels of reality, and transcendence. It was a unity to be found at the end of a search, a pilgrimage, a holy journey.

What still remains for us of the Gothic vision of wholeness is the legacy of a search, now transposed to a world whose transcendent markers have been dwarfed by new vertical strivings for power, achievement, knowledge, and accomplishment. Our skyscrapers and rockets take our reaching into the heavens, not to meet there the hope of a gift of meaning but to celebrate striving itself. How is the search for a sense of wholeness to be achieved in a world whose specialty is specialization, whose language is linear and literal, and whose sense of the symbolic is derived from cartoon and caricature? How is the search for wholeness to be expressed in a world made horizontal by the sheer immensity of our knowledge about this world?

The achievements of science and psychology in rendering this world understandable have stretched the cosmic landscape into spaces of such intense interest and relevance that they rivet our attention. And justifiably so. The medieval worldview was true to its scientific and psychological landscape; a current search for a new synthesis can do no less than honor the highest insights from our own surrounding landscape, too. We no longer inhabit a universe capable of being represented vertically alone; the embeddedness of us all in an intricately interrelating dance of energy and spacetime, of connection and change, has become the inescapable heritage of our time. We must reach out for horizontal metaphors which speak the language of embrace and interconnection, rather than striving and rising above. The images needed are images of immanence, of meaning within and through what we know, not solely of transcendence. The path of wholeness must take us through and within, rather than leading us upward and outward alone.

The Gothic cathedral could absorb the variety of different facades; it was a source of coherence transcending the sum total of its imagery. Its perfection lay not in its literal structure, but in the direction toward which it pointed the seeker; its imagery was a symbol for a higher unity. Thus the cathedral at Rouen is a reminder of the multiplicity of viewpoints to be integrated in a contemporary search for wholeness. If science, psychology, and religion today speak different languages, inhabit different mindscapes, traverse different terrains, they are all nonetheless crucial for a unifying synthesis. If we seek metaphors of wholeness which can lead us beyond their differences to a coherent totality, it can not be at the expense of neglecting any of the rich uniqueness within each realm. The cathedral was a powerful external statement in stone of an inner reality. The task for our scaffolding is to allow and facilitate the construction of an equally sustaining inner worldview to reflect the experienced scientific, psychological, and spirtual insights and realities of the current age.

As the medieval world once turned to stone, we must turn to metaphor, the inner building blocks of the mental landscape, to evoke a living expression of the unity available in our time. Each field offers its own conditions and assumptions, its own metaphors. If we seek a unifying level of metaphor, it must emerge from the fields before us and carry us into new ways of thinking and connecting. Its usefulness must be measured not only by appropriateness within its own field but by the capacity to "carry us beyond," which is the root meaning of metaphor.

The fundamental impetus of this book is integrative, holistic, and constructive. It traverses intellectual terrain necessary to see the outlines of a viable contemporary worldview, and as such traces the shifting landscape of late twentieth-century intellectual history. In some ways it is an intellectual autobiography, and to this extent one hears the concerns of a psychologist voiced in the direction of dialogue with science and religion. Though inherently interdisciplinary in its concerns, its discourse is grounded in the psychological and in the search for a broader view of human beings that does justice to our inextricable interrelatedness with each other, with the environment, and with the wider reality. It crosses the landscape of contemporary psychology from epistemology to transpersonal concerns, bearing witness to the relevance of these issues for the field of religion. If we are to find an image of wholeness that can actively inform our lives, we must seek metaphors that function with integrity across the realms we inhabit as we step from one aspect of life to another.

I begin this task from the standpoint of psychology, not only because this is my home of professional origin, but because it stands as a bridge between the sciences and humanities and is the place where scientific and religious pursuits of truth uneasily meet. It is in the context of this epistemological tension regarding the validation of knowledge that metaphor emerges as a perspective by which to facilitate dialogue. This book will focus on the three fields of psychology, science, and religion, not only because they span the range of human exploration of life's mysteries and share the passion and immediacy of this pursuit in very different ways, but because the attempt to take into account three different spheres of influence can help us avoid the simple polarization that follows too easily from treating two contrasting approaches.

Yet the focus is on these three fields also because my heart and mind are planted in each of them, and the voice I wish to release is a voice that seeks a level at which these three might communicate more fully with each other. My hope and conviction is that the paths of truth, whether scientific, psychological, or spiritual, might find a basis by which to see separately, uniquely, yet compatibly. I believe that an exploration of metaphor can serve this purpose. The special viewpoint this book offers results from ways in which it utilizes metaphor and symbol to reveal a "systems" perspective congenial to the three diverse fields of psychology, science, and religion.

If any metaphor could replace the Gothic cathedral for our time, I believe it would be the image of Indra's net, the cosmic web of interrelatedness extending infinitely in all directions of the universe. Every intersection of intertwining web is set with a glistening jewel, in which all parts of the whole are reflected, mirroring the intricate interconnectedness of all reality and its intercausality. Indra's net captures the web, network, pattern, tapestry, textured imagery of our time, yet perhaps needs to be seen as a more dynamic field of energy, revealing a shimmering and ever-changing holarchy, where each part reflects the whole, and where nothing exists apart from the whole. Though this image comes from the Chinese Buddhist heritage, it is rich in associations for a world that has come to see the earth in its blue planetary wholeness and integral embeddedness in the universe. Indra's net is an image highly compatible with the more active and dynamic systems metaphors we will be exploring, and opens out into transpersonal and ontological richness.

Following this guiding image in tracing and integrating the various voices that inform a systems metaphor of interrelatedness, the book is organized according to the metaphor of network or web. Each chapter forms a node from which a critical strand in the web is hung, each node providing a point of departure for constructing a relevant strand, and bearing the content and voice appropriate to its discipline and concerns. As a network, the book reaches both backwards and forwards, across planes and terrains relevant to the construction and expression of a systems worldview.

It can be read forward, from its underpinnings in the struggle to escape the constrictiveness of an antitheoretical psychology based on logical positivism. Part One provides the background for an attempt to ground intuitions regarding wholeness and complexity in a philosophically more adequate framework and an expanded experimental research program. The earliest chapters in Part One, being the barest and closest in structure to philosophical discourse and psychological experimentation, offer an introductory overview of the claim that knowledge can only be an approximation. It is within this context that metaphor emerges as an effective and critical tool of inquiry, and broader definitions of acceptable methodology and content become possible for empirical research. Chapter 1 examines issues in "metapsychology" and epistemology concerning the limits of objectivity and certainty in inquiry. Chapter 2 develops this theme in the context of theory-building, illustrating the importance of metaphor in the process of inquiry. Chapter 3 samples the expanded range of empirical research in psychology deriving from and exemplifying a paradigm increasingly informed by the importance of metaphor and nonlinear modes. These early chapters in Part One thus provide the reader who is less familiar with the rapidly growing body of literature on these themes with a critical summary of issues relevant to the task of constructing a worldview more adequate to the complexity of the concrete interrelated world. They also summarize for the reader the rationale and importance, indeed the necessity of metaphor to this task. Readers who are already familiar with these arguments from the philosophy of science and other disciplines are encouraged to move more swiftly to the consideration of metaphors of interrelatedness in Part Two.

Part Two situates the pursuit of metaphors of interrelatedness more specifically within the context of metaphors of the self, the territory of theoretical controversy most readily accessible for appreciating their importance. Thus in the process of constructing and evincing a systems understanding of psychological issues, in chapter 4 we explore alternative metaphors of personality and the self that provide a point of contrast for the arguments to follow. Chapter 5 provides a discussion of models and metaphors of wholeness from contemporary science, with particular emphasis on systems theory as a promising model for cross-disciplinary dialogue. Chapter 6 seeks to clarify and explore the implications of systems theory for the fields of personality, clinical, and transpersonal psychology.

The perspectives developed in Part Two issue forth in abundant implications, and given the nature of a metaphor of interrelatedness, readily move beyond strict disciplinary boundaries. Thus in some ways Part Two returns us to the importance and predicament of metaphor use discussed in Part One, but also introduces us to questions of extending a systems viewpoint toward a broader understanding of ontology or metaphysics in Part Three. Chapter 7 raises issues regarding the role of metaphor in religion, the ontological potentialities within systems theory, and the kind of spiritual worldview with which a systems ontology might have affinities.

Prologues to the three major parts of the book trace the movement of the discussion from the bare bones of philosophy and experimental psychology, to the tissues and complexity at stake in metaphors of interrelatedness, to the promise of a worldview embodying the wholeness of Indra's net. The prologues present natural metaphors that reflect the tone and content of each of these domains, moving from desert to tropical profusion to the oceanic realm of the horizontal god.

This book is intended to introduce lay and professional readers to the role of metaphor and models in psychology, science, and religion; and to argue the case for systems theory as a contemporary unifying metaphor across domains. Abundant resources now exist, following a long period of neglect, for exploring the importance of metaphor in inquiry; the recently appearing collection *Metaphors in the History of Psychology* (Leary, 1990a) is a notable addition for that field. However, the task of extending this analysis to systems theory and the importance of metaphors of interrelatedness has remained to be done.

As articulated by one of the major contributors to the recent collection (Gergen, 1990a), systems theory offers some of the leading contemporary metaphors for understanding human experience. In addition, by virtue of its status as a metaphor, systems theory further contributes to challenging conventional linear and positivistic epistemological assumptions of experimental social science. Despite these fruitful implications, systems theory has remained largely inaccessible to the general reader, to professionals from fields for whom the implications of a fuller understanding would be profoundly heuristic, and even to psychologists themselves. Systems theory has been particularly underutilized as a resource for transpersonal psychology, and due to its roots in modern science, it has tended to be misunderstood in ways that have prevented the appreciation of its potential roles for mediating discussion in science and religion.

This book, then, is centrally an attempt to lay the groundwork for and sketch out a systems theory of psychology by integrating many of the key voices central to this task. It will be relevant to courses in systems and theories of psychology, philosophy of science, psychology of religion, transpersonal psychology, and related courses in philosophy and religion.

It is also written for those who seek to live coherently, beyond the compartmentalization of our twentieth-century intellectual mindscapes, and who seek a synthesis from which to think, imagine, and live. This book is an invitation to dialogue and discovery, written in the conviction that intellectual, psychological, and spiritual wholeness is possible. It is an affirmation of the power of metaphor to carry us into new and unifying insights.

Part One

BARE BONES

PROLOGUE

At the edge of the canyon, right before sunset when all the people are off to the west for a better view, you can find a place very close to the rim on one of the deserted spokes of land left behind after dark. It is possible to sit very still and listen to the sounds of the canyon welcoming back its solitude. The orange sun shrinks to a golden line across the horizon and Vishnu's peak fades to a lavender, then grey, and disappears. Time returns, or timelessness. Peace. Expanse. Emptiness. Carried in the wind that haunts the nesting spot, sending a new chill and shudder, a gratitude for a warm jacket, a feeling of privilege to remain for a few moments past human time and sense the return of eternity.

Not everyone likes the desert, its starkness, its extremes. The heat of its burn can sear the soul; its coolness at night can taunt the memory of a day without relief from the sun while it drives you to the comfort of down clothing. Yet the desert is a place of immense clarity, against which illusions emerge with a watery insubstantiality to meet the test of time and confrontation. The desert drives the illusions into focus, offering them to our eye in frontal assault. No outer ambushes here, only the shadows cast by the inner enemy. In the desert you yourself are prey. The desert returns you to yourself, to your own resources, with a knife and compass and canteen. There are few distractions here. We are driven to look within or beyond. There is no lush and verdant foliage to catch our senses and invite, distract from the task at hand. We can go to the foundations, the bedrock, without fear of moisture or decay. It is a time for beginnings, or endings. It is dry, hard, difficult. One can lose one's way. There is risk here. Every thought counts.

Yet in the clarity of a desert night you can see the earth turn against the stars. The blackness of a mesa cuts across the path of the moving sky. Time becomes space. Solitude pulls you to the heart of the universe. The mind, clean honed and crystalline, shimmers in cool starlight. It is a time of seeing.

Chapter One

KNOWLEDGE AS APPROXIMATION

Not long ago, one could sit in a psychology class where the professor would ring a buzzer anytime a student used the word "mind." Mind, of course, was a heresy more preferable than speaking of soul or self, but all such explanatory intervening variables, intervening presumably between observable stimuli and responses, were taboo. Anything unobservable was suspect, including such constructs as personality or motivation, wiping out in one fell swoop much of the vocabulary and questions that had drawn people to the study of psychology in the first place.

Under the reign of strict behaviorism that dominated much of the twentieth century, the legitimate domain for the study of academic psychology was external, observable behavior. Data were obtained through measurement using the five senses augmented by instruments or apparatus. Questions not capable of testing via sensory-grounded empiricism tended to be dismissed as non-meaningful. Behavioral psychologists argued that psychology needed to free itself from philosophical speculation, hypothetical constructs, and intervening variables, returning to what could be observed and seen.

Scientific laws were conceived as simply summarizing relationships between the observed data. The role of theory was to be minimized by avoiding hypotheses about "why" *X* and *Y* are related. Some "theory" would be necessary in order to form hypotheses and propositions to test experimentally, but the goal was to stay as close as possible to the data, moving from data to minimal "theory" to a prediction and gathering of new data, with no pause for global speculations or formation of concepts to explain how two events are related. Theoretical statements had the status of "ghosts" (Pirsig, 1974) haunting the "black box" or no-man's-land between stimulus and reponse, about which behaviorists did not wish to speculate.

This set of assumptions reflected the model of classical science, and argued on behalf of the existence of actual facts that could be known about reality "out there," derived in trustworthy fashion by the senses. Such a view of science was grounded through the first half of the twentieth century on the assumptions of logical positivism, which insisted on the primacy of sense data as the starting point and measure of all valid knowledge. The dominance of behaviorism's demands to avoid theory and philosophical speculation led to a singular blindness toward acknowledging and examining its own philosophical underpinnings in logical positivism. And as increasing criticism became directed in philosophy toward logical positivism, psychology was effectively shielded from this debate. Thus as the second half of the twentieth century began, psychology continued to model itself on a science and philosophy of science that had long since been collapsing.

Much has happened in more recent years to challenge these positions, though it is clear to those working in the field that these issues are by no means dead. To those outside psychology, questions about the limits of objectivity and certainty, and fundamental epistemological doubts about truth-seeking and what if anything we can know for sure, became familiar issues in the discourse of postmodern language communities. It has been within this context that increasing appreciation for the relevance of metaphor to issues of epistemology and knowing has become widespread in philosophy, religion, and the humanities.

Psychology has not been immune to this debate,[1] and it is indeed a major achievement of philosophical psychology and "metapsychology" that metaphor is fast becoming an accepted topic.[2] These arguments in contemporary philosophy of science regarding the limitations of objectivity, knowledge as approximation, the importance of theory, and the necessity of metaphor are directly relevant to the task of seeking to explore a systems model of reality. To the extent that systems theory represents a departure from positivistic assumptions, and a challenge to linear behaviorism, it is valuable to understand the nature of the criticism in philosophy of science which has opened up a more serious appreciation of theory and model in the process of inquiry. Further, to the extent that this book represents a quest for a model of wholeness that can inform our perspectives and guide our practices, it must address questions of the adequacy of any model and the special relevance of metaphor in this process of inquiry.

The claim of systems theory to offer a large-scale unifying model for understanding "reality" must negotiate a path through the serious concerns that have been raised regarding the limits of knowing. At the same time, the possibilities of systems theory as an informing metaphor are enhanced by a fuller understanding of the limitations of the logical positivist and more linear behavioral models with which systems theory contrasts. Systems theory, with its metaphors of interrelatedness, seeks to do justice to the complexity and connectedness it confronts in the domains of science and psychology. By providing an interdisciplinary metaphor system that invites dialogue across the fields of psychology, science, and religion, systems theory stirs up issues in epistemology across this range of concern. These issues need to be taken up by way of introductory overview, to allow for the full emergence of systems theory as a unifying model across domains. Such is the task of the first two chapters, the first addressing issues in knowledge as approximation and the second, the crucial role of metaphor in theory-building.

> Desiring to know the sizes of fish inhabiting a newly discovered mountain lake, enthusiasts went out to the lake with large 12-foot nets, the holes varying in size from two inches up to six. Systematically covering the lake, they dipped their nets into the water and counted and measured the fish they drew up. The official report submitted to the town council evidenced surprise that although there were an abundance of fish of varying sizes over two inches, not one fish under two inches appeared to be living in the lake.

The Limits of Objectivity

Perhaps the most powerful legacy of the twentieth century for science and philosophy has been the steadily accumulating challenge to the possibility of "objective" knowledge, uncolored by assumptions or interpretations. The core implication is that there can be no such thing as neutral fact or finding: there are no "raw" data (Grover, 1981, p. 8). All data are affected by theory, method, or interpretation. "Data" are really "capta" (Laing, 1967, p. 62), seized according to some framework rather than neutrally encountered. No scientific fact exists apart from a value decision, a choice or interpretation about what is worth studying and how this should be done.[3]

The perceptual process itself models this problem of interpretation. Even in the very act of seeing, there can be no such thing as "immaculate perception" (Laszlo, 1987, p. 109). Perception is an interpretive process in which the raw data of sensation are organized and transformed in the process of yielding a final impression. The process of sensation is already a data-filtering system which receives only that type and degree of input capable of being selected by the physiological limits of the sense receptors. Of the vast electromagnetic spectrum, we can only identify those wavelengths for which we have receptors. Abstraction or data reduction is a hallmark of the sensory act, and the process of perceptual interpretation begins almost immediately in the first codings the received input is given on its way to the cortex.

Past experience, context, cultural expectations, and other factors create a "perceptual set," an interpretive matrix through which the sensory input is understood by the organism. The schema or categories available for assignment of incoming input depend on past experience and affect the ease and accuracy of the process of interpretation. For example, persons who watched pictures of playing cards flashed on a screen at extremely high speeds were often unable to identify accurately aberrant combinations such as a red six of spades. Instead they might see this as a black six of spades, a red six of hearts, or even a purple six of spades, if the unassignable combination did not disrupt perception altogether (Bruner & Postman, 1949). The influence of perceptual set and expectations on pain perception is even more dramatic.

Our knowledge from its onset is also embodied, embedded in our kinesthetic relationship to reality and in the connection of our bodies to the physical world (Johnson, 1987; Berman, 1989). We understand causality at least as much due to our bodily based experience of moving and interacting in the world as due to abstract intellectual understandings of the concept. The body as a context for knowing, and the sense of touch as a way of taking in information, illustrate the interactive nature of perception even more tangibly than vision, which often misleadingly encouraged for philosophers of science a sense of neutral distance between perceiver and perceived (Gill, 1982).[4]

Polanyi calls this bodily based backdrop to formal knowledge "tacit understanding." Tacit understanding consists of the assumptions, subjective values, and preverbal, peripheral awarenesses that direct our attention when we seek to understand something in a more formal, explicit, and abstract way. There would be no science without the tacit understanding that there is something to be discovered, that something of value exists to be studied. Personal participation or "indwelling" is the fundamental basis for human knowledge. Not only do our rather hazy apperceptions of the importance of a discovery witness to the role of value and choice in directing inquiry, but our very passion for truth, beauty and comprehensiveness is a critical guide to the integrity of research. Rather than an enemy of inquiry, passion becomes a clue to significance and an irrevocable part of inquiry. Involvement, not detachment, characterizes the discovery of the new.[5] The knower participates in the shape of the known. "Reality seems to be a kind of alloy between perceiver and perceived" (Maslow, 1966, p. 111).

The role of perceptual set and tacit understandings at the individual level is paralleled at the cultural level by the role of basic assumptions, presuppositions, guiding models, or paradigms which characterize an age. Remaining seductively hidden from consciousness, those presuppositions by which we operate are often the last to be examined, just as the fish proverbially are the last to discover water. Kuhn (1970) argued that science can best be understood, not as the accumulation of individual discoveries or "facts," but as a series of revolutions or changes in its ruling "paradigms."[6] Periods of "normal science" are dominated by an acknowledged paradigm which provides direction to two basic types of questions: (1) What aspects of reality deserve attention; what questions are interesting and worth asking; what shall we study? and (2) How will we study these questions; what methods or procedures are appropriate or adequate to this task? Seen from this perspective, the scientific method is itself a set of assumptions about how to discover knowledge rather than a neutral process.

Normal science proceeds under its relevant paradigm until a persistent anomaly or exception in the data is observed and cannot be fit into the old paradigm. Although paradigms are highly resistant to change, an inconsistency found repeatedly will eventually trigger a crisis for the science and a search for a new paradigm and subsequent revolution in worldview. Shifts in paradigms usher in a new phase of normal science and assumptions again recede into the background, shaping awareness and methodology but only too often out of awareness themselves.

> Returning home from a late evening gathering, a young couple notice their neighbor stooping over the curb under the streetlight. Suspecting that he might have lost something and willing to offer assistance, they inquire. Indeed, replied the neighbor, I have lost my keys. Where exactly do you think you lost them? the couple asked. Over there by the garage, motioned the neighbor, pointing away toward his house. Then why are you looking for them here in the street? they asked with surprise. Because, my friends, the light is much better here.[7]

Although the history of psychology has not been unified under one sole paradigm, the major schools have held differing "miniparadigms" regarding the nature of what is worth studying and how this varying content should be studied. As we have seen under behaviorism, what we are to study was defined as external, observable behavior. Areas of human functioning like willing, thinking and feeling were considered irrelevant to explaining causation, at most acceptable among clinically oriented pursuits on the fringe of mainstream academic psychology and only recently relegitimized in altered form under the rubric of cognitive-behavioral psychology.

Under the same behavioral miniparadigm, how we are to study behavior was answered in favor of the experiment. Naturalistic observation, case studies, and correlational data were considered inferior sources of data or new hypotheses. The emphasis on empiricism and the importance of direct observation of data became translated into a near-exclusive valuation of experimentalism as the acceptable form of empiricism. In being "method-centered" rather than "problem-centered," psychology risked committing "methodolatry" (Maslow, 1966, pp. 16, 145) or "method-fetishism" (Koch, 1981, p. 260), with methodological and statistical considerations often dictating the types of questions worth studying or even considered studiable (Bakan, 1972, 1973). Whatever did not fit with ease into the dominant methodological designs was often dismissed as overly vague and unworthy of study, with the result that the focus of study was determined by method rather than by the essential, rich complexity of the problem area itself.

The behavioral paradigm carried another important assumption that was made doubly powerful and thereby less obvious by being shared by the psychoanalytic school with which it otherwise fundamentally disagreed. The emphasis for both was on the analysis of complex behavior or experience into component parts, whether chains of stimuli, response, and reinforcement or ego, id, and superego dynamics. The first challenge to this analytic emphasis on parts came from Gestalt psychology which championed the maxim that the whole is greater than the sum of its parts. In fact the paradigm most likely to be emerging today is a holistic one, in which systems theory carries even further the Gestalt emphasis on wholeness.

As starting points for observation and thinking, assumptions play a further role in psychological research through the formation of operational definitions for what we are going to study. An operational definition in psychology is a definition or explanation of a construct or concept in terms of how you are going to measure that quality. Thus if we wish to study anxiety we must specify in observable terms if possible how we are going to measure anxiety, whether by a specific questionnaire or other more behavioral measure. There are often several alternative ways one might choose to measure a concept, depending on what assumptions one holds about the construct.

Once love is included within the realm of acceptable concepts to study, a process which has taken much of the twentieth century for example, it must be operationalized. Love might be variously defined in terms of "the amount of eye contact between two persons" or "the extent to which one person puts the interests of another above his or her own." Each choice may lead to different observations and discoveries about love. The scientific method is intrinsically bound up with choices in how one is to measure and define one's target area of study. The critical issue is not to determine which operational definitions are more true, but to stay aware of the role each set of assumptions and definitions plays in determining specific observations and reflections upon reality.

In the realm of personality theory it has been long argued that every theory is linked and supported by a set of philosophical assumptions characteristic of the theorist in question. These assumptions may only be implicit in the theory, as in the case of Skinnerian views of human behavior which embody a certain set of philosophical assumptions despite a typically deliberate attempt to avoid theory. William James (1963) called attention to what he labeled the "tough" versus "tender-minded" philosophical or personal leanings which underlie most theoretical debates and differences of opinion in philosophy and psychology.[8] Projections, selective attention, and differences in values also have the potential to color theory. Any process of classification or categorizations provides a set of blinders, useful for purposes of extracting order and simplicity from complex phenomena, but potentially detracting from a more complete vision.

Probably the classic testimony in psychology and the social sciences to the power of assumptions and expectations has been the phenomenon of self-fulfilling prophecy (Merton, 1948) and the accompanying issue of experimenter bias (Rosenthal & Fode, 1963; Rosenthal, 1966). Demonstrated in a wealth of different experimental and naturalistic observation contexts, self-fulfilling prophecy represents the way in which our assumptions and expectations about other people or ourselves actually affect what they or we become. In research settings, expectations from experimenters can be transmitted unwittingly to participants in experiments, a concern underscoring the importance of double-blind procedures in research and other methodological precautions. Though attention is now being directed to qualifying the limits of expectancy effects and noting a greater role for accuracy in social judgment in educational settings (Jussim, 1989; Wineburg, 1987a, 1987b),[9] concern for the dangers of diagnostic categories and labeling in families, schools, hospitals, and juvenile justice systems continues to be a vital issue.[10]

Within the field of physics, an even more profound implication of the role of the observer can be found in Heisenberg's uncertainty or indeterminancy principle. This principle was derived from the finding of quantum physics that an observer cannot know both the position and the momentum of a subatomic particle with precision at any one point in time. Both position and momentum can be known approximately, but the more information is known about one, the less one can know about the other. This observer-observed dilemma reflects the problem that measurement at this level involves high speed particles fired at other particles, which affects and changes the trajectory of the particle being studied. To leave the particle alone is not to see it at all. One cannot observe without changing the phenomenon; discovery involves interaction. This and other related findings have suggested and underscored the emphasis in modern physics on probability statements about reality rather than a claim for perfectly predictable and deterministic events at the subatomic level. In addition, the finding has stressed the impossibility of objectivity at this level, for by choosing where to focus, one "creates" a new situation where what is observed "is not nature in itself but nature exposed to our questioning" (Heisenberg, 1958, p. 58).

There is considerable debate as to the appropriateness of extending this argument derived from the subatomic level to more complex levels of reality. Great caution always needs to be exercised when extending a concept beyond the domain from which it was derived. Suffice it perhaps that this law of physics be a profound reminder from another level of reality of the danger of observational methods affecting the findings of a study, a principle already demonstrated at the psychological level of reality.[11] By remaining relatively unexposed to the principle of indeterminancy and the inevitabilities of observer influence, however, much of psychology has too often been caught in the position of trying to "outscience" science in its pursuit of unqualified objectivity.

Another major finding in modern physics has served as a reminder of the ways in which the questions we pose in science actually affect and mediate the types of answers received. This discovery has been termed the principle of complementarity and is derived largely from Bohr's formulation of a way to conceptualize the classic wave-particle debate in nuclear physics. Energy has been found to travel in discrete packets or quanta, yet a quantum appeared to have both wave properties and particle properties, depending on how the study was set up to measure the issue or how the question was posed experimentally. According to the principle of complementarity, both alternative viewpoints can be seen to hold validity depending on the point of view assumed. The principle underscores the role played by questions and assumptions in affecting the nature of what will be found in inquiry.

Again it is valid to use caution in extending such a principle from the level of quantum physics to molecular levels such as found in psychology, but the principle provides a useful example at another level and domain of a principle found independently in psychology, in particular in such issues as operational definitions. There is a growing suspicion, for example, that mind/body dualism is a problem at least partly resulting from the types of questions asked. One of the potential strengths of systems models and metaphors lies in challenging such dualisms and subject-object dichotomies that are also called in question by contemporary philosophy of science.[12]

It is not surprising that psychologists, faced with the great risks of subjectivity in a field where humans study themselves, have been concerned to make psychology as objective as possible through emphasis on experimental control, observable behavior, etc. This emphasis was a critical and valuable contribution of behaviorism. However, this desire for objectivity has often been pursued with a conviction that such a goal was in fact totally reachable, and any deviation from it was judged as suspect. It is this absolute use of the concept of objectivity that is under criticism in psychology, physics, and philosophy of science today.

Although knowledge can be seen as involving participation, embeddedness, and interaction, there is still an important role for public validation and replication in science, which is another meaning of the term objectivity that should not be lost. Even if there is no absolute guarantee of objectivity in the sense of a glass wall or one-way screen behind which psychologists can stand, without contaminating the phenomena on the other side, there can still be an attempt for publicly repeatable and shared observations; and there must be an attempt to avoid subjectivity, in the sense of private idiosyncracies, in data collection. However, it is an error to confuse this public meaning of objectivity with an insistence on only collecting externally observable or so-called "objective" data, for complex, subtle, and internal data can also be submitted to tests of replication and public validation. Data derived from personal internal experience pose greater challenges to research, as in such concepts as a state-specific science (Tart, 1975a), for example; but to neglect these sources of knowledge can be as idiosyncratic and "subjective" as the decision always to give these sources priority (Rychlak, 1968, p. 24). Thus, while absolute objectivity may be a myth in the field of inquiry, this does not mean that science is impossible or that the community of scholars cannot protect against idiosyncratic subjectivism. It must also be remembered, however, that the body of scientists themselves may share a common basis for subjectivity that remains unrecognized due to positions of majority vision.

In an experimental animal therapy program, a young trainer brings an elephant to a group of blind children. Eagerly they each approach the new experience, to be able to share their information with the others. But soon they are arguing. It is like a wall, says the one standing up against the elephant's side. It is like a rope, says the one at the tail. No, you are both wrong, it is like a pipe, shouts the one at the trunk. How silly you all are, argues the one at the ear, it is like a huge fan.

Doubt and Certainty

Even if we acknowledge the limits of objectivity, we come up against the more challenging issue of whether there really is a "reality" out there to know. In other words, if all we can know are our limited perceptions, how can we be sure there "really" is an elephant "out there"? Responses to the question of whether there is a reality to be understood external to the observer typically have been split into two competing and presumably mutually exclusive orientations. The "realistic" argument assumes the existence of an external world independent of the observer and known by the orderly, sequential, and largely passive process of building up more complex ideas from simple sensory input. The "idealistic" approach assumes that one cannot get at an understanding of reality in itself, and in its most extreme form idealism argued against the possibility of profitably and validly conceiving of a reality apart from the perception of the perceiver. In this view knowledge could only be an approximation in which the active human mind, with a priori categories and transcendent qualities of intellect, brings its own or a created structure to experience. Knowledge is thus seen in idealism as a creative act, a shaping of reality and not a mapping out of sense data.

Contemporary philosophy of science has dealt the strongest blow to realism, particularly in criticizing the "correspondence theory of truth" whereby our constructs can be said to derive from and parallel "reality" out there (Rorty, 1979). Our view of the world does not function as a mirror, the postmodern argument goes, and perspectives must be deconstructed to reveal their biases. Yet there is no absolute standpoint or center that can be appealed to in establishing priority of perspective or in evaluating bias. The legacy of Wittgenstein has been to render questions of ultimate truth beyond capability of resolution, and thus to challenge even the perspective of idealism. The growing field of "metapsychology" directs attention across the range of these philosophical controversies, including: the impossibility of objective verifiability of knowledge through empirical observation, the difficulty of grounding descriptive psychological language for human behavior and experience in objectifiable event, the dependency of meaning on sociohistorical context and construction, and implications for evaluating or differentiating theory in light of these challenges to objectivity.[13]

Much of contemporary philosophy leaves us with the dilemma of competing language communities (science, philosophy, art, history, psychology), each playing its own language "game." According to the sociology of knowledge, science and all inquiry are conducted within communities of scholars who share certain language and conceptual patterns, norms, paradigms, and politically and economically motivated dilemmas—all of which factors influence and inform knowledge as much as the nature of the phenomenon under inquiry. Each discipline has a social history and shows an inextricable embeddedness in its communal discourse.[14] By implication, we enter an age of multicentered perspectives, none of which can claim to be seriously concerned with Truth seeking. Often the only protection from using power to adjudicate competing claims is seen to reside in maintaining a maximum of differing perspectives, so that no minority position is excluded.

Such a philosophy perches on the edge of relativism, and contributed greatly to the depreciation of metaphysics, that branch of philosophy that seeks to construct a view of ultimate reality. Both trends have been criticized. The concern to avoid the danger of "uncritical relativism" (Sampson, 1987, p. 43) is reflected, for example, in Gergen's commitment to finding a basis for theory evaluation and comparison that can replace that of "objectivity." He suggests the alternative criterion of "generativity," or the capacity for a theory to open up "alternative metaphors" which can transform culture and society in keeping with chosen values.[15] Furthermore, proponents of the revaluation of metaphysics and others note that relativism as a truth claim fails prey to its own criticism; it too can only be a relative claim.[16]

In addition, the argument that we can never know reality in itself and must settle for approximations does not mean that there is no reality to be sought or experienced. It is possible, and fruitful, to be a realist in affirming that there is a reality "out there" or simply "here" to be confronted, interacted with, understood, sought, encountered (Manicas & Secord, 1983). Some "isness" exists—perhaps not recoverable or representable in nouns or concepts, or perhaps even in mathematical formulas or laws—yet worthy of study. This assumption in some form must be the fundamental tenet of any search for knowledge or process of inquiry. Second, we can affirm with idealism that knowledge can only be an approximation of what is ultimately real, an act of encounter inherently affected by the creativity and subjective character of the inquiring mind. Such an affirmation does not preclude the possibility of science, or necessitate a totally relative view of knowledge, but it tempers the claim of any human search for knowledge as capable of absolute certainty. This kind of realism, tempered by this insight of idealism, resembles critical realism (Barbour, 1974).[17]

The claim to take the possibility of truth and reality seriously, yet acknowledge the necessity of approximation in our expression of it, can rest on several bases. First is the claim to direct intuition of reality, a claim which has much in common with revelation as seen in world spiritual traditions (see H. Smith, 1976), and hence is the least likely to be used by psychologists. Second is the claim that truth statements derive from experience, in the sense that any persons following a set procedure or practice (e.g., meditation) might evidence the same insight and experience of the world (see Wilber, 1983, 1984b). Johnson (1987) also defends a realism based on our bodily grounded experience which gives rise to structures reflecting this embodied understanding. Third is the pragmatic argument that truth is evidenced in the transformative effects certain perspectives and beliefs have on living (see James, 1963) or in predicting ways of operating in the world. And finally there are the "axioms of faith" that the world is real, and that we can in some sense come to know it, which surprisingly, come closest to the perspective that has guided modern science (Barrow, 1988, p. 26), augmented by pragmatic appeal to the usefulness of its formulations in predicting and controlling events.

Perhaps these seem slim underpinnings, but they are a starting point. As we are reminded in all cases of formal proof, one can never prove one's initial axiom. We begin always with certain axioms or principles which we assume, which in themselves cannot be proven. Truth may lie beyond provability of a given set of axioms, in that "provability is a weaker notion than truth" (Hofstadter, 1979, p. 19). Metaphysics returns to relevance not only in philosophy, but psychology too (O'Donohue, 1989). The challenge lies in becoming aware of fundamental postulates and remaining open to possible alternative conceptualizations which lie outside the current frame of reference.

> The students sit with great anticipation of their first class in college chemistry. Half of what I will be teaching you in this class will not be true, announces the professor to their great surprise. Unfortunately, their teacher adds, at this point in our knowledge I am not able to tell you which half.

We are never far in contemporary philosophy of science from concerns with the limits of knowledge. The fundamental challenge of science and inquiry is to walk the tightrope of doubt and certainty, allowing both to be measures of integrity in the pursuit of understanding. Absolute certainty is not the qualifying measure of science in the sense that knowledge can only be approximated in human language, concept, or scientific law.

Psychologists in particular must recover their capacity for experiencing ambiguity, perhaps becoming more like their introductory psychology students who feel inundated by contradictory paradigms. It is only too easy to teach and represent these paradigms compartmentally, immune to a full wrestling with their implications. Pointing to the intrinsically paradoxical and contradictory quality of all great questions and answers, Koch (1981) criticizes much of the history of psychology for "cauterizing away the quality of ambiguity" (p. 269). The meaningful questions in life do not issue into safe and certain straightforward conclusions, but have a quality of mystery and complexity and are in turn embedded in larger questions affecting more encompassing levels of phenomena.

The search for secure, cognitive boxes which protect against ambiguity leads to "epistemopathy" (Koch) or "cognitive pathology" (Maslow, 1966). This cognitive style can affect science and all forms of inquiry, creating a tendency to avoid anxiety, defensively cling to findings as fact, and deny a realm for the intangible or unquantifiable. Among these cognitive pathologies Maslow (pp. 26–29) includes the "denial of doubt, confusion, puzzlement"; "intolerance of ambiguity"; "the need to conform"; "overrespect" and "underrespect for authority"; a "flight" into categorization; and uncontrollable "dichotomizing." In contrast, the world of experience is always judged to have more alternatives than the simple A or not A choice of classical logic. As seen in "quantum logic," reality does not inhabit only the two ends of a line, but all the points in between.[18] Science must include stages open to hunches and new ideas; knowing must be measured by degrees, not absolute certainty. Maslow (p. 135) reminds us that the heart of science is its commitment to the "empirical attitude," the commitment to observing for oneself rather than depending on authority, but science does not have to remove wonder and mystery. In fact at its highest, science issues in increased awe and wonder.

Even the bias of scientific questions in the direction of usefulness, prediction, and control may need to be challenged (Needleman, 1965). As long as the motivating question we direct towards the earth is how can we control and use what we find to enhance our own security, we will not discover all that the earth has to teach us. The utilitarian and fear-ridden nature of our questioning predicates certain types of findings and blinds us to other insights into the interrelatedness of our acts and the ecosystem of which we are a part. Questions focused on independently chosen, separate targets will rarely lead to insights into a total system.

Though the emphasis of this chapter has been on the limitations of knowledge, it is important to recall that we began this inquiry in search of an exit from the absolutism and narrowly conceived focus of a psychology steeped in radical behaviorism. Though this perspective has already been supplanted by a cognitive-behaviorism far more open in its assumptions, the philosophical issues at stake have not received wide enough attention. The result for psychology has been a tendency to carry over many habits from positivism into current mindsets. By reminding ourselves of the limits of knowledge, we also paradoxically liberate ourselves to more fully examine our assumptions, widening the possible scope of both content and methodology considered appropriate for psychology. Thus the import of this self-examination as a field is the celebration of new avenues for exploration, a wider range of possible hypotheses to be taken seriously, and a promise of new metaphors more adequate to our time. In chapter 2 we continue this exploration, focusing on the importance of theory in scientific inquiry and the inevitable role of symbol and metaphor in stretching knowledge into new understandings.

Chapter Two

THE NECESSITY OF METAPHOR

If knowledge is approximate, there may indeed be alternative ways to conceptualize and approach the nature of what is to be known. Within the freedoms of imagination opened up by this inevitability and the limits posed by the interface of theory and experimentation lies the terrain where metaphor and model become the tools of science and inquiry. Theorists are the architects and synthesizers in the process of inquiry, and metaphor becomes an aid to creative theorizing and hypothesis construction.

A full appreciation of systems theory and its metaphors of interrelatedness requires consideration of the role and power of theory itself in the process of inquiry. Systems theory richly illustrates the assets and challenges of theory-building and brings into immediate focus the ways metaphors and models of interrelatedness can play a vital role in guiding intuitions of wholeness and complexity into responsible dialogue with ongoing theoretical and research traditions. While theory always embodies a perspective and tone, theory is as rigorous an intellectual exercise as experimentation and involves a disciplined type of critical thinking. Theories do not run wild in the dark; they are to be judged by their own set of criteria related to the multiple functions of theory.

Theories are intended to define and delimit relevant constructs in terms of the particular level of interest to the theorist. Note again that the data do not really impose their own structure and limits on the perceiver, but the theorist is active in choosing between alternatives. Operational definitions carry the signs of their formulators. Theories may open up certain vision, but they also can be blinders. Further, theory dictates the level of description we are interested in targeting, e.g., physiological or psychological, and whether a level is to be understood in terms of any other level. Reductionism to the most molecular level is not necessarily a laudatory goal for all purposes; it may blind us to the levels of complexity inherent in the data. When one switches domains or levels of reality, an entirely new theory may be required to do justice to the complexity at this new level of phenomenon, just as Einsteinian theory and quantum theory complement and augment Newtonian theory, which remains valid but only in its more limited domain.[1] One of systems theory's strengths is that it allows for ever increasing levels of complexity within its explanatory scope, yet also avoids reductionism.

Theory at its best is heuristic, serving to generate new hypotheses and stimulate further inquiry into the relationship between constructs. Theory is positively valued if it stirs up thinking and controversy, spurs research and allows predictions which can be tested. In this view, theory is not to be judged so much in terms of whether it is ultimately true, which may in fact be an impossible claim, but rather in terms of whether it can provide useful questions to pose, useful models by which to function in approximating truth. Chapter 5 explores the range of new issues opened up for exploration by systems theory and the fruitful way systems theory avoids traditional dichotomies like mind/body dualism.

Finally, theory is integrative, organizing empirical findings and bringing together constructs and principles in a unified framework. The aim is internal consistency and a balance of comprehensiveness and parsimony. It is in these areas that systems theory makes its most powerful claim to theoretical excellence.

Comprehensiveness and parsimony pose a paradoxical challenge to the theorist, demanding maximum breadth and complexity adequate to the domain, yet requiring that integrations be given the simplest possible formulation to do justice to the phenomenon in question. Parsimony at its worst encourages simplicity at the price of adequacy, and may reflect the preference for clarity and streamlinedness rather than the data themselves. While many of the most complex truths can be expressed in terms of the simplest principles, this does not mean that the principle of parsimony is an infallible guide. A model must be "adequate to the characterization of our data—no more, but *no less*." The question at stake is "not *how* the phenomenon must be turned and twisted . . . to appear explicable . . . but—*in what direction* we must enlarge our thoughts in order to stand in fit relationship to the phenomenon."[2]

The issue of parsimony is a caution against unnecessary abstraction in theorizing, yet ironically the appeal to parsimony may camouflage degrees of abstraction as well. Abstraction is a chameleon-like phenomenon which does not just accompany effusive theorizing. Even in an approach which claims to be very atheoretical and concrete, concepts like stimulus and response can jump up and down levels of abstraction every bit as fast as in a less ostensibly data-based approach.[3] Newtonian science, in its "fallacy of misplaced concreteness" (Whitehead, 1925), presumed to study "concrete" phenomena as if they existed independently in three-dimensional space, ignoring the extent to which this resulted from abstracting phenomena from their embeddedness in process and spacetime.

Western science has actually tended to favor mathematical abstraction and "theoretic" law over a qualitatively oriented empiricism derived from immediately sensed or intuited nuances of complex pattern, the latter more typical of Chinese science.[4] This tension between the phenomenological richness of experiential knowledge and abstract knowledge has characterized modern psychology as well, and is potentially best understood as a type of "sensuous-intellectual complementarity." Science and psychology face the twofold task of acknowledging the concreteness of phenomenological detail and binding that experience together in larger frameworks through increasing abstraction and organization. To correct for the tendency in Western science to be overly attached to the abstract step requires more emphasis on the receptivity phase, what Maslow (1966) calls a Taoist complement to Western science, where the immediate apprehension of a field of inquiry is allowed to take precedence. Only in this way can we be sure to be dealing with a phenomenon in its own integrity and not distorting it to fit our methodologies for knowing. Such receptivity also promises to restore to psychology the capacity for awe and mystery, too often sacrificed in the move toward abstractness.[5]

Attention to the full complexity of what is to be described is a necessary step toward adequate comprehensiveness in theory,[6] and remains one of the most fundamental characteristics of systems theory. Systems theory in fact is a theory aimed specifically at conceptualizing the profound interrelatedness of levels across the full spectrum of domains in the universe. Its categories, while abstract in the sense of applying to all levels of systems, incorporate and do justice to fundamental details and potentialities characteristic of each level.

Comprehensiveness also holds the key to adequate prediction. Science often takes the strategy of creating partially closed systems by experimentation and seeks to understand causality in terms of abstract relationships observed in these closed systems. If, however, scientists seek to apply this knowledge of abstract laws to explain and predict particular effects in a world of complex, interrelated systems, they must use strategies that take into consideration the full complexity of the open system in which the event of interest is embedded (Manicas & Secord, 1983). Actual prediction of individual events requires a knowledge of biological, physiochemical, psychological, social, and other levels or domains relevant to a full understanding of concrete phenomena. Abstractions can emerge from closed system experimentation, but predictions and applications must involve a re-immersion in complex systems of analysis and interpretive (hermeneutical) inquiry.

In the interests of objectivity and the clearer pursuit of deterministic relationships, positivistic and reductionistic science and psychology ironically often eliminated from consideration those very degrees of complexity necessary for actual precise prediction. Yet greater accuracy requires consideration of the profound complexity of factors impinging on the events of interest. Models must do justice to the level of empirical and phenomenological detail present; they must be adequate to the level of complexity we are attempting to describe and understand.

As Rychlak (1968, 1977) reminds, there are many ways to construct theory. Theories can be guided, as has been traditionally the case in contemporary psychology, by empirical observations and data collection, with theoretical statements following the lead of experimentation. In this "demonstrative" approach, theory is derived totally from available sense data. There is another well-established "dialectical" tradition in which theory building issues forth from the human capacity to reason via polarities, going beyond given data in the pursuit of hypotheses. The dialectical approach acknowledges the role of the creative mind in inventing pathways to truth. Behavioristic psychology has been unduly and prematurely critical of the dialectical approach to theory construction, trapping too much of psychology into studying only those areas of knowledge which could be put in demonstrable form and exploring hypotheses that became virtually trivial from following only too obviously from previous data collection. This unnecessary restriction tempted psychology into neglecting the role of serendipity, creative hunch, visualization, and intuitively derived hypothesis in the pursuit of science.

This neglect is being remedied by increasing attention paid in science and psychology to the range of potential sources for theory construction that are derived from the active use of the mind and imagination. Rather than being limited solely to empirical derivations of theory from sensory based observations, theorists can reason via opposites and move beyond knowns to hypothetical alternatives, as in "Janusian thinking," the generation of new hypotheses by simultaneously conceptualizing two opposite images or concepts. Increasing recognition is being given to the role of intuition and holistic thinking, hunch, speculative insight, creative incubation, and serendipity in the work of great scientific breakthroughs, such as the often cited discovery of the structure for the benzine ring by Kekulé. The importance of visualization and imagery in creative and scientific discovery has likewise been given new emphasis. Image is built into the word "imagination" and is particularly conducive to generating metaphors. Visual illustrations, mental designs and models were crucial in the historical advances of technology, and are returning to importance today by way of computer technologies.[7]

Any source or idea is admissible for theory construction, although logical consistency, comprehensiveness, parsimony, and heuristic value may place some strictures on unbridled speculation. However, as Rychlak cautions, the context of theory construction differs from that of theory testing.[8] For academic psychology, the critical hypotheses of theory, no matter what the source of the formulation, must be submitted eventually to testing via the scientific method. The challenge of a newer field like psychology is to engage in creative theorizing and avoid unnecessary conceptual restrictions derived from a concern for this context of validation. The task of rendering constructs operationalizable and empirically testable, and the integrations of theory formal and clear is crucial and necessary; but the need for adequacy to the types of questions of interest to us as human beings is equally crucial.

Systems theory is an interesting example of a theory that has both demonstrative and dialectical aspects to its derivation. On the one hand its categories emerged by induction from data collected across a variety of domains, with heavy emphasis on the scientific domains in particular. Yet systems theory belongs in part to the dialectical tradition with its rich indebtedness to analogy, visual images (e.g., nested hierarchies or embedded spheres), and its capacities to see similarities and transcend domains, thus opening up hypotheses for further exploration and speculation about such areas as the nature of the self and the universe as a whole. The far-ranging heuristic quality of systems theory and its capacity to promote "systems thinking" is a feature that has much in common with the dialectical tradition of theorizing, and receives much emphasis in this book. In fact, the way in which systems theory is considered demonstrable from the scientific side and yet heuristically rich in implications for other realms give's it its special status and merit as an integrative metaphor in our time, deserving of further empirical investigation and application.

An enterprising merchant who lived near the border between two kingdoms was stopped every day as he wheeled a wheelbarrow full of straw across the border. The customs officials could not help thinking that he was smuggling something, but even as many times as they searched through the straw, they could never find a single thing. Years later, one of the officers left his duties. Thinking that the merchant, who now also was an old man, might confide in him, the retired official asked him what it was that he had been smuggling, since he still was convinced something had been askew. The merchant paused. Wheelbarrows, he replied at last.[9]

Metaphors and Models

We arrive at the importance of metaphor, model and analogy as tools for grasping and suggesting connections between new and as yet unrealized aspects of reality in the search for theoretical understandings. Metaphor involves the use of images or concepts from one field of discourse or experience to describe some other field of experience in such a way as to suggest certain parallels, commonalities, or useful paradoxical connections between the two areas. In their root sense, metaphors transfer or carry meaning across ["phor" from *pherein*] and beyond ["meta"], from one context to another. Metaphors are "meaning transports" which extend our level of understanding by comparison, or some might argue by smuggling extra dimensions into our analysis. In either case they enrich the field of potential comprehension.

Though metaphor has been among the first targets of "semantic positivism,"[10] metaphor plays a significant role in all discourse (Lakoff & Johnson, 1980). Metaphor ranges from its use in daily thinking, where constructs and schemas are formed by seeing similarities among differences, to the "root metaphors" of worldviews.[11] Metaphor characterizes science as well as the humanities, and provides a nexus for approaching issues of truth.[12] Human thought is indebted and dependent on reasoning from comparisons and relationships between known and unknown, and that subsequent inevitability and reliance on metaphor occurs not only with respect to verbal but also mathematically or visually represented knowledge (Leary, 1990b). Metaphor may even open up a new vehicle for understanding the thought of other cultures and "speech communities" (Potter, 1988).

The power of metaphor resides in its capacity to hold in interactive tension both similarities and differences between two compared objects or events, the two poles of the metaphor. This assertion within metaphor of both an "is" and "is not" is crucial in mediating understandings. As a "tensive symbol," metaphor is a kind of "semantic impertinence" or "innovation" which draws out new dimensions of reality. The power of analogy opens up fruitful contrasts and comparisons; an inappropriate metaphor can even be useful in suggesting more precisely how two fields in fact do differ. Negations play as crucial a role as affirmations in "analogical imagination."[13]

Metaphor is a type of contrast or comparison that draws on imagery or affective associations as part of its power for sharpening thought. Metaphor "carries us," allowing the rich subsidiary meanings we bring to both points of contrast to be organized around the creation of new meaning. Metaphor creates "semantic resonance."[14] In turn, through introducing a new view of the world, metaphor plays a role in changing culture (MacCormac, 1985). In fact metaphor may be centrally valued in terms of its capacity to contribute new insights and promote social critique (Gergen, 1990a).[15]

Metaphor enters the field of inquiry as a tool for approximating knowledge in new areas and seeing "new connections" (Black, 1962, p. 237). It suggests the inevitability of reasoning from one's background toward new and unknown fields, of applying metaphorical language to expanding views of the world (Hesse, 1966). As such metaphor can carry implicit and unrecognized assumptions, but often metaphor actually serves to bring into relief and consciousness many of the unconscious assumptions already present. Metaphors and their more structured progeny, models, taken from one field into another, help tease out the similarities and differences through this juxtaposition.

The term model refers to a specific use of metaphor in a carefully delineated and circumscribed way. A model can be understood as a blueprint, a paradigm, a representation, a pattern, a standard, or an ideal. If theories are maps of a terrain, models are the ships that take the inquirer into the specifics of a certain unknown (Judson, 1980). A model is a "rehearsal for reality" (p. 112), a chance to select critical parameters out of a wealth of possible alternatives, paring the problem down to a workable format. Models offer "stepping-stones to theories," a kind of intellectual "scaffolding" crucial for the construction of an understanding but needing to be dismantled and abandoned when the new theoretical structure can stand on its own (p. 186). A model can only take us to the "doorstep" of reality (Jeans, 1943, p. 203); it is not a picture of reality, but rather an aid in imagining.

It has been an important reminder to psychology, recognizably concerned with the risks of subjectivity in exploring human content, that the physical and biological sciences have made frequent use of analogy, metaphor and model in the pursuit of knowledge. Computer and information-processing models are only some of the models in psychology which have ties with the other sciences.[16] The Copernican revolution was at least in part a revolution in models judged most useful and accurate. The data themselves may not even make the critical difference in whether one model versus another may hold sway. As Crick wrote regarding the famous DNA double helix model, it was just as critical to temporarily discard some of the apparent data as to pay attention to each facet: "There isn't such a thing as a hard fact when you're trying to discover something. It's only afterwards that the facts become hard."[17]

In the realm of inquiry, there is a constant need to find new concepts to do justice to new findings (Heisenberg, 1958). Science continually faces the dilemma of translating into the realm of language and discourse. Mathematical language is the only one capable of the clarity and precision required by science, yet it is a language of abstraction and we do not know how far it can actually be applied to concrete phenomena. Ordinary language must eventually be resorted to, for it alone makes an attempted connection to phenomenological experience.[18]

The "necessity of shuttling between the two languages," argues Heisenberg (1974, p. 120), represents "a chronic source of misunderstandings," however. Ordinary language cannot be used to describe mathematically derived principles without ambiguity. Reality defies easy conceptualizations and confounds clarity. New visions and concepts of reality necessitate new words, new images, new language, yet even these new concepts are capable of distortion and the dangers of reification. In physics, for example, expressions like atom or wave function, are only too easily represented as things, nouns, entities. Jeans (1943, p. 200) would add "matter" itself to the list of misleading concepts. Bohr's original model of the planetary atom with nucleus of protons and neutrons and electrons in orbit, while useful in its own time, has given way to a model involving vibrational patterns with various tendencies to exist. We forget only too easily that atoms are "hypothetical" explanatory devices which attempt to help make sense of empirical investigation. The word atom is an idea, an idea which cannot even be visualized. If modern physicists speak of "massless particles," of the concept of "spin" without the parallel concept of something to be spinning, they have in fact entered the realm of paradox, of the koan which poses puzzles that defy rational understanding and the rules of classical logic.[19]

The language of the senses must dissolve before the insights of modern physics, and science must continually reach for new language systems, metaphors and models by which to portray its mathematical insights. The problem is compounded when attempting to reach an understanding of the whole or the entire fabric of reality. For Heisenberg (1974, pp. 120–121), the inadequacies of both mathematical and ordinary language in describing ultimate truths and unified knowledge must yield before the language of poetry and image, the language of "images and likenesses." Like the physicist Pauli, he notes the relevance of Jung's concept of archetypes, primordial patterns for cognition and consciousness, rich in symbolic imagery and emotion, as a "bridge" and "precondition for the emergence of scientific theory" (p. 180).

Sign and Symbol

The importance of symbol in human inquiry promises to shed light on an old dichotomy. Often the sciences and the humanities have been separated by assumptions that these fields represented two mutually exclusive approaches to inquiry: a rational cognitive method of knowing based on empirical fact, sense-data, and logical derivation, and in contrast, a non-cognitive, more intuitive, affective form of knowledge.[20] Neither the sciences nor the humanities have been willing to surrender the insights and commitments provided by the mode of knowing most utilized and defended by itself, and the debate between these two alternatives, represented also within the field of psychology, has often been stalemated in a rather rigid controversy.

The debate between cognitive versus non-cognitive modes of knowing, however, is in fact a false dichotomy. All expressions of knowing involve the process of "symbolization" and in this sense, whether "mystical, practical, or mathematical" (Langer, 1942, pp. 19–20), all knowledge and meaning is mediated via symbol. The human is a symbol-creating and symbol-using creature, and symbolic thought is fundamental in human life (Cassirer, 1946). This is true not only for such domains as art and literature, religion and myth, but also for the sciences. All knowledge that attempts to interpret reality is essentially symbolic and participative in the creation of that knowing. This becomes even more true when fields attempt to grasp the whole, to understand the world in its completeness, and must rely on images and metaphors for the larger picture. Language must be adequate and precise relative to the domain to be described. However, if the nature of reality is paradoxical, language itself must stretch and perhaps be rendered less precise.

Signs and symbols are typically differentiated, yet both are forms of symbolization and represent modes of language best understood on a continuum rather than as a dichotomy. A sign has a one-for-one correspondence to another event or object and stands for that other experience as a tightly defined equivalent. For example, a stop sign and a traffic signal are signs with prescribed, specific meanings. In contrast, a symbol has the qualities of a one-to-many relationship in that a symbol has a surplus of rich meanings, none of which are exact equivalents but rather hint at and suggest the nature of that which is represented symbolically.[21] Symbols point beyond themselves, participate in and open up dimensions of knowing, and are themselves organic in quality, growing and dying beyond the power of the knower (Tillich, 1957).

In Jungian thought, symbols emerging in dreams are not so much to be interpreted or decoded, but rather are circumambulated, walked around, appreciated and interacted with through active imagination. Unlike signs which can be isomorphically translated into another equivalent image, symbolic modes of thought respond to an implied analogy, allowing a linking of reality or resonance between more than one image or association.[22] For example, the moon does not stand for a specific experience, but suggests multiple meanings and significances to be appreciated, not decoded with an eye to one perfect message.

If science emphasizes signs and humanistic fields lean more toward symbols as mediators of knowing, psychology in a sense stands as a bridge field in which clinical, phenomenological insights (more along the nature of symbol) and experimental findings (more of the nature of signs) meet.[23] Even science itself shows examples of complex symbols with "one-to-many" relationships in situations where an abstract law can apply to a great range of phenomena. The biological sciences especially face increasing issues of symbolization in attempting to honor the complexity of life.[24] Perhaps the central reminder is the extent to which both sign and symbol are forms of symbolization, and the process of inquiry, even in its most abstract mathematical formulations remains indebted to symbolic forms for expression.

The intriguing aspect of systems theory as symbol and metaphorical system is its birth in scientific language, yet its potential for extension toward the humanistic fields. The extent to which systems theory is more like sign or symbol depends on the contexts in which we explore its explanatory power. Its flexibility in spanning domains allows it to walk the full range of sign to symbolic thought, appealing both to data-based derivation of significance and explanatory power and to symbolic implications for deeper realms of meaning. Systems theory thus appears particularly apt as a vehicle at the psychological level of discourse. As a holistic model, it draws from a wide variety of metaphorical domains and is thus both integrative and rich in implications.[25]

Metaphor, Symbol, and Validation

As we have seen, metaphor as symbol mediates between knower and that which is to be known, providing hints and glimpses from the world of what is known that suggest analogies to aid the apprehension of the new. Symbols and metaphors provide the "fictional constructs" for the process of knowing (Vaihinger, 1924, p. 15), the way to explore "a hidden likeness" between two phenomena in scientific and creative discovery (Bronowski, 1965, p. 19). Metaphor is fundamental to systems theory which draws explicit analogies between levels of complexity in the phenomenal world.

Metaphor and symbol are not merely emotive expressions, however, but carry genuine ontological status as statements which mediate a partial vision of reality (Wheelwright, 1954). Symbolic or "expressive language" and related experiential knowledge is "vector-like" (p. 75); it carries a truth claim and objective referent, yet the nature of what is to be apprehended at times includes the fundamentally "enigmatic" (p. 74) and contradictory. While all knowledge inextricably involves the knower, the degree or intensity of involvement may differ between fields and this in turn affects the degree of precision in the language possible in each field. The closer one comes to a comprehensive vision, a search to understand wholes, the more participation or "indwelling" is required of the knower and the more one must rely on the symbolic mode to mediate the knowledge.[26]

The ideal of an objective reality out there to be studied independently of an observer and the idea of a transcendent unity between knower and known provide two poles for understanding reality. They stand in a kind of tension, irreducible to each other, yet complementary, held together by their common passion and commitments to knowing.[27] It is interesting to speculate that perhaps these two paths of knowing resemble the planes of a Moebius strip which appear as separate searches in separate domains, yet if one follows each plane around the strip one finds that in fact it is one dimension they are exploring—one unified plane. We will see how systems theory is particularly apt as a unifying metaphor to carry us between the two poles.

Psychology in particular faces the challenge of the tension between these two poles of knowing, for it tends to address issues falling within both the traditionally scientific and humanistic dichotomies. It is therefore essential to recall that all forms of knowing show great similarities in moving through stages of intuition, to discovery, to symbolization and theorizing, to a form of validation (Havens, 1968, p. 65). If science and psychology have tended to overemphasize the traditional criteria of "verification" almost to the exclusion of a legitimate place for hunch, insight, and symbolization in the process of science, the neglect of criteria for validation among humanistic pursuits has been an equally problematic trend. Rather than rendering the humanistic pursuits invalid as avenues toward truths, the challenge is to search for ways of turning toward the context of validation in even those areas of inquiry which most defy precision and demand the most participation (Barbour, 1974; Tracy, 1981). Although verificationism in the strict sense has gone out of science with the critique of positivism, the language and concern of validation is still widespread with respect to evaluating the heuristic function of theory.

A broader understanding of validation becomes critical at this point, however, beyond tests of internal coherence of the symbol system or translation into operationalized concepts that can be submitted to experimental test. These include standards of validation appropriate to the level of symbol per se, prior to and significant apart from this translation process.

Royce (1964) suggests that the clue to the validation of symbol lies in the extent to which a symbol is capable of opening up new insights about the nature of reality not otherwise available. This overlaps considerably with Gergen's (1978) proposal of a generative criterion of theory evaluation, by which a metaphor's potential for bringing new and constructive understandings ,for society becomes definitive in assigning value. Existential criteria for knowledge examine the extent to which the metaphor can provide insight that "enhances" rather than "diminishes" human experience, that conveys a sense of the "unmanifest." Polanyi also sees a role for "heuristic passion," "elegance," and a sense of "beauty . . . and . . . profundity" as criteria for "validation" in distinction from the traditional experimental context of "verification."[28]

To be valid, metaphoric approaches to knowledge must be adequate to the total experience of the fully involved participant or seeker of understanding; the metaphoric insights must lead to continued growth toward authentic living and must be in keeping with the body of facts and concepts discovered by other processes of inquiry (Havens, 1968). Inferences, hunches and insights from the humanistic-phenomenological realm need checking against these criteria in the same sense that scientific hunches and theories need elucidation in the traditional context of empirical and potentially experimental investigation. Systems theory in its implications for human living and its extensions as an ontological system need processing against these criteria.

In summary, the pursuit of knowledge—whether in the fields of science, psychology, or the humanities—involves to varying degrees a reliance on symbol and metaphor, the importance of theory as well as empirically based experience, a role for the knower in the process of knowing that intensifies proportionate to the comprehensiveness of that to be known, and finally the necessity of evaluating the insights of discovery within the context of a form of validation adequate to the form of knowledge. The issue is not to create a methodological dichotomy, however, between the context of experiential knowledge and experimental investigation, but to suggest a hierarchy and complementarity in the two processes by which neither is rendered the exclusive mark of valid knowledge (Maslow, 1966). Models and metaphors that can answer to both contexts of validation and can speak across disciplines might deserve our particular attention. Interdomain metaphors may even create new domains for exploration (Post, 1987, p. 237). It is precisely here that systems metaphors will capture our attention.

The Buddhists argue that when you take a raft to cross a river, it is important not to drag it up onto the land and carry it on your journey, but to leave it on the other shore.[29]

Cautions and Limits of Metaphor

The extent to which modern physicists discuss and understand their scientific theorizing and pursuits in terms of approximation, the search for new metaphors, the guidance of intuitive insights, beauty, and feeling as clues to unified theory—all convey a very different image of science than that carried by classical positivistic assumptions. However, it is important to conclude this analysis of the importance of metaphor and intuitive modes of knowing with a concern for the limits of metaphor. As in the premise made famous by Korzybski, the map is not the territory. However useful, models and metaphors must not be mistaken for the phenomena in themselves. In addition, models can turn active processes into static nouns which take on a life of their own.[30] Degenerating into literalism is the chief danger of all metaphor and model (McFague, 1982), the "loss of tension between model and modeled" (p. 74).

Second, models outgrow their usefulness but are difficult to surrender. Note the outmoded worldview carried by our language of "sunrise" and "sunset," for example (Fuller, 1972). By staying attached to a positivistic view of science, psychology too has carried an outmoded model as its judge for validity in theorizing and empirical study. Note also how long it has taken psychology to critique the nearly exclusively analytic approaches of both structuralism and behaviorism to search for more holistic ways of knowing, approaches represented by early Gestalt perceptual researchers and by current systems theory. Kurt Lewin (1931) was critically concerned with this question of the adequacy of our models for contemporary psychology in arguing that psychology had in many ways not yet undergone the revolution in scientific worldview from Aristotelian to Galileian premises. He argued that psychology was often unduly bound to Aristotelian conceptualizing via polar classes rather that continuous gradations of concept and by statistical group averaging of data rather than the study of the individual case as equally lawful. Newtonian views of the mechanistic, billiard ball model of the universe, with its linear chains of causation, have given way before the Einsteinian and quantum physics view of a complexly interrelated universe, a network or web of energy transformation in which matter has essentially disappeared in a flux of energy patterns. Yet this shift in scientific worldview is only beginning to be felt in fields like medicine or economics (Capra, 1982). Philosophical arguments, too, are often based on outmoded scientific understandings (Jeans, 1943), as seen particularly in issues regarding causality and determinism or materialism and mentalism.

A third danger in the use of metaphor involves the concern for the limits on generalization and appropriateness that must be observed. The capacity to move between levels of analogy and not get trapped at inappropriate comparisons is a critical issue for science (Judson, 1980). Scaffolding must be surrendered to new experimentation and testing. Model and metaphor may prove to be misleading, yet heuristically that very discovery may be just as valuable.[31] Computer analogies to brain/mind functioning that prove inadequate as paradigms may direct the search to new levels (Pribram, 1980). A particular danger is that of overgeneralizing a term or concept beyond its original domain. This has been a concern of many physicists regarding what they perceive as possible overuse of the term "energy" outside the definition of the capacity to do work. While it is important to note that the use of metaphor and analogy is precisely an issue of extension of a concept to a new field of inquiry, this extension must be fully judged in terms of its limits and the rigors of the testing to which this use of the model can be put. Extension per se is not wrong or invalid; it is in fact part of what science is about. However, precision and adequacy must be tested and metaphors must be refined.

Finally, metaphors are most dangerous if they give permission for overly sloppy and loose thinking. Theorizing and empirical evaluation are equally rigorous processes, however different they may also be. Metaphors are aids to thinking, not substitutes for thinking. Too much of the popularization of modern physics concepts has given license to fuzzy claims which thoroughly psychologize reality. In the efforts to point to the limitations of science, indulgence in unbounded emoting and claims of proof for metaphysical statements have followed. Global excoriations of outmoded paradigms can be no substitutes for disciplined science and psychology. The overextension of the research on left and right hemispheres of the brain is only one, though widely witnessed, testimony to the dangers of unbridled metaphor which however provocative and useful, becomes extremely misleading in some of the uses to which it has been put (see also Corballis, 1980). As we approach the study of systems metaphors, we must stay alert to the possibility of these dangers while still mining their significance.

Metaphor plays a powerful role in theorizing, and because of its special status and relevance to all forms of human inquiry, it has the potential for facilitating communication between fields. Contemporary metaphors will be at their strongest if they open up interdisciplinary dialogue. It is in the interests of this premise that the contemporary metaphor of systems theory will be explored as a unifying metaphor in our time.

Chapter Three

BROADENING THE RESEARCH PARADIGM

The importance of metaphor and model for theory construction joins contemporary psychology as part of a more general reaffirmation of the need for broadening its research paradigm. This concern has addressed not only issues of methodology, but also has included attempts to broaden the range of acceptable content researched in the discipline, particularly to include greater recognition of the significance of nonlinear modes in psychological functioning. In a field dominated for so long by the logical, sequential, analytic process of experimentation, with its scientific emphasis on rationality, mastery, and control (Keller, 1982), the intuitive and symbolic modes in both human experience and scholarly discipline became diminished in value, lying within the academic "shadow" of a psychology more attuned to simpler taste, right angles and clean lines, the three-dimensional hard-core "call-em-as-you-see-em" world of sensory reality. Yet there are major signs of change, not only in currents that occasionally sweep through the field, challenging paradigms or offering insightful criticism from a minority position, but in mainstream experimental psychology as well. As psychologist Jerome Bruner (1966, p. 3) foreshadowed, walking the delicate line of metaphor, "the artificial separation of the two modes of knowing [i.e., the scientific and poetic] cripples the contemporary intellectual. . . ." He challenged the "right-handed psychologist" to:

> tame the metaphors that have produced the hunches, tame them in the sense of shifting them from the left hand to the right hand by rendering them into notions that can be tested. . . . Because our profession is young and because we feel insecure, we do not like to admit our humanity. . . . We place a restrictive covenant on our domain. Our articles . . . have about them an asceptic quality designed to proclaim the intellectual purity of our enterprise. (pp. 4, 5)

Bruner added optimistically that "perhaps the moment is uniquely propitious for the left hand, for a left hand that might tempt the right to draw freshly again" (p. 8). It is within this broadened set of possibilities that systems theory, as a metaphor and model offering new perspectives on interrelatedness, emerges as resource for our time.

In relegitimizing the role of the metaphorical and symbolic dimension as an inevitable part of all search for truth including science, we are entering an important period of reaffirmation and widening acceptance in culture and scholarship. As the importance of theory to the process of science has returned to a more legitimate position in psychology, other trends and currents in the field of psychology have also drawn empirical attention to the importance of symbolic modes in human functioning. Increasing appreciation for creative ways of bringing these nonlinear areas into the context of validation has also accompanied this broadening of interest. We will explore these currents and signs of change in experimental psychology at greater length in this chapter, noting an increasing openness to new models of inquiry and a relegitimization of a range of content areas bearing a family resemblance to symbolic expression, metaphor, and nonlinear modes of processing information. These areas include an emphasis on broader research methodologies and a number of content areas receiving increasing experimental attention, particularly within cognitive psychology: visual imagery, metaphor itself, creativity, cognition and emotion, cerebral-hemisphere functioning, mind/brain models, consciousness, and cognitive approaches to teaching and education.

Research Methodologies

The impact of new insights provided by philosophy of science into the nature of inquiry and the inevitable involvement of the knower in the process of knowing has been accompanied, as we have seen, by a renewed valuing of theory[1] in complementarity with empirical exploration and experimental quantification, as well as by a stronger recognition of the importance of intuition and symbol in the formation of theory. Along with this process of relegitimization have come expanded interpretations of what constitute appropriate methodology and focus for research and a renewed emphasis on alternatives to the near exclusive valuing of experimental methodologies in psychology (Hoshmand, 1989). As Bakan (1972, 1973) and Rychlak (1968) have pointed out, psychology had risked making an ideology out of its methodology, confusing experimentalism with empiricism and allocating less controlled forms of empiricism to an orphaned status. Thus the case study, the phenomenological approaches to clinical investigation, and naturalistic studies were placed with historical and remedial emphasis in introductory textbooks of psychology, but the major training for graduate students remained the experimental method and its related series of statistical and methodological paradigms acceptable in current journal circles. Modern psychology still seemed in danger of assuming the value of "incrementalism," the assumption that progress can be guaranteed by accumulating data, and "mensurationism," the tendency to value numbers disproportionate to theoretical perspectives as the basis for scientific advance (Robinson, 1979, pp. 276–278).

Discussion of the superiority of the experimental method over correlational forms of inquiry has typically involved stress on the ability of experimental method to enable one to make conclusions about cause and effect. A careful philosophical analysis of causality, however, drawing from Hume and others would argue the impossibility of proving causality beyond correlations or associations in a certain time order of two regularly and repeatedly associated events (Eacker, 1972). In fact, all conclusions are really correlational or can be described as functional relationships between independent and dependent variables.

One of the important ways science and psychology have tried to do justice to the full complexity of empirical data has been the growing choice of multivariate as opposed to "single-variable" designs, particularly in the biological and behavioral sciences (Royce, 1965b). Linear designs where one looks for simple relationships between one independent variable and one dependent variable fail to do justice to complex systems or natural settings (McGuire, 1973), nor can they predict to the individual case (Manicas & Secord, 1983).

Phenomenologists, expressing a concern for qualitative richness and the complexity of individual variation and uniqueness, insist on pursuing empirical methodologies compatible with the needs of both phenomenology and experimentation (Giorgi, 1970). Researchers focusing on women in a variety of fields also have argued on behalf of methodologies compatible with new phenomenological and experiential content (Carlson, 1972), preferring to speak of participant-collaborators rather than the traditional "subject," or emphasizing oral history, journals, and letters as sources of data.[2] This emphasis harkens back to Allport's classic *Letters from Jenny* (1965), and his defense of the idiographic approach to research in complementarity to nomothetic approaches based on statistical averaging.

The return of the idiographic case study is of course not only the province of phenomenological and feminist experience; ironically it is also the favored domain of figures as varied as Skinner and Piaget. "Discovery-oriented" research in psychotherapy is receiving more attention (Mahrer, 1988), as are concerns for articulating the contrasts between qualitative and quantitative research emphases (Patton & Jackson, 1991). In addition, the debate between experimental methodology and phenomenological approaches has not been a pure dichotomy at all times, for room has been granted for initial exploratory searches to have recourse to a less rigorous methodology. The door is thus open for a fuller honoring of both approaches to inquiry, with mutual respect for theory construction and validation.

A particularly significant line of approach follows from the developing field of historical social psychology (Gergen, 1973; Gergen & Gergen, 1984), which critiqued traditional social psychology for its neglect of the historical embeddedness of events. Traditional psychology, by favoring the controlled experiment with its "independent" variables (M. Gergen, 1987), has contributed to a truncated understanding of events frozen at "synchronic" cross-sections in time. Advocates of an historical social psychology have supported a contrasting "diachronic" perspective with more emphasis on longitudinal studies, the role of narrative, and the social embeddedness of constructs like the self. Further openness to methods of historiography and ethnography are also suggested as vehicles for enriching psychological research.[3] Highly noteworthy is Hoshmand's (1989) inclusion of "cybernetic" or "high-context" methodologies drawn from systems theory dynamics among major contemporary alternate research paradigms.

Imagery

A major area that has received considerable experimental attention recently is the role of imagery in cognitive processes, a direction of research and area of interest anticipated and announced by Holt in a critical article in support of imagery as early as 1964. Block (1981, p. 1) argues that imagery is "one of the hottest topics in cognitive psychology, after fifty years of neglect." Under the influence of Watsonian behaviorism, which emphasized thinking as subvocal motor responses and ruled out discussion of conscious experience as non-meaningful and taboo, such phenomena as mental imagery had been judged as "sheer bunk" (Watson, 1928, p. 76). It is noteworthy that Tolman's critique of behavioral learning theory eventually led to the construct of cognitive "maps," a concept which foreshadowed a possible role for some analogue of imagery as an important aspect of cognitive behavior. Milgram's work on mental maps of cities could also be seen as a recognition within social psychology of the importance of such visual analogues in cognitive experience.[4]

With the return of imagery within cognitive psychology as a topic meriting experimental attention, much debate has focused on the role of words or linear propositions versus imagery as central "thinking" modes. Paivio's (1971) model of imagery provided a major alternative to S-R behavioral traditions, proposing two coding systems: a verbal, propositional system which processed information sequentially and a visual system which could process information in simultaneous or parallel fashion. There is considerable insistence, however, that visual modes do not imply any literal, internal picture in the head.[5]

Significant support for cognitive research on imagery as a mode of information processing has come from the work of Kosslyn (1980, 1983) at Harvard. Though emphasizing that imagery represents only one mode of thought among many, and has no "privileged" status (1980, p. 456), Kosslyn insists that imagery is not an epiphenomenon, reducible to other modes of internal representation. He argues that there is "nothing mystical or unscientific about the concept of a 'mental image'" (p. 173), and has designed a computer model for representing, storing, and retrieving visually coded information. In this model images are discussed as "quasi-pictorial" structures for processing information that differ from verbal, propositional modes in being more concrete, spatially oriented, and directly parallel to the data being represented (p. 31). Kosslyn also speaks of surface versus deep levels of image representation, at least somewhat analogous to parallel concepts in verbal, grammatical modes.

The strength of Kosslyn's model lies not only in the careful description of imagery processing in terms of a possible computer model, but in terms of the extensive experimentation that he and related workers have brought to this task. This direction of research has complemented the classic work of Cooper and Shepard (1973), one of the major studies instrumental in returning credibility to the interest in imagery in human information processing. Cooper and Shepard found that the mental rotation of alphabet letters in a experimental task took time proportional to what might occur if participants were actually rotating some mental analogue to an internal image of the letter. While the Cooper and Shepard study should not be used to suggest the presence of literal images in the head, it has stood as a hallmark of research on imagery.[6]

Kosslyn and colleagues have also proceeded in presenting participants with experimental questions which might be processed in visual or verbal modes and studying the conditions under which different strategies appear to be used.[7] Kosslyn has also been interested in exploring a developmental model for visual processing, and tentatively hypothesizes that children compared to adults rely more on visual processing.[8] Finally, in an intriguing and provocative possibility, Kosslyn (1980) suggests that an imagery representational system may serve a role not only in the commonly studied areas of problem solving, learning, or memory, but also as a bridge linking unconscious processes to consciousness, as in Freudian or even perhaps Jungian theory. While Kosslyn does not choose to elaborate much beyond these assertions, his statements represent a remarkable integrative and open-minded approach to the potential exploration of symbolic representational systems of interest historically to clinicians. Kosslyn cautions us, however, that "it is a long road from the present fragment of a theory to one that specifies how this kind of 'symbolic' representation operates" (1980, p. 456).

The clinical experimental interest in imagery as a tool for change has also increased significantly in recent years and representatives of a wide variety of clinical perspectives have become interested in the role of imagery in therapeutic change. As a natural extention of the role of cognitive variables in behavioral approaches to change, imagery has always played an important role even in such traditionally behavioral approaches as desensitization and certainly in the more dramatic form of Stampfl's implosive therapy. Guided imagery techniques have played a role in many forms of humanistic therapy like psychosynthesis, although other approaches insist on the primacy of the client's own imagery as guide to change (e.g., active imagination in Jungian practice and much of Gestalt use of imagery). Imagery is playing more of a role in the human potential movement, in body work, and in sports psychology where athletes receive training via extended fantasy periods of internal mental imaging and skills practice. Imagery has been instrumental in new approaches to healing drawing on visualization, particularly in cancer treatment. Research interest in imagery includes not only eidetic imagery, the rare skill of being able to sustain an image once seen for several minutes, but a much broader range of imagery phenomena. Increased professional attention to mental imagery has also been reflected in collections of empirical research and theory (Sheikh, 1983) and interdisciplinary conferences and workshops on guided imagery for clinicians.[9]

Metaphor and Symbol

A second major area of investigation which has been returned to a position of legitimacy in recent times concerns the role of metaphor itself in human functioning (Ortony, 1979). Metaphor has been defined in a variety of ways in psychological research, though some variation on metaphor as comparison or interaction predominates.[10] Bracketing the debate within linguistic circles regarding the distinction between metaphor and simile, etc., typically psychologists investigating such phenomena have included all forms of speech which draw from analogy under the rubric of metaphor.[11] Much of the work in this area has involved calling attention to the importance of metaphorical thought in human experience as a legitimate if somewhat different form of thinking typical of human cognitive thought. Much work has been directed at the problem of studying metaphorical, figurative modes and demonstrating that many of the same techniques used in studying the formation and decoding of literal propositions can be applied to metaphor (Kreisler, 1982). Metaphorical thought need not lie outside the domain of psychological investigation (Ortony, Reynolds, & Arter, 1978).

Perhaps the greatest challenge to those interested in metaphor as a field of study has been to establish the importance and pervasiveness of this mode in human thought. Thus Leary (1990b) demonstrates that in the history of science and the social sciences, metaphors have been borrowed back and forth from society to science. For example, Newton drew from the idea of social solidarity or "sociability" in devising his concept of gravity, a concept which once formed was then borrowed back again to explain social structure in terms of physical gravity. Metaphors have been important in the natural and biological sciences, in Descartes' use of a mechanistic model of automatons to understand the human organism itself, and in Freud's abundant use of metaphors from physics and biology. Metaphors can have both visual and verbal components, and different metaphors may encourage totally different ways of conceptualizing the same set of data. L. D. Smith (1990) adds a provocative argument regarding the impossibility of avoiding metaphor even in those theoretical positions which decried metaphor. In a kind of a tour-de-force, Smith calls attention to the presence of metaphor in logical positivist writing and the work of "neobehaviorists" Hull, Skinner, and Tolman. Biofeedback metaphors as well as modern computer analogies and recent holographic models of mind/brain functions (Pribram, 1990) are further examples of the role of metaphor in psychology. The pervasiveness and importance of metaphors in the history of psychological theory and research on motivation, emotion, cognition, and abnormal behavior also have received excellent documentation and discussion in Leary (1990a).[12]

Metaphor is not solely the province of linguists, psycholinguists, and theorists. It is also the language of everyday speech, although people differ of course in the extent to which they engage in metaphor, especially in a culture which does not provide explicit training and encouragement in these modes. Lakoff and Johnson (1980) call attention to the wealth of metaphors by which American culture represents such basic experience as time, thought, love, and many other realms of experience. In contrast to more linear, quantitative, literal, observable and detached ways of describing experience, metaphor uses one thing or aspect to understand another in a symbolic way, yielding an affective understanding as well as a cognitive one. Metaphor is couched in imagery and feeling as much as it is a purely rational process; metaphor reveals in subtle ways that skirt around the fringes of reality, surrounding an idea rather than pointing a finger straight at one particular aspect of interest. Thus, we might linearly discuss time in terms of seconds, minutes, lifespan, historical dates, holidays, appointment times, or we might speak of time flying, dragging, flowing like a river, ebbing, branching into alternative worlds, or time as money to be spent, wasted, "borrowed," "lost," or bought (pp. 7–9). In similar fashion, we might operationalize love as the amount of time spent together, the number of communications exchanged, the amount of time engaged in mutual eye contact, or we might metaphorically speak of love in terms of raging fires of passion, disease metaphors of pain, lovesickness, pining away, or "journey" metaphors for love relationships: being "at a crossroads," "not going anywhere," "spinning . . . wheels," "off the track" (pp. 44–45, 49, 141).

Contrast linear expressions of brain physiology and brain waves with the wealth of metaphorical expressions for mind: those emphasizing spatial locations (storehouse of knowledge, nothing upstairs, rooms, filing cabinets, library card files); conception, as in the brain-child; the mind as "machine" (cranking out, grinding out, "little rusty," "running out of steam"); mind as "brittle object" (easily broken, "crushed," "shattered," "going to pieces"); ideas as "food for thought," leaving "a bad taste," spoon-fed, simmering; ideas as "plants" (coming "to fruition," "budding," having "many branches," "a fertile imagination"); and ideas as "commodities" in the intellectual marketplace (pp. 27–28, 46–48). Lakoff and Johnson note also the abundance of war, conflict and competitive metaphors in discussing modern society, and we might add the organic metaphors of life, death, crisis, and turning points which have begun to characterize discussion of change.

The challenge for psychology has been to become aware of the profound and broad presence of metaphor in human speech and conceptualizing and to regain an appreciation for thinking via metaphor in human functioning. We have been slow to see the importance of metaphor in daily experience rather than merely as a tool of expressive rhetoric. The profoundly "metaphorical character of psychological life" has been elaborated most extensively by Romanyshyn (1982, p. 143) in his phenomenological account not only of psychological functioning, but also of the birth of psychology as a field, its paradigms and construction of reality. Research on metaphor also plays an exciting role in extending cognitive theory in ways adequate to account for the human capacity to create metaphor (MacCormac, 1985). Research on metaphoric capacities and deficits associated with different patterns of brain damage, as well as with schizophrenic and borderline states, suggests a promising tie to ongoing research on brain/mind functioning.[13]

Another area of research has focused on developmental studies of metaphor use through the lifespan, with Gardner and Winner's (1978, 1982) work an early example. The interpretation of metaphor appears to be a skill that increases somewhat parallel to the ability of children to engage in ever more abstract modes of thought, with four-year-old children already possessing some "rudimentary metaphorical competence" (Vosniadou & Ortony, 1983, p. 154). As predicted by Ortony, Reynolds, and Arter (1978), research on the development of metaphoric competence has proliferated (Vosniadou, 1987), addressing a range of issues that help clarify some of the paradoxes of widespread spontaneous metaphor use in preschoolers, yet difficulties or inconsistencies among this group in metaphor interpretation in research settings (Gentner, 1988, p. 47). Continuing research has served to further refine criteria for identifying metaphorical use in children, and at times brought previous findings into question.[14]

Metaphor has been gaining attention in clinical work in conjunction with the growing importance of imagery and other symbolic, analogic modes of communicating (Haley, 1976; see also Watzlawick, 1978). Metaphor and the related concept of models are specifically emphasized in Neuro-Linguistic Programming. This approach emphasizes that humans form cognitive maps or models which represent their experiences of the world according to their preferred modalities for taking in and representing information, e.g., visually, auditorially, kinesthetically. Models are distinct from the 'reality' they represent, however.[15] Drawing an analogy between surface versus deep structure in linguistic grammar, Bandler and Grinder (1975) suggest that the surface structures, used by a client in talking about his or her world, are clues to the type of deep structure or fundamental model by which that person's world of assumptions is organized. The person can be assumed to be making the best choices based on their current model of alternatives, and the task of therapy is to help the person widen their model of reality to allow more options for viewing, experiencing, and acting in the world.

In this view, therapy is a process of challenging and rebuilding models, and metaphor can be a conscious tool toward exploring ways for expanding models. Metaphor and storytelling are modes of communication broad enough to allow clients to listen and fill in concrete details from their own experience, thereby enriching their understanding of the issue being explored. Metaphor seems connected to that part of a person often called "the unconscious," and thus allows access to change on many levels (Gordon, 1978). The very definition of primary process thinking comes very close to image-based, preverbal, analogical or metaphorical thinking. A range of other related approaches to metaphor use in therapy, including ones indebted to Milton Erickson, are described by Barker (1985).[16]

In the clinical fields, nowhere are the role and power of metaphor so amply demonstrated, however, than in their very capacity to define and create the categories of "psychopathology" and "mental illness" that characterize our present diagnostic system. In their controversial arguments, Sarbin (1990) and Szasz (1961) trace the way in which unwanted or deviant behavior becomes treated in "as if" fashion by an analogy with physical illness, partly in response to the humane desire to help suffering people. The metaphorical transform on nonconforming behavior then becomes reified as "mental illness," hysteria, or schizophrenia, unleashing a whole set of social roles both for patient and therapeutic agent, with tremendous social consequences.[17]

Creativity

The relationship between imagery, metaphor, creativity, and imagination is another area receiving current attention in psychology (Forisha, 1983; Rothenberg, 1979). Imagery has a long association with art and creativity, and some of the earlier proposals of imagery as a form of visual thinking came from work in the arts. Visual thinking is receiving more attention as a complement to linear thinking styles, and an aid to breaking through creative blocks or facilitating problem solving. Skills in working with analogy appear as critical and remediable components of intellectual functioning. Computer capabilities have augmented the role of imagery in facilitating imagination in science and other areas.[18]

In addition to its relevance to problem solving and creativity, other more clinically related implications of imagery have been explored. Imagery and imagination facilitate not only cognitive and social areas in child development, but affective learning as well, helping a child develop a sense of confidence and identity, regulate emotions and arousal, learn to delay gratification, and handle stress (Tower, 1983). The importance of daydreaming and accompanying imagery as cognitive/emotional tools for planning, creativity, and other dimensions of mental health has also been documented in adults (J. L. Singer, 1975). Rather than a sign of aberrance, daydreaming can instead be seen as a rich internal skill enabling internal processing of material. Giambra (1974) notes that the majority of daydreams in adult men are focused on problem solving, suggesting their direct relevance to daily coping.

Imagery has also received emphasis as part of the renewed interest in fantasy, make-believe and imagination. Play as an important facilitator of cognitive development (Bruner, Jolly, & Sylva, 1976) has also been described as foundational to the process of scientific experimentation (Bronowski, 1978).[19] Fantasy and imaginative components can be seen in children's play, and possible implications of imaginative skills in play and creativity for healthy psychological functioning are also receiving attention.[20] If play provides the child with opportunities for cognitive development via imagery, an adult equivalent may involve the role of creative visualization. Increasingly, in fact, the role of visualization has become a popular topic in books describing tools for self-change (Gawain, 1978).

Cognition and Emotions

Metaphor and symbol are often described in terms of feeling-filled imagery or affect-laden thought, suggesting the importance of both cognition and emotion in an understanding of their impact. While emotion has received attention in the history of psychology, and is informed by a wide variety of metaphors (Averill, 1990), it has often been subordinated to the importance of cognitive processes within the field of cognitive psychology. Much of modern psychological theory on the relationship between emotions and cognition has been profoundly influenced by the important role for cognition in the labeling of emotions in Schachter and Singer's (1962) classic study.[21] Participants receiving injections unidentified as epinephrine apparently looked to the modeled emotional behavior of experimenter confederates for cognitive clues to interpreting their own unexplained arousal as a specific emotion of euphoria or anger. Affect has tended to be considered a response that follows substantial cognitive judgment, although the precise theoretical relationship has been profusely debated.

Zajonc (1980) in a provocative argument proposes and defends instead the case for the separate functioning of affective and cognitive systems, with affective systems having the capacities for immediate and possibly more rapid response than cognitive systems. This model has been challenged by Lazarus (1982) who argues that rudimentary cognitive processes begin to mediate emotional responses at points far earlier than the full-blown cognitive judgments Zajonc refers to in defending the separation of the two systems. The debate has continued (Zajonc, 1984; Lazarus, 1984), with Lazarus (1991) increasingly clarifying a possible role for modes of unconscious appraisal.

What seems most important in Zajonc's research, however, is the growing respectability and interest in the emotional judgment pattern per se and his effort to give it an important role if not absolute primacy in terms of human mind/brain processes. Symbol, metaphor and image appear to be highly related to emotion as well as cognition, and the emotional component has an importance in human thought and experience that cannot be fully ruled out or replaced by sheer rational intellect. Thus the importance of emotion as a research topic within the field of cognitive psychology, which already carries the danger of focusing too exclusively on rational problem solving, seems an important sign of openness to new types of experience as psychologically valid and researchable. And if Zajonc errs in exaggerating the separation of feeling and cognition, he has made a substantial contribution in stressing just how powerfully and immediately the emotional response system moves into action and how important it is to trace its discriminations ("preferenda") if we are to fully understand human judgment (Zajonc, 1980, p. 159).

Left and Right Hemispheric Functioning

An area of mind/brain research drawing extensive attention to nonlinear modes of processing information as a potential within brain functioning comes from the widely discussed split-brain experimentation. These research findings generated hypotheses regarding two different modes of knowing or skills in information processing represented by left and right hemisphere functioning. The left hemisphere, which governs the right side of the body in terms of motor functions, houses the speech center in the majority of right-handed adults, and is associated with linear, sequential modes of information processing such as that typified by language and mathematical formulations. The right hemisphere, governing the left side of the body, has been characterized as processing information in a holistic, simultaneous way and demonstrates special skills in pattern recognition and spatial judgments.

These two different types of information processing suggested by the initial work of Sperry, Gazzaniga, and others provided for Ornstein (1972, 1973) a metaphor for extending and validating a wider range of modes of consciousness than was currently accepted within mainstream psychology. He analogized these differences in left and right hemisphere functioning to contrasts between a number of other polarities, for example: the contrast of active, controlling, manipulating consciousness and receptive, holistic, intuitive modes (Deikman, 1973).[22] In a new metaphor for consciousness, the capacity for two different and equally legitimate modes of consciousness operative within the human brain could be seen as a model and argument for the importance of both these modes of knowing within the process of science and psychology itself. Neither mode was to be judged superior to the other, and psychology was challenged to find valid room for the holistic, intuitive realm of hunch and image within the normal process of theory building and scientific investigation. The role of left hemisphere functioning, in accounting for inputs from a variety of subsystems within us including the right hemisphere, provided even a potential model for coping with the effects of "unconscious processes" within brain functioning (Gazzaniga, 1983a).

The interest in hemispheric functioning has generated considerable research (Springer & Deutsch, 1981), and thus has played a very valuable heuristic role in cognitive psychology. In addition, the extension of the right and left hemisphere metaphor offered a stimulating and important critique of current psychological practice in its time, and has made an important contribution in broadening the scope of inquiry both in terms of the content studied by psychology and the acceptability of a variety of steps and intellectual processes in the pursuit of knowledge. However, the metaphor and subsequent popular extensions of the right-brain/left-brain terminology erred in a particularly dangerous way in neglecting to stress the fact that the separation of functions in each hemisphere was found in persons for whom the corpus collosum was severed. That the two hemispheres actually function separately in an intact brain was highly improbable, and much controversy has been surfacing to address these and other oversimplifications.[23] Kinsbourne (1982), for example, stresses the importance of the two hemispheres' activities as reciprocal parts of the same global activity, separated as opponent processes to prevent mutual interference within such close proximity, but simultaneously active in contributing to one overall process. The emphasis is on specialization as a way to allow harmonious relationship between components of one activity, rather than the more popular stress on the two hemispheres functioning in terms of two totally different types of activities. Unity and coordination of component parts in total functioning is the metaphor which is more accurate to brain evolution and function.

Mind/Brain Models

Research on mind/brain paradigms, perhaps more than other areas of recent psychological theorizing and research, draws extensively on metaphor as a tool for conceptualizing, and therefore speaks to the importance of metaphor in scientific process. "Mental metaphors" used in psychology over the years from 1894 to 1975 show a U-shaped curve in overall frequency, with metaphors least common in the middle years 1925–1945, a phenomenon probably reflecting the dominance of behaviorism during that time (Gentner & Grudin, 1985). There has been a decreasing emphasis on "animate-being" and "spatial" metaphors and a significant increase in a variety of "systems" metaphors. Classical Cartesian brain/mind dualism is receiving challenge, and advances in physiological psychology have opened up relationships between cognitive psychology and physiological research, so that models developed in one field can be tested and explored from the perspectives of the other. Considerable examples exist of the relationship between cognitive metaphors and theory or research on memory, pattern recognition, perception, and attention (Hoffman, Cochran, & Nead, 1990).

Pribram has been one of the chief theorists and researchers to address the history of changes in analogy, metaphor, and models used in describing human mind/brain functioning, changes reflected in his own work.[24] An early historical model came almost exclusively from communications and information-processing theory, provided by such inventions as the telephone. Thus researchers began to talk of bits of information, channel capacity, noise in the system, etc. A second emerging model drew from cybernetics and the concept of the thermostat. Cybernetics, with its simultaneous emphasis on information feedback and homeostasis, provided a model still very much alive in the concepts of systems theory. Cybernetics feedback models were incorporated to some extent in computer models which continue to dominate much current thinking on brain/mind functioning.

The computer metaphor, with its related vocabulary of information processing, feature analysis, software programs, and reprogramming has filtered not only into scientific models but into popular speech and has been very compatible with current cognitive psychology paradigms. Miller, Galanter, and Pribram's (1960) classic book, *Plans and the Structure of Behavior,* gave impetus to this movement and recent speculation and reformulation of old mind/brain/self controversies are couched often within the framework of computer analogies and models. The computer metaphor has proven to be extremely heuristic, stimulating not only empirical research but considerable theorizing and debate regarding the nature of the self and mind/brain issues.[25] Its chief neglect has been to forget the extent to which computer analogies are embedded in cybernetics assumptions in explaining organism-environment interactions.

A model which brings back the sense of embeddedness of mind/brain functioning within a larger systems model, and reflects great compatibility with the metaphors of modern physics, is provided by Pribram's work on the holographic model in brain/mind functioning.[26] A hologram results from the interaction pattern formed when two sets of vibrating fields intersect, as when for example one throws two pebbles in a pool, or when one illuminates one object from two different light sources or directions. The hologram represents a special kind of mathematical summary of this pattern information called a Fourier transform. In a holographic pattern or transform, most commonly seen in a holographic picture formed by split laser light, the essential pattern is coded throughout the image such that each fragment bears the imprint of the whole pattern. Recognizing the importance of Lashley's (1950) work suggesting the nonlocalization of memory in the brain, the hologram provided a stimulating analogy for explaining not only this phenomena but others as well. In the holographic model, Fourier transforms of incoming stimulus input are encoded and stored holographically; the brain becomes a receptive field for receiving pattern input and the patterns are enfolded in a sense within the entire brain field.

The holographic model changes not only our understandings of brain/mind functioning, but may also imply that the entire realm of external reality might be composed of vibrational fields rather than objects in the traditional sense (Wilber, 1982). This concept relates to Bohm's work in physics on the "implicate order" of the universe, a hypothesized dimension or level of reality existing as a kind of dynamic backdrop, implicit in sensory-based or "explicate" reality.[27] In this wider perspective, the brain becomes a lens capable of receiving impressions of fields in the surrounding universe, and one might go so far as to say that the distinction between individual brain as receptive field and the universe as field becomes "blurred" (Pribram, 1980, p. 34). Pribram, however, is explicit about the inadequacy of models in and of themselves; he urges repeatedly the necessity of following up the creation of a model with the thorough testing of its properties and feasibility in laboratory settings. He proceeds to test the holistic and holographic model, committed to experimental precision, yet hoping to correct for the dangers of "pre-(s)cission, the analytic severing of part from part" (p. 34).

Consciousness Research

The return of consciousness as an acceptable term and content for psychological investigation has been a hallmark of recent psychology, and psychologists have directed increasing attention to its importance within the field.[28] Sperry (1988) goes so far as to argue that the mentalist paradigm that legitimizes the study of "inner experience" (p. 607) opens up new possibilities for dialogue between such fields as science and religion. As Hilgard (1983) reminds, however, consciousness never entirely disappeared from the place of importance it once held in structuralism, for such currents as functionalism and William James' contributions to the importance of consciousness never entirely disappeared. This was true particularly within the more clinical fields of psychology, but also within research on sleep and dreaming (Dement, 1976; Cartwright, 1978) and

Hilgard's (1977) own work on hypnosis. What seems clear, however, is that while the field of cognitive psychology may be opening itself to the possibilities of exploring consciousness, being itself a newcomer to a place of legitimacy, it is likely to be cautious in its approach.[29] Consciousness research is thus likely to focus on phenomena and concepts related to existing subfields of cognitive psychology such as attention, brain/mind models, relationships between cognition and feeling, and mind/body issues.

There exists within the field of transpersonal psychology, however, a considerable amount of theoretical analysis and research on a much broader range of states of consciousness than those traditionally receiving attention.[30] Tart's (1975a) proposal for the development of a state-specific science, a highly trained modern version of introspection for exploring different states of consciousness, represents an alternative methodology for exploring such domains. Much work in the field remains theoretical and speculative, as in Jaynes' (1976) tracing of the concepts of consciousness and the individual self as the evolution of a metaphor, missing in ancient peoples. Work, however, is shifting toward the experimental context, as cognitive psychology begins to provide an increasingly accepted model for a rigorous combination of openness to theory and commitment to empirical research.

An area of consciousness research reflective of a dramatic increase in empirical attention can be seen in the research on meditation. In studies directed at a range of meditation techniques and using different methodologies, researchers have found changes in a variety of physiological and psychological variables associated with experience in meditation, although the research record is not without controversy.[31]

Metaphor, Cognitive Imagery, and Educational Psychology

The cognitive value of metaphor in learning is emerging as a topic for educational theory and discussion,[32] and metaphor has been argued to play an important and useful role as a tool for organizing information and facilitating new understandings (Sticht, 1979). Visual imagery and nonlinear modes of presenting and processing information also have been receiving increased attention with respect to possible roles in facilitating learning. The use of imagery in mnemonic devices to enhance memory storage and retrieval has been a classic topic in introductory psychology textbooks and has been emphasized in foreign language learning (Delaney, 1978). Greater recognition of visual modes holds promise for individualizing teaching strategies to better meet the needs of a variety of nonlinear learning styles, as well as offering more visual strategies for teaching problem solving (Kosslyn, 1983). Experimental evidence from a variety of sources suggests the importance of such factors as visual analogies, textbooks using words high in imagery, and imagery strategies of problem solving for enhancing learning or other desired outcomes such as originality.[33]

Within the lecture format itself, the importance of visual modes of organizing and presenting information has also been receiving increasing emphasis. The use of pictorial or graphic modes in lecture notes, or diagrams in teaching, can provide alternatives to traditional linear organization for both teacher and student. Explicit use of models and analogies also seems to promote clearer understanding of theory for students.[34] Hampden-Turner (1981) makes extensive use of visual models, for example, in his survey of central theories and systems in psychology, *Maps of the Mind.* Such visual and diagram approaches may have fruitful implications for the teaching of a wide range of cognitive fields. In classes in Theories of Personality, for example, where students have been assigned the task of creating drawings or diagrams to represent major concepts of personality theorists and demonstrate how these concepts are interrelated, exciting implications for learning are suggested by qualitative impressions of the students' work and students' own reports (Olds, 1985). The potential benefits of adding an imagery-rich dimension to traditional and linear cognitive approaches to material seems an area worthy of further experimental attention.

Conclusion

While we will proceed in later chapters to a summary and analysis of the role of metaphor in personality theory and clinical psychology, with special emphasis on the emergence of the unifying metaphor provided by systems theory, the work in cognitive and experimental psychology on imagery, metaphor, and related areas of nonlinear thinking provides a ground and backdrop by which to measure progress in understanding the importance of metaphor and symbol in psychology. Without the balance provided by significant growth in experimental openness to broader methodologies and content areas, much of the fruitful clinical and theoretical exploration of metaphor would risk an existence cut off from significant dialogue with mainstream psychology. It seems particularly noteworthy that trends in the traditionally separated fields of experimental and clinical psychology are providing a common ground for unity in conceptualization and research strategy, made possible in large part by the growing dominance of cognitive over strict behavioral models. Thus, when such writers as Capra (1982) decry outmoded Newtonian models in the practice of psychology, we can go much further than a simple plea for diffuse holism in psychological theory and practice. Psychology already offers an emerging history of concern with broader models than S-R behaviorism. The emphasis on metaphor, symbol, and nonlinear modes is part of a larger sensitivity to the demands of a more comprehensive science addressing the complex interrelated variables characteristic of human behavior and experience.

Part Two

FLESH AND TISSUE

PROLOGUE

It is midnight. The stars are so bright they almost cast shadows on the black waters. Not too far away dark shapes toss in the warm wind, silhouettes of palm trees. It is an hour for wonder as the tropical night sky embraces the questions of the mind, somehow embodying them with a new density and significance. The sky always asks the largest questions.

They are the old familiar questions from the evenings back home, when a quick glimpse up at the heavens seemed to give a breath of pause in a day too filled with human scale. Yet here, in the tropics, where vacation days roll back at night to uncover the great emptinesses, here is where the questions are imprinted in my mind. Perhaps when one need not bundle up against the cold, where you can sit on the damp sand and feel into the night, here there is time to get lost in the skies, the wonder, the infinite stretches away from this warm, green planet. There is no teacher of time and space as great as the evening sky, no greater prompter to the question why, no greater courier to the sense of majesty, of great and small, no greater dwarfer of one's own significance. Yet comforted in the sand and balmy air, one can perhaps forgive the ache and turn back to the melody.

The wonder of the tropical sky is that by night it pulls one to the universe, by day it draws you back again to the earth, in a giant rhythm and cycle of life. If we seek shelter from the sun, it is in the opulence and extravagence of a jungle of living forms, orchids breathing air, and moist verdant earth. Everywhere water seems to be in transformation through patterns of life and sound and fragrance. Waterfalls spill from heights of hazy green, against cliffs whose skin still shows the folds of creation. Water is busy getting back to being water, passing through the air, the plants, the moisture on our bodies, back to the ocean and the sea. We share in the process as carriers of droplets, salt water on its way home, passing through the profusion of organic forms we call the world.

The wonder is also that nature is so munificent, so lavish with detail, with color, sight, and shape. Each seashell bears the markings of gratuitous splendor, of unnecessary design and beauty. Who would have thought the world could be so spectacular and abundant in variety and form. Shapes curl in spirals, etched with bands of coloring, offering sheer delight as they founder on early morning beaches after a more functional lifetime in other service. Recycling in reverse, the sea brings its refuse to the soil, a peaceful exchange for the returning rains that drop past pollen, plant, and earth to bring minerals and molecules back to the sea mother of us all. Stars, shells, sand, and seed—a living museum of wonder and time, following the cycles of the night and day in unceasing succession.

Chapter Four
METAPHORS FOR THE SELF

Metaphors can be understood as ways of imaging reality, or portraying in concept, image or symbol something about the nature of what one is trying to understand or express. As we have seen, metaphors intervene often as analogies, models taken from one aspect of experience, attempting to bridge a gap or see something new in another field. Metaphors are the language of the inexpressible or difficult to express. They are the "as if" language of the imagination or search for truth. Metaphors have been suspect in contemporary psychology under the influence of behaviorism for they hint at possible ungraspable terrain, at tentativeness in the pursuit of knowledge, at choice of perspectives in interpreting reality. Yet although they may sound elusive, metaphors serve to construct the framework of what is claimed as real. Metaphors are the tools of the overriding concept, the backbone of the bottom line, the blueprint for the blueprints. And metaphors and models are often the last to be seen by those who frame them, so deeply embedded are they in support of the system they hold together.

For personality theorists, the central metaphors are the metaphors for self—an array of constructs, concepts, images, and vocabulary to describe what is essentially human in life. The concept of metaphor applied to the field of personality theory is a surprisingly new perspective on a very old phenomenon, beginning to receive attention.[1] Metaphors of self span a variety of viewpoints. Some theorists turn to cognitive dimensions and the conscious ego for a central theme; others choose the concept of identity, the self as an answer, a commentary on who we are. Existentialists and related thinkers turn instead to the primacy of active process in defining selfing, refusing to objectify through nouns the sense of human agency, an active choosing process of becoming. For others the focal theme is wholeness, understood in a variety of ways, all of which stretch, challenge, or embed the concept of individual self in the direction or context of a larger wholeness. In still other perspectives, the self as active process or as participative in a larger whole gives way paradoxically to the metaphor of no-self.

Such metaphorical understandings of the self are by no means universal in psychology, however. In the history of psychology, a critical step was taken when the focus and methodology of structuralism was challenged and replaced by the growing school of behaviorism. Rather than study the contents and structure of consciousness via the rigorous internal observation and analysis of introspection, behaviorists focused instead on external behavior, stimuli and response chains, and brought the experimental method to a position of dominance as adjudicator of significant findings. Words and concepts like "mind," "feeling," "mental" became unnecessary explanatory fictions (Skinner, 1971). The critical events in understanding and explaining behavior were argued to be external to the organism, reflecting interactions between behavior and environmental consequences in the presence of external stimuli. By setting perceptual priorities, behaviorism sharpened the focus for analysis; and explanatory, predictive power and control were also increased.

In Skinner's view, "self" as a nonbehavioral term is void of meaning, to be eliminated, along with id, instinct, unconscious, anxiety, mind, and free will, as mentalisms, intervening constructs which are essentially unobservable. For Skinner (1983), it is not so much that feelings, for example, are nonexistent, but they are irrelevant to examining what is central in human life and behavior. They are unnecessary for explaining the causation of human behavior. It is misleading to focus on a concept like self as a locus of change for the individual; instead one needs to focus on the reinforcing consequences or contingencies which shape behavior, not on any hypothesized inner motivation. "Self knowledge" is only valuable as an awareness of one's own typical reinforcement contingencies.

In *Beyond Freedom and Dignity,* Skinner (1971, p. 189) refers to "a self" as "a repertoire of behavior appropriate to a given set of contingencies." Identity results from a pattern of similar contingencies over a span of time. We can explain what people do on the basis of observing reinforcing consequences that follow behavior. It is fallacious to give credit or blame in explaining behavior to individual or internal causation. We must proceed therefore to design better environments, reinforcements, and technologies of behavior, not better human beings with stronger senses of self. We must not attempt to make humans more "moral," for example, but set up reinforcers to induce and reward desired behavior. Note despite the emphasis on the power of the environment in shaping human behavior, that Skinner provides a model of essential individuality based on each person's unique pattern and history of contingencies, and in addition offers us a profoundly optimistic vision of social and behavioral change. If we are controlled by the environment, it is an environment largely of our own making and potential remaking.

Despite actively denying the validity of self metaphors, radical behaviorism was not able to avoid metaphor altogether.[2] The result of the classical behavioral approach was a rather focused, stripped down, tangible vision of the human being, a kind of skeleton of behavior and responses, interacting at least in part in a billiard ball universe. In this view, actions do have reactions, but there are no causal actors or agents, only antecedents and consequents ticking off their own kind of impersonal karma. It is a marvelously simplified, austere and clean lined world, an abstraction from internal complexity which still carries much respect for detail. The eye indeed can be trained to perceive behavior pathways, tracks, and lines of action much like a flow chart of city traffic, an x-ray of body movement, or an interstate road map. It is an extraordinarily useful road map, in fact, as long as you are interested in getting to the destinations described by its map. Behaviorism brought a language system and a new currency (complete with tokens) to allow one to function in the new culture/worldview independently of outmoded models. Like its modern and more complex counterpart, Neuro-Linguistic Programming, behaviorism offered a new way of seeing, a new method for organizing and differentiating foreground and background. Like its Western roots, it was agentic, goal-oriented, pragmatic and as with most forms of science—utilitarian and useful, interested in prediction, control, and potential change.

The behavioral setting we have inherited is a tremendous gift. Its very simplicity and elegance is a reminder of the way in which theory directs vision, language guides perception of relevance, and constructs structure what we will accept as data. Although less often examined with reference to behaviorism itself, the reminder of the danger of constructs in diverting attention and in creating false premises is an important teaching of behaviorism. Nowhere in psychology is this reminder perhaps as relevant as in our constructs about the human "self." It is no wonder that behaviorists recognized this construct as construct, perceived it as unuseful and vague, and operationalized what they perceived to be its essence as a sum total of interconnected and reinforced stimulus-response bonds, ever changing in response to environmental stimulation and consequence. In this model there is no self (Skinner, 1990, p. 1209); there is no fixed essence. The multitude of subjective emotions, feelings, needs, wants experienced by most humans was only to be considered so much chaff, noise, flack in the system. The important thing was to train and keep the eye on what a person does—if you are truly to understand or change them.

The self as construct, however, did not disappear. In fact, in the hermeneutical and constructivist tradition gaining influence in psychology, the construction and interpretation of the self becomes a central focus for understanding.[3] Cross-cultural awareness of the diversity of self-understandings again echo and enhance this emphasis on the self as constructed against a sociohistorical background.[4] The self is a very persistent fiction, a powerful model in the history of being human. To live "as if" we were a sum total of responses and consequences is a powerful and useful model in its own way, but it is only one model, one metaphor. Alternative metaphors do not thereby disappear. As we have noted, the role of metaphor in determining choice of theory in psychology until recently has been a relatively unexplored area, but current psychology is beginning to stretch its metaphors. Terms like consciousness are beginning to be heard lurking in cognitive psychology laboratories; cognition itself is very much in vogue, the new bride of behaviorism. Systems theory, cybernetics and chaos models, holograms, modern nuclear physics, depth psychologies, and research on imagery and cognitive styles are beginning to jostle against each other in currents like floes of ice broken off the melting glacier of alternatives frozen by behaviorism. Metaphors long dormant in the field of psychology, although still active in other areas, are thawing, stretching, and making their way to claim relevance.

For personality theorists, the central metaphors clamoring for dignity and attention are the metaphors for self, and it is to this exploration that we turn now, as a way of setting the scene for the powerful relevance of systems models of the self. Although offering a wide range of insights for reconceptualizing humans, nature, and issues of ultimate reality, nowhere is the impact of systems theory so direct and telling as in its challenge to most reigning metaphors of the self. These currently competing metaphors of the self deserve closer attention in order to note more clearly in chapters 5 and 6 the radical implications of a systems metaphor based on interrelatedness.

What have various theorists meant by their metaphors for self? What aspects of being human have they tried to capture, to portray? And what about those theoretical approaches which have argued against the relevance of this metaphor, who have raised in its stead the metaphor of non-self, no-self? In what different but powerful ways can behaviorism, Eastern thought, and systems theory, as we shall see later, be seen to dissolve the metaphor of self and thus share ironically in a kind of provocative vision for Western psychology?

If we examine in depth the concepts of "self" present in major approaches to personality and learning, it is possible to abstract some areas of priority or qualities of self judged most essential by each theorist. It is important to note, too, that not all theorists even use the term self. The very choice of terms by which to describe concepts central to personality becomes itself a critical issue. Thus when I use the term "self" in this general way, I am referring to the variety of responses posed by each theorist to the questions: "Who are we? What is most essential to know about being human?" It remains immensely difficult to even raise these abstract questions without dragging along a variety of presuppositions. Perhaps that is why the search for the right question has been at least if not more critical in the search for knowledge than the search for a series of answers.

Self as Rational Ego

One of the first approaches to self metaphors we encounter places emphasis on the mental and cognitive capacities of the human being, the ego functions as they are termed in modern psychoanalytic terminology. Who are we? We are essentially beings who struggle to perceive, to test reality against the oppressive and insatiable demands of both unconscious needs and internalized social rules. It may perhaps seem surprising to recognize Freudian concepts within a section on the importance of the rational ego, for Freud is known widely as the champion of the unconscious dimensions of life. Typically and accurately, Freud is seen as portraying the essential human predicament as an eternal conflict between a tripartite division of psychic energy consisting of id, ego, and superego. The dynamic tension and conflict between these three forces becomes the structurer of personality.

For Freud (1965, p. 65), the id referred to "the dark, inaccessible part" of us, the chaotic realm of instinctual libido and thanatos, the "cauldron full of seething excitations." For the id there was no recognition of time, or moral judgment, of good or evil. The instincts pressed for immediate expression according to the pleasure principle, seeking gratification by wish fulfillment and incapable of formulating any distinction between means to a desired end other than the spontaneous image of primary process thinking. The id remains largely unconscious, embedded within the individual as an essential guarantor of absolute inviolable primacy of instinct against any encroachments from civilization's rules and sanctions (Rieff, 1961). For Freud, the ego evolved in the service of the id as the system capable of assisting in the differentiation of reality from fantasy, capable therefore of discriminating effective means of gratification from purely wish fulfillments. The necessary capacity for delay to enable such discriminations becomes an important hallmark of secondary process thinking or reality testing. With the development of the superego as the successful resolution to oedipal conflicts, the child internalizes the rules of society through identification with its parents and carries within itself its own trigger for obedience or repercussions through guilt. With the appearance of the superego, the ego receives an upgrading of duties, a new job description to include the arbitration and mediation of potential conflicts between id and superego demands. Thus the ego with its functions of problem solving, organizing, control, and perception, becomes the agent of compromise, protecting the organism through a delicate process of balanced frustrations and disguised gratifications in the form of defense mechanisms.

The emphasis with Freud is always on the drama of this tension and orchestration between conflicting forces within us, and it is his genius that he relied on a tripartite division of energy rather than a simple dichotomy of consciousness and unconsciousness to suggest the struggle of being human (Rieff, 1961). Yet while Freud certainly placed emphasis on the power and provinces where unconscious processes held sway, his central appeal was to the hope of the ego functions, the third-party negotiator of the opposition of id and superego, the dogged heroic agency that struggled against ultimate impossibility in order that rationality and consciousness could gain some foothold against an unconsciously ruled life. In Freud's (1965, p. 71) famous metaphor of "draining" the Zuider Zee, the task of analysis and perhaps even life were described with the aphorism: "Where id was, there ego shall be." And it is in this sense that Freud's metaphors for self can be seen to privilege the rational ego.

Despite Freud's emphasis on the derivation of the ego from the defensive service of the id, and the ego's consequent and inextricable involvement in unconscious conflict, it is his very emphasis on the ego's critical role that has become the greatest legacy for modern psychoanalytic theory. The articulation of the ego functions, i.e., problem solving, organizing, and cognitive adapting, became primary with the ego psychologists like Hartmann and even with Erikson and his stress on the adaptive ego in society. Hartmann's idea of a conflict-free ego sphere, a dimension of conscious, rational thought not in the service of unconscious need, brought psychoanalytic theory more into dialogue with theorists like Allport, who stressed the conscious determinants of personality almost exclusively, or Kelly, whose portrayal of the human is almost totally a cognitive one.[5] Modern object relations theory has moved also in an increasingly cognitive direction, with more and more compatibility with the insights of Piaget's theory of cognitive schemes as essential developmental markers (Rizutto, 1979). Object relations theory stresses the importance of the first "objects" of emotional attachment and awareness, usually the mother or primary caretaker of the child. The critical issue of early development becomes the process of separating one's early ego consciousness from these objects of attachment.

Self as Identity

For other theorists, the central metaphor of self is not consciousness but identity. For them, the question "Who are we?" in fact already poses the critical issue as one of identity. The "self" is an answer, a commentary on who we are essentially. We need to know centrally how we hold together. For Allport (1955), the central question of our lives has to do with the unity and uniqueness of who we are, and he gave the term propriate functions to those aspects of our experience or behavior which give us a sense of distinctness, by which we recognize ourselves. Kohut, too, argued that Freud had left no term for central identity. By analyzing our behavior into id, ego, and superego components, he neglected a construct for totality, for total me-ness, a concept Kohut reintroduces in his use of the term "self." Kohut (1977) argues that the sense of identity or self evolves in parallel to an evolving sense of a separate "other," without which the person is trapped in narcissistic inability to be independent, whole, and validated in separate selfhood. The profound shift from experienced unity and oneness with the mother to this sense of separateness is a process facilitated by the child's capacity for the formation of transitional objects, such as the cherished teddy bear, which can carry both a sense of self and of the loved "object" to ease the learning of independence (Winnecott, 1971). As in object relations theory, the differentiation and eventual integration of good and bad facets of the perceived "other" helps facilitate parallel integrations in one's own sense of self (Klein, 1957).

The modern psychoanalytic emphasis on self is thus one grounded in both concepts of ego and identity, rooted in the importance of rational, cognitive capacities as well as the ego's achievement and sense of separateness. The ego self is born in the tension of relinquishing the rich, sensuous, nonverbal immersion in total relatedness to another being for a hoped for independence, somehow less tarnished by the loves, hates, frustrations, and deprivations of an infancy totally dependent on another. It is a hero's identity, wrested from a matrix of connectedness remembered as a golden dream of oneness or nightmare of subjection to another's will. It is, in addition, an identity wrested with the potential price of fear, guilt, and loneliness to complement its gifts (Neumann, 1954). The very birth of the self-reflexive subject, the "I," is inextricably bound to the creation of "me" as "other," as in Lacan's mirror metaphor, whereby we both see and construct ourselves in this recognition, moving from a grounding in biology to the formative context of linguistic reality (Kugler, 1987).

Feminist theory has been particularly incisive in noting the metaphorically masculine tone of this model of ego development in analytic writing. Dinnerstein (1976) and Chodorow (1978) trace the implications of these early processes for female and male development and cultural value. In different ways for men and women, the qualities of relatedness found in our early embeddedness with mother become the source of longing or fear as we carve out the path of ego development. In a culture which honors the qualities of independent rationality more than the relational, intuitive ones we left behind, development becomes a drama of conflicting drives for separation and connection. Feminist theory has challenged the understanding of self in terms of a hard-shelled, rational, bounded ego identity (Keller, 1990) and sought to validate a relational theory of self (Huff, 1989). Yet feminist discourse in general tends to reverberate all too often between the poles of these alternatives of individual selfhood and the relational legacy we left behind or kept for women, rather than moving toward models inclusive of autonomy and interdependence,[6] although Keller's (1986) attention to Whiteheadian or process views of self represents a noteworthy move toward transcending this dichotomy. It rarely occurs to us to question whether we are caught on the horns of a Western dilemma resulting from positing selfhood as an existing identity or "thing," whose very separateness may create dichotomous struggles like belonging versus independence (see also Klein, 1987). The extent to which historical images of the independent self, or even models of self-in-relation, further reflect models of power and control is confronted by Lykes (1985) and Sampson (1987).

Theories that anchor the self in the concept of identity face another irony, for with every aspect of ourselves we come to accept as identity, we thereby exclude other aspects from our self-definition or even awareness. Thus theories of "identity" generally note that there is more to who we are than what we claim in our identity. Rogers' stress on the way in which self-constructs come to dominate our awareness of who we are (ideal self, actual self, etc.) is an example of this emphasis on identity. Resembling George Herbert Mead's (1934) theory of development in which the self evolves as a product of social interaction with others, Rogers argues we learn to show different aspects of self depending on the changing social context of approval or appropriateness. It is because of a tendency toward creating a reduced identity from the fullness of who we are that Rogers stressed the importance of unconditional positive regard as the nexus for growing and total acceptance of onself.[7]

Sullivan's (1953) concept of the "self system" also highlights those personifications of "me" that help us defend against the interpersonal anxiety of unacceptableness. Jung's (1966, pp. 157–158) concept of the persona, or the public and conscious role we present to others and often to ourselves, also places stress on acceptableness to some extent. Thus identity often ends up as an emphasis not only on who we are—but also who we are not, just as the underscoring of conscious processes raises questions about dimensions of unconsciousness as a kind of shadow, acknowledged or not, by the theorists who focus on rational, cognitive processes. Each metaphor for self pays its price for what it chooses to affirm and what it thereby neglects or anchors in as a dichotomy. Thus identity and alienation may go hand in hand (Berman, 1989).

Other theorists have also challenged the concept of identity as locus for self with the caution that we in fact cannot be said to have one essential self system or core. This is not the criticism more familiar from social learning theorists like Mischel (1968, 1973) who have challenged the notion of an enduring, consistent self apart from contingencies of the environment, but rather it is the voice of a different kind of challenge. The critical contribution to the discussion comes from those theorists raising the possibility of a pluralistic view of self, of many shifting selves within us all. Thus Hillman (1975) speaks of the need to develop a polytheistic approach to psychology and the many forces within us rather than seeking the monotheistic psyche or ego. Assagioli (1965, 1973) in psychosynthesis speaks of a variety of subpersonalities which vie for control, though he does distinguish these subidentities from a wider centering force he calls, like Jung, the Self.[8]

For Gergen, although self concept is independent of empirical grounding, a variety of self-conceptions may be generated in the context of different social realities, with each actively subject to ongoing renegotiation. The self-not self boundary may be continually elaborated through a lifetime. The self is historically situated and socially constructed, thus creating space and even necessity for a variety of perspectives in understanding the self.[9] Ogilvy (1977) takes a perspective focused on social change. He speaks (p. 117) of the need for a new self that is "heterarchical, many dimensional," a decentralized self for a nonhierarchical world and characterized by a "multipolar" (p. 111) rather than bipolar consciousness (see also Verhave & van Hoorn, 1984). Whatever their differences, the heuristic contribution of these theorists is to question the concept of one sole identity as locus of self.

The understanding of the self in terms of identity provides the point at which traditional self theory and critiques from hermeneutical or constructivist interpretations most intersect, for the very notion of self as "identity" has a constructivist ring to it. The notion of construing the self as identity paradoxically receives both affirmation and negation from constructivist understandings. This view anchors the self in the framework of a created identity, much as individual selves are created by narrative or story-telling. Yet with the recognition of the wider cultural embeddedness of this self-construction process, the impossibility of understanding the self as a timeless, unitary essence or identity is also established. Thus these understandings of the self further "distribute" the self interpersonally (Bruner, 1990, p. 138), opening up relational understandings of the self (Gergen, 1988, 1990b, 1991) that can be seen as highly compatible with systems metaphors.[10] In addition, these views of the self necessitate attention to the ways the notions of the self or identity are shaped in time. Self constructs of identity are not the only self constructs vulnerable to this type of critique, but they have received much of the criticism.

Constructivist notions of the self need not be devoid of ontological reference or be infinitely variable, however. Drawing on the widespread spatial metaphors of self-reference (e.g., within/without, up/down), Taylor (1988, 1989) locates the changing conceptions of the self in a "moral topography" emphasizing the ontological moorings for the construction of self. Taylor traces the way in which emerging modern cultural constructs of the self reflect increasingly internalized portrayals of the individual in response to relocating the source of moral responsiveness. Taylor's articulation is particularly relevant in suggesting the potential ontological reference points for the notions of the self built around fundamental moral conflicts and issues, even if affected by historical change concerning these referents in moral topography.

Systems metaphors of the self emerge at a time in history when cross-cultural awareness not only highlights the limitations of individual models of self, but when models of reality in both science and religion are opening up increased appreciation for interrelatedness as a fundamental quality of the way the universe works. Thus systems models of the self will be able to benefit from the constructivist critique particularly of the self as identity, without ruling out the potential for reflecting or suggesting ontological possibilities. Again, we see the unusually rich nature of systems metaphors which will be introduced at greater length in the next chapter.

Self as Active Process

A third approach to metaphors of self chooses to focus on self as an active process, i.e., on "selfing." Allport (1955) tried to do this in his stress on the propriate functions as essentially active processes and his emphasis on agency, the individual as essentially active and proactive. Yet, by the unfortunate choice of a noun "the proprium" (p. 40) to comprise the propriate functions, he offered others a tool by which to misunderstand his intended emphasis. The substitution of nouns for verbs, reification or nominalization is an old danger in psychology as well as life (Bandler & Grinder, 1975). Freud struggled not to reify id, ego, and superego as internal homunculi; Jung's view of the unconscious had more of the sense of a verb, an expression for unknown energy processes, but the collective unconscious often has come down to us more as a reservoir or repository of cultural heritage, a cultural "trunk" of missing treasures, a noun once more. Adler (1956), in his emphasis on the "creative power of the individual" (p. 177), on living toward the future goals of one's choices, comes close to affirming the self as active process, but does not entirely escape the danger of reifying the "style of life" as a choice that may last a lifetime, once formed (1937, p. 44). It is perhaps the existentialists who most cleanly escape noun-metaphors with their insistence on the experience of "aming" (Keen, 1970, p. 25), the subjectively experienced present choice and moment, and the nonobjectification of "me" into some essence, some self-as-object. For them, the self-as-subject, as process is centrally affirmed, despite the limits of a noun-based language system.

There are other theorists who insist on the primacy of active process, theorists like Rogers, Jung, Lewin, Bateson (1972), yet their choice of metaphors goes beyond this emphasis on activity to a portrayal of the self in terms of the metaphor of wholeness, and it is in terms of this broader metaphor that I will later discuss their contributions. The theoretical approach which extends the understanding of self the furthest in the direction of active process, though, is probably the heritage shared in most Eastern psychological and philosophical perspectives. The most extreme expression of this emphasis on self as process indeed dissolves the distinction between individual and universal process, thus denying the very existence or validity of the separate self or ego. The Buddhist concept of anatman (no-self) radicalizes even the Hindu perspective which saw an ultimate identity of the highest self (Atman) and divine reality. With Buddhism we come to understand the self as a construct of the mind grasping for identity through attachment to its ego needs. The self is a label placed on the flow of experience and has no status except as mental and distorting construct, interrupting awareness of our essential identity with the ever changing flow of experience.[11] This is the sense of oneness described as nirvana, glimpsed with the "beginner's mind" (Suzuki, 1970) in which all is seen as new, without preconception, labeling, or possession by any I-ness. This portrayal is perhaps the ultimate of self as active process, where only process remains and we are that process in its totality. We will see that systems theory will have much in common with this construal of selfing also.[12]

Self as Wholeness

The theorists we will examine from Western psychology who move most consistently in the direction of metaphors of wholeness, unity, and integration, and who thus most prefigure systems theory, are Rogers, Jung, and Lewin. Their various views of self convey a sense of movement toward a unity of personality and being through the evolution of a lifetime. The common metaphor is one that portrays selfhood or selfing as a process of becoming more whole, of interacting with larger wholes or of being embedded in larger systems. Thus, Rogers describes the total personality in terms of the more encompassing viewpoint of the "organism," the sum total of all we are capable of experiencing in response to the "phenomenal field," uninterrupted by any labeling or judgment of acceptable or nonacceptable parts. The experience of the organism is contrasted with the partial, conscious self concepts which we cling to in fear of trusting the larger organism. Thus the self construct or self-structure is only a part of the larger organism whom we truly are, and movement toward actualization is in the direction of experiencing increasing congruence of the perceived self and the full range of experience of the organism. Increasing trust in the organism means more openness to total experience.[13] The organism is "wiser" than conscious thought, and represents for Rogers the "formative tendency" evidenced in the entire universe as a movement toward increasing consciousness, complexity, interrelatedness, and transcendent unity.[14] Thus, toward the end of his life, Rogers was moving in a direction paralleling many of the insights we will see in systems theory and thinking.

Jung also describes a kind of two-level process of selfhood, in which the conscious, rational ego built during the first half of life learns in the second part of life to surrender to the broader sense of its total potentiality which he calls the "self." Jung understands the personality in terms of both conscious ego functions and identity and powerful resources emerging from what he calls the collective unconscious. The conscious part of ourselves is the product of the birth of the ego and its struggle to develop the ability to think critically and analytically, solve problems, set goals, and develop a strong sense of personal identity and independence.[15] The ego reflects the values of society and the criteria for success in the paths of this world, and represents the major achievement of the first half of life. The ego is an achievement of immeasurable worth and value, though its limitations and habits of focus remind us that it is not the whole of who we are (Jung, 1966, pp. 73–79; 1968b, pp. 3–6).

In addition to his insistence on the role of the ego in the process of becoming a conscious human being, Jung held in profound respect the role of mystery and the unknown in human experience (Jaffé, 1971). He believed that great wisdom lay in some dimension of our beings, transcending individual learnings, and holding the keys to balance and healing needed in reaching wholeness in human life. The archetypes of the collective unconscious (Jung, 1968a; 1966, pp. 65–72), mediated by symbols and images shared across vast differences in cultures, provide the patterns which reflect and nourish the elemental features of human experience—birth, death, the mother, father, divine child, fool, wise man and woman. We experience these archetypal experiences in powerful, numinous moments when we sense the experience of reality beyond our ordinary preoccupations. We cannot experience the archetypes in themselves, however, but only through the agency of image, metaphor, and symbol. In an age which has lost touch with the symbolic dimension, the task is difficult indeed.

Jung taught that the great motivator of life lay in what he called the transcendent function, the urge to become all that we are, to develop both ego and access to the collective unconscious in a kind of spiral process of communication. This great task of life he called individuation, a never-ending journey accentuated in the second half of life when ego turns to a recognition of its own partiality and surrenders itself to a new center of consciousness, the self. The process of individuation involves the construction of an ongoing dialogue between conscious and unconscious parts of ourselves and the recovery of all that has dwelt undeveloped in our psyches. For every quality accepted by consciousness as part of our self image, its opposite lies relegated to the shadow, Jung's term for the undeveloped parts of ourselves, lying in the shadow cast by the light of focused consciousness. To move toward individuation is to move toward recovery of the shadow, a perilous journey, though the shadow contains undeveloped positive help as well as darker regions.[16]

Confronting the shadow is only the beginning of the long process of learning to transcend all one's polarities, embracing opposites, enlarging one's psychic container to allow space for all of human experience. The Jungian goal is completeness, not perfection (Jung, 1968b, pp. 68–69); the aim is wholeness not judgment, although an authentic capacity to act out of this wholeness also characterizes this path. The self, for Jung, is the experience of the totality of who we are, social roles or persona as well as shadow, conscious and unconscious, ego and archetype. The self in a sense is both the center point of the sphere of who we are as well as the totality. It is that perspective from which we are whole and united with ourselves, from which the cycle of life does not constantly turn us at the periphery, but we remain centered at the hub of the wheel of life's fortunes. The self is an experience of great awesomeness.[17] It lies at the threshhold of the holy, containing within its circumference the guiding metaphors for the full spectrum of human values, including the metaphorically masculine qualities of logic, rationality, and assertiveness and the metaphorically feminine values of relatedness, intuition, and receptivity. Jung raises the metaphor of wholeness or unity to the most accentuated expression we have encountered thus far—a unity of conscious and unconscious, a transcendence of polarity, an image of completeness which includes both dark and light sides. The term self expands to include all that is known or unknown in human potential as focused through the process of individuation, in which my ego personality is a lighted patch on the surface of the larger sphere of self.[18]

From here it is but a short step to enlarging the metaphor even further, a step taken by those theorists who consciously attempt to explore the intersection of individual and environment, human and universe. This is an emphasis ironically forged by the behaviorists who, without the metaphors of conscious ego function, identity, active processes, or wholeness, nonetheless zeroed in on the critical index of interconnectedness. In a sense it was the behaviorists who crossed the barrier of individual, isolated response to link behavior with environmental consequence, perhaps in a limited and stereotyped way, but in their own manner they made a heroic statement about the embeddedness of human behavior in a larger arena. Thus we find a rudimentary concept of system, stripped to be sure of all but the essential hardware of a simple circuit, but relevant to issues of interaction and environmental influence.

It is not surprising then, perhaps, to come to the work of Lewin (1936) whose interest in social phenomena was an important guide to his research. Lewin's metaphors for self also come from physics and topological mathematics and launch us via scientific metaphors into a field theory of personality. He embeds the differentiated "person" within a relevant psychological "environment," together comprising the universe he calls the "lifespace."[19] While Lewin's "person" lacks the complexity and richness of the Jungian concept of self, he adds the critical interactive medium of the lifespace, encompassing the rest of the universe in relationship to the person. Thus Lewin offers a potentially wider vision of interconnectedness between individual and larger whole, which Jung implies, believed in, but left undeveloped as part of his broad concept of "psychoid" reality, the parallel between internal and external reality which Jung felt characterized the relationship of psyche and universe.[20] Lewin thus makes explicit the embeddedness of human behavior in external reality, and leaves the path open for a more sophisticated systems and cybernetics theory to reintroduce the complexity earlier behaviorism left behind. The metaphors have become thicker, so rich in fact in nuance and tissue that the skeleton of behavioral S-R connectedness almost moves beyond kinship and recognition. We will follow this pathway paved by Lewin toward the increasing complexity of systems theory models and the metaphor of the interrelated self.

Chapter Five

MODELS OF INTERRELATEDNESS: THE EMERGENCE OF SYSTEMS THEORY

Few of us can escape a sense of wonder at the new images of the world made possible by modern science. Nor can we avoid contemplating the precariousness of our existence on the planet, threatened as we are by such global challenges as nuclear armament, poverty, starvation, pollution, overpopulation, and political conflict. Though we have been exposed to new models in science which might contribute to creative solutions, we have not found sufficient ways to translate these models into daily life to inform decision making. Likewise these models have not been translated adequately into the psychological context where they might better inform behavior and consciousness.

If the Newtonian worldview of a mechanical billiard-ball universe composed of independent atomic building blocks is crumbling, we still lack habit patterns to conceptualize a vision of interrelatedness we can live by. Rarely are humans capable of relinquishing a well-tried and familiar model of the world without another to replace it. We do not live easily without the planks which underpin and buttress our assumptions and daily decisions. Nor do we sustain the glimpses of greater realities and alternative possibilities without a consistent sustaining image to keep us focused during the all too frequent times when the vision fades. If Needleman (1965) is right, that we live in a period between dreams, the importance of finding a new model is particularly crucial, not only for its possibility of soothing the anxiety of disrupted expectations, but more importantly for its ability to guide and encourage imagination. Again, a model, a metaphor is less crutch than vaulting pole, less security than springboard for new alternatives.

Capra (1975, 1982), Zukav (1979), and Pagels (1982) led the way in directing popular attention to the shift in vision made possible by relativity theory and quantum mechanics in modern physics, although much writing in this vein has ensued.[1] Our images and language for the ways we see and describe the world have not caught up with scientific discovery and theory. Even concepts like time and space are metaphors which guide our vision (Jones, 1982). The concept of empty expanses of space, for example, accentuated and perhaps even created a feeling of isolation and individual differentiation in post-Enlightenment periods, in contrast to assumptions of connection and belongingness characteristic of earlier organic worldviews. Space is not something in which the universe exists, but space itself came into creation with the creation of the universe (Davies, 1984). Its status as an independent construct is a misleading product of the power of words and metaphors to reify commonsense perceptions as if they were the final appeal.

What then is the image opened up to us by moving "through the looking glass" in exploring the world of the infinitesimally small and the infinitesimally great, traversing beyond normal levels of perception to encounter new dimensions of experience?[2] To do so, we are asked to relinquish our attachment to the level of discrete object, of edges and separateness, of hard matter versus empty space. As I look at the proverbial philosophical table with its surfaces and edges I no longer ask whether it is real, but whether I can allow myself to conceptualize, perhaps even see it as part of a constant interchange of energy patterns coming in and out of existence. And if I can succeed in this retranslation with the table, can I then extend this boundary-lessness to another person, to myself, to that edge of skin by which I anchor my identity in this worldview of separateness? The exercise in perception of objects quickly runs into resistance at the edge of personhood, yet where does one draw the line? Skin is no less a physical surface than wood, or plastic or steel. And if I do succeed in staying for more than a moment in the wonder of the subatomic world, how long can I sustain this perception to allow the shifts in implication that can follow from this perspective? How soon will I run back to familiar territory and separateness? How long can I retain the vision and not idolatrize the insights from physics, which refer always to nonvisualizable mathematical properties which escape our direct experience.

Our vocabularies are challenged to move beyond "thing" language, nouns. Constructs like gravity and matter disappear in a certain sense through radical redefinition. The demonstration that mass and energy are interconvertible, translatable into each other, becomes a cornerstone for the shift in worldview which dissolves matter into transformations of energy. In the four-dimensional geometry of spacetime in Einsteinian physics, gravity becomes a phenomenon of topology and geography, no longer best conceived of as a force or attraction. With the fourth dimension we cross the line of visual analogy and the threshold of metaphor, beginning to move into nonconceptual space such as an eleven-dimensioned universe (Davies, 1984), stretching even metaphor beyond its limits.

The atom and other aspects of concrete reality become more "idea-like" rather than "matter-like." The electron cloud which replaced the idea of orbiting electrons becomes a mathematical construct of probability waves which may not "exist" in the classical sense. Matter and substance thus dissolve into probability wave. Yet it is distorting to speak of waves, just because we can no longer talk of substance and thing, for the waves of quantum physics are not material but waves of probabilities. In a sense only the field is real, the matrix of probable reaction channels by which certain subatomic particles are more or less likely to come into and out of being. Each particle potentially exists as a certain probability of coming into being out of the combinations of other particles. Drawing from gravitational analogies, matter becomes a warp, ripple, or condensation in the field. It has no discrete separateness as object; no part of the pattern has separate status or even substantive existence. Even the classical electromagnetic and "strong" forces can be retranslated as an exchange of virtual photons or pions respectively.[3]

Time, change, pattern all become as real as matter. In the bootstrap hypothesis, no law or part of the interwoven pattern of probability functions becomes any more fundamental than any other part, reflecting a state of evolving "interpenetration" by which the universe as a whole is determined by every other part. The metaphor of web or network replaces the idea of fundamental building blocks.[4] With these perspectives, the philosophical underpinnings of modern physics begin to resemble idealism more than realism (Heisenberg, 1958). What we can know of reality begins to appear more as reflecting the shape and way our minds operate, formulate questions, measure reality. As Jeans (1937, p. 186) has affirmed in a frequently quoted line, "the universe begins to look more like a great thought than like a great machine."

In sum, there is no empty space or vacuum, but rather particles appearing and disappearing out of the void according to certain probabilities. The subatomic zoo comprises a pattern of particles constantly being emitted and destroyed and recreated. The universe is dance, an interconnected web, a field of energy. Antiparticles interact with particles, accompanied by an ambiguity of time that ushers in imagery which extends to discussion of simultaneous universes. The Feynman diagrams that track the patterns of change, for example, can be read in two directions of time and space, as positrons moving forward in time or as electrons moving backward in time. The dissolving of a standard time frame wrecks havoc with conventional linear causality, and notions of "before" and "after," yielding another perspective on the meaning of an interrelated universe.[5]

In this conceptual universe, koans abound, puzzles as fierce as the best of Zen. There is the dilemma of Schrödinger's cat who inhabits a closed box of probabilistic existence and can be said to be neither alive nor dead at any point until the very split second when one opens the box and the actual event happens. There is no such thing as an event in the abstract, only a certain range of probabilities, a puzzle which has been resolved in a variety of theoretical ways including an hypothesis of alternative worlds corresponding to each possibility. In any case the cat's deadness or aliveness is not to be detected as an external event apart from my own interaction with it, although as a thought problem, the puzzle is posed on a level of material existence far from the quantum level which gave it expression. Further koans are posed by Bell's theorem of non-locality which attempted to explain the apparent connection between two events which technically should be predicted to be independent of each other's causal influence, in this case the spin of two particles separated by design. Bell's theorem has led to positing a deep interconnectedness to reality, rendering it non-independent or non-local in its effects such that events seem to be connected even though not spatially contiguous (Herbert, 1987, pp. 211–231).

Other modern theories in physics reflect also on a vision of interconnection and interrelatedness and carry philosophical implications as well (Schumacher, 1981). Computer modeling has further enhanced understanding in the new "sciences of complexity" (Pagels, 1988). "Theories of Everything" begin to emerge, such as superstring theory which attempts to unify all the classic forces of physics into one system (Davies & Brown, 1988). Chaos theory opens new discoveries regarding the patterns which emerge in complex, dynamical, nonlinear systems, such as characterize constantly changing systems like the weather, or living systems such as the heart and potentially brain functioning (Gleick, 1987; Peterson, 1988). Small differences in initial conditions in complex events can trigger chaotic and disordered conditions with substantial unpredictability, yet which at a deeper level show coherence, predictability, and the presence of anchoring patterns called attractors. Chaos models predict that dynamical systems will tend to undergo long stable periods with sudden periods of rapid transformation, a phenomenon basic to contemporary theories of "punctuated equilibrium" in biological evolution, and also receiving emphasis in theories of social change. Chaos models are also already finding extention to such fields of personality theory as archetypal psychology.[6]

David Bohm's (1980, 1985) model of wholeness hypothesizes that beyond the material, visible or explicate order of the universe lies an "implicate order" or dimension which is infolded latently within what we see, representing the pattern that makes all form come into and out of being. Bohm might explain the paradoxical connection between two seemingly unrelated events observed in Bell's theorem as two perspectives on one implicate and whole reality, coming into view simultaneously from very different vantage points. Matter in Bohm's view rides like an enfolded ripple on the sea of energy; the dynamic process of wholeness as backdrop to all incarnate reality dissolves the distinction between animate and inanimate.[7] If implicate order were another term for consciousness, enfolded throughout the universe, as Briggs and Peat (1984, p. 267) ascribe to Bohm, the metaphorical point for another fruitful dialogue with psychology is born.

The extent to which we can borrow these metaphors and models for psychology must observe the cautions of all metaphor use when shifting domains. Perhaps the greatest immediate gift of modern physics is that of restoring wonder, awe, mystery to the heart of science. Probability, field, process, energy, change—these are the concepts of the worldview we are given, backdrop to a new vision by which to begin to resee ourselves, our relationships to ultimates, to action in the world. The incredible complexity of this planet, of this universe, of even the objects before us must surely speak of a beauty and patterning to be matched at other levels, perhaps in their own unique languages and visions, but matched at least for complexity, for awe, for a choreography at least equally intense. As we turn to the next level of complexity, the biological life sciences, we will seek the metaphors this level speaks.

Metaphors for Life: Models from the Biological Sciences

The metaphor of world as organism is not without precedent, but the shift to a mechanistic model of the universe with the rise of modern science has made the recovery of organismic models in modern biology a significant achievement. As Merchant (1980) traces so provocatively in her book, *The Death of Nature,* the shift in the "root metaphors" (pp. 227, 234) from world as organism to world as mechanism rendered nature and matter inert, passive, devoid of the sense of living energy or spirit that characterized earlier relationships to nature (p. 193). As windmill and clock on the town hall provided technological imagery to buttress this shift of the imagination, nature received more of the projections from a rationalism intent on ridding itself of emotional, unpredictable elements. The ruling association of nature and femaleness shifted from positive to negative associations and laid the groundwork for rationalizing the subjugation and exploitation of the earth in place of earlier respect and awe. The drawbacks of a mechanistic model have taken a long time to surface. Not only can the ethical abuses of the earth so often decried arise with our distancing from nature, but distortions of understanding are engendered by a model which neglects the inherent interactiveness of the cosmos, with no part immune to interpenetrating influence.

The path back to a new model of wholeness complex enough to do justice to the nature of organism and life cannot come solely from what Berman (1984) calls the "reenchantment of the world." It is ironic that Berman (p. 273) himself tries to avoid this simplification by calling for a "post-Cartesian paradigm" rather than a return to a "premodern" infusion in an animistic world of spiritual presence within matter. Yet despite his appeal to modern systems theory, he himself seems close to suggesting the need to celebrate the preverbal, pre-ego state of Eros and sensual wholeness as a path back to a balanced worldview, a kind of Norman Brownian, Marcusian, Reichian search for sensual holism. A new feeling-ful relationship to nature would indeed follow from a shift in metaphor, and it is to be celebrated, but the path to such a change must be grounded in more than emotional appeal.

The "reenchantment of science" is accompanied by new models that do more justice to wholeness in the natural world and by the emerging ecological paradigm and Deep Ecology movement.[8] Sheldrake argues, for example, that organismic understandings of nature are more basic than mechanistic models. Mechanistic models of natural law may more accurately be seen as describing secondary accretions of habit formation derived from more basic organismic processes. Mechanism represents the extreme possibility for behavioral regularity rather than a mechanical base from which organismic actions are an exception.[9] Likewise biological process is looked at increasingly in terms of its connections with cognitive processes and potential. In a paradigm shifting work, Maturana and Varela (1987) trace the emergence of social relatedness, language, and concepts of the self as part of the way an organism creates its world to maintain adaptive correlations between sensory and motor input, an evolution continuous with all biological process of adaptation and self-reproduction. The framework of modern systems theory and cybernetics likewise emerges as an intellectually and emotionally provocative schema for understanding the life sciences and all levels of organization. It is to this model we turn in an effort to understand the promise of metaphor in biology as a tool for opening up new ways of hypothesizing and conceptualizing issues of wholeness in the biological sciences and by potential extension to systems in general.

> Gradually I discovered that what made it difficult to tell the class what the course was about was the fact that my way of thinking was different from theirs. A clue to this difference came from one of the

> students. . . . At the end of the session, one resident came up. He glanced over his shoulder to be sure that the others were all leaving, and then said rather hesitantly, "I want to ask a question." "Yes." "It's—do you want us to *learn* what you are telling us?" I hesitated a moment, but he rushed on with, "Or is it all a sort of example, an illustration of something else?" "Yes, indeed!"
>
> But an example of what?
>
> And then there was, almost every year, a vague complaint which usually came to me as a rumor. It was alleged that "Bateson knows something which he does not tell you," or "There's something behind what Bateson says, but he never says what it is." (Bateson, 1972, p. xvii)

Systems Theory

The approach to systems theory which we will be exploring draws largely from the work of Ervin Laszlo (1972, 1973) and Gregory Bateson (1972, 1979), who have addressed their attention to systems theory as a bridge between conventionally separated domains. The concept of "general systems theory," however, is most widely credited to the work of Ludwig von Bertalanffy (1955, 1962, 1968, 1975), whose emphasis on the scientific exploration of organized wholes and wholeness could be seen to constitute a model transportable across fields with different levels of focus, whether chemistry with focus on the atom, biology with emphasis on the cell and organism, psychology with focus on the mind and human, or sociology with emphasis on the social system or society.[10] The concept of system was a tool for analysis potentially applicable far beyond its biological context of origin and the mathematical contexts within which it grew rapidly as a means of solving problems involving complex, interacting wholes.

It is significant that the emergence of systems theory was rooted in an epistemological critique of the limits of the analytic method and reductionistic assumptions in science, as well as in an affirmation of the necessity for new ways to study wholeness and "organized complexity."[11] From its onset, it has raised philosophical issues as a critical part of its empirical heuristic, and has directed attention to constructs which involve isomorphic analogies across domains.[12] Thus systems theory is an interdisciplinary model or metaphor which seeks to address a science of wholes at different hierarchical levels. With the exception of Capra (1982, 1988) and Berman (1984), who devote sections of their books to this topic, however, and early links to communication theory in the behavioral sciences, systems theory has not tended to reach beyond the biological sciences to other disciplines or the general public in the same way that modern physics has been made available to a wider audience than physicists. This process of translation of the core concepts of systems theory is a key objective of this chapter and the next.

Perhaps the clearest definition of a system comes from Laszlo (1973, p. 38) who defines a system as "an ordered whole in relation to its relevant environment." Systems are embedded within surrounding environments with which, in open systems frameworks, they continually interact. The metaphor here is one of process, of organic imagery, of field theory: "fields within fields . . . within fields" (Stulman, 1972), all in a dynamic state of change. Key in the set of assumptions that define systems theory is the notion of synergy, a term chosen by Buckminster Fuller (1969, p. 71) to refer to the phenomenon that the operation of a total system is not reducible to or predictable from the behavior of separate subparts within the system. In other words, the Gestalt notion that the whole is greater than the sum of the parts holds here. Laszlo (pp. 36–37) contrasts the notion of a "non-summative system" from the concept of unrelated "heaps" or "aggregates" of events, as in the contrast between an intact building and a heap of bricks. Like the vision offered by the space missions and the view of the earth as blue and white whole, it is a gift of perspective which can bring wholes into focus with an immediacy that allows for new acknowledgment of complex interconnectedness.

Equally characteristic and fundamental to systems is their tendency to be arranged in hierarchies, with systems embedded as we have seen within systems (Laszlo, 1973): electron within atom, within molecule, within compound, and so on up the levels of complexity to include crystal, cell, organ, organism, community, society, ecosystem, planet, solar system, galaxy, and universe. Hierarchies become key to understanding ecological complexity (Allen & Starr, 1982) and evolution (Salthe, 1985; Grene, 1987). In the rich imagery of Lewis Thomas (1974, p. 2) that captures a sense of this systems embeddedness at the human level, "we are shared, rented, and occupied" by mitochondria with separate DNA, "stable and responsible lodgers" in the mini ecosystem that forms our cells. What we are given is a new kind of unit by which to approach the universe, the dynamic system or "holon" (Koestler, 1967, p. 48), a two-sided Janus-like concept reflecting that each level system is a whole relative to its constituent parts and a part relative to the next larger level whole.[13] Holons higher in the hierarchy in a sense constitute the environment for those lower in the hierarchy.[14] Laszlo (p. 30) suggests the name "natural system" to refer to the systems unit. Thus atoms, organisms, societies are reconceptualized as one variety of natural system, and we can begin the process of comparing systems as systems to see what they have in common at this level. This opportunity for seeing similarities across levels opens up many possibilities for fresh conceptualizations of old puzzles.

The behavior of self-regulating systems can be described by principles of cybernetics, a term created by Wiener (1948, 1950) to refer to the complex interrelationships between systems and environment via inputs and outputs to the system and information exchange.[15] Hierarchy can be understood as a system of communication between levels, allowing degrees of freedom within constraints provided largely from higher levels (Allen & Starr, 1982, pp. 11, 15, 37). As Laszlo describes, systems are self-regulating, adaptive entities which show two fundamental ways of adapting to the information and changes in the surrounding environment. The first he calls adaptive self-stabilization, a process of using negative feedback about deviations from a steady state level by which the system maintains itself at a kind of equilibrium (p. 39–41). This process is basically one known as homeostasis in biology, whereby the body tends to return to a set level of functioning after temporary disturbance, operating much along the analogy of a preset thermostat for regulating temperature. In a relatively unchanging environment, such a mechanism is particularly adaptive.

The second mode of system functioning Laszlo calls adaptive self-organization or self-reorganization, where positive information about a change in the environment is used to reorganize the system in entirely new ways, adapting to a relatively stable new level of environmental demand (1973, pp. 41–47).[16] Thus by analogy, in summer we might leave our thermostat at a set level and adapt to temporary coolness by a change in what we are wearing, putting on a sweater or taking it off, but in winter we are more likely to raise the set point of the thermostat rather than constantly rely simply on a shift in clothing. This analogy, however, falls short in that it may seem to locate the self-reorganizing change externally to the organism; perhaps more helpful is the phenomenon by which a move to higher altitudes will eventually promote the increase of red blood cells, rather than relying indefinitely on increased breathing as the sole means of enhancing oxygenation. Again the essential point to be illustrated is the capacity of systems not only to adapt to change in small homeostatic variations around a set point, but in the capacity to create larger changes, for example in that very set point, or in a variety of adaptive reorganizations to help facilitate survival under such new conditions. What we are tracking here is a new perspective on evolution and change as a process inherent within systems.[17] Allen and Starr (1982), for example, describe ways that enzymes, which speed up chemical reactions, create a change in time scale for holons relative to larger suprasystems. This enables holons to escape certain constraints and allows more self-organizing structures to evolve (pp. 67–68, 91).

An equally critical characteristic of systems is their tendency to be arranged in increasing levels of complexity. Laszlo (1972) differentiated the systems perspective as one of "organized complexity" in contrast to Newtonian "organized simplicity" (p. 15). Although a less complex suprasystem may emerge at a higher level of organization and control more complex subsystems, once formed this higher level system will tend to become progressively more complex (Laszlo, 1987, p. 25). Such increase in levels of complexity would appear directly derivative from the capacity for self-organization which systems possess. The higher levels of complexity are structurally less stable since they are more complex and less probable of occurring, but functionally they are more adaptive to that very complexity in which they are embedded and hence can be seen as possessing greater "cybernetic stability" (Laszlo, 1973, p. 109). Systems, argues Laszlo, show progressive organization and order, and thus can be seen to reduce entropy. This phenomenon associated with living systems has received considerable attention as it occurs counter to the expectations of the Second Law of Thermodynamics for energy to move in the direction of equilibrium or increasing disorder and dissipation as heat. The overall law, however, is not violated by the capacity of special subsystems to show non-equilibrium conditions (Morowitz, 1972), and thus life systems constitute a kind of negative entropy situation. Thus in a rather rough analogy, there is an easily noted tendency for the order in a room at home or in a carefully stacked pile of paperwork to revert constantly toward clutter or disarray, were it not for the reorganizing efforts made to maintain the ordered system and perhaps even make it more efficient through a more structually sound filing or shelving system. A highly complex system holds more information, is more adapted, more "negentropic."[18]

Finally, systems as we have seen appear to develop in the direction of increased hierarchical structure, a phenomenon which also seems related to the tendency for increased complexity and adaptive self-reorganization (Laszlo, 1973). Rather than starting over from scratch at each shift in environmental challenge, systems can build and evolve more rapidly from intermediate levels of subsystems lower in the hierarchy. Likewise systems sharing a common environment are likely to combine already existing systems into larger systems rather than reverting to self-reorganizations on an individual level (p. 48). Hence the tendencies toward complexity and hierarchical arrangement seem to work complementarily in the process of evolution of new form. It is important to note that these tendencies in systems toward complexity, order, and hierarchy are natural properties of systems according to this analysis. Laszlo argues (p. 261) for the "telic" nature of systems as opposed to the teleological, where often supernatural reference is implied beyond the system. The fact that evolution in complexity is a characteristic within the framework of this natural systems model is in fact one of its powers as a heuristic in our time, a possibility we will explore later in this chapter.

Transcending Traditional Dualisms

Just as we can speak of "energy-processing" physical systems, we might also speak of "information-processing" mental or cognitive systems, using the concept of system to open up new avenues of comparison between these typically contrasted levels (Laszlo, 1973, p. 143). Laszlo argues that cognitive systems show the same tendencies of all systems toward adaptation and change. Cognitive self-stabilization resembles the intellectual process of equilibration described by Piaget as the active testing and refining of schemes in interaction with feedback from the environment (Laszlo, pp. 126–127). Adaptive cognitive self-organization is represented more in the process of learning new constructs or in Bateson's (1972) stress on the evolution of new levels of rule and metarule as information from two levels is compared. With more complexity comes more role for the selection of "programs" and more flexibility at this level (Laszlo, pp. 190–191).

Traditionally the mental and physical systems have been conceptualized via the Cartesian mind/body dualism which has frustrated attempts to see through to the unity that somehow also marks their functioning. Laszlo (1973, p. 154) suggests that we adopt the concept "natural-cognitive system" to help bridge the intellectual gap we have created between these two types of systems by treating them so separately rather than stressing their similarity "*qua* systems." Thus the emphasis is placed on one single system observable from two points of view. Laszlo (p. 154) calls this perspective biperspectival, as opposed to dual, stressing the possibility that when "lived" or viewed internally, such a system can be seen as a cognitive system of mental events, but when viewed externally the system is seen as a system of physical events. The systems are identical as systems, but correlated at the level of how they are experienced. The identity is not due to their substance but the "isomorphy of the theories mapping the systems" (p. 163).[19]

A tremendous array of exciting theoretical possibilities are opened up by this concept of natural-cognitive system, which becomes the basic unit for addressing any system of sufficient complexity to fold in on itself so to speak as a complex information-processing unit dealing with dual levels of input. First is the rather dramatic possibility that the line we have classically drawn between mentality and non-mentality in the universe is a logically arbitrary one (Laszlo, 1973). Mentality might in fact be a correlate of all physical existence, argues Whitehead (1978) who stresses the possibility of a kind of prehension rudimentary in material entities which is continuous with the kind of processes later seen as apprehension and consciousness. Bohm (1985) speaks of the "soma-significance" of all reality whereby events tend toward both somatic and meaning expression. For Laszlo, the critical issue is one of degree of complexity and organization as a criterion for mental-events. Sufficient organization, including both the capacities for differentiation and integration would be necessary to support mental correlates to physical systems. In this viewpoint one would not attempt to derive higher order mentality from a non-mentality ancestry, but rather from rudimentary potential for such complexity already latent within any evolving system. Consciousness would emerge from more basic levels of "subjectivity."[20]

For Bateson (1979, p. 234), "'mind' is immanent in certain sorts of *organization* of parts."[21] For mind to be present, there must be sufficient levels of complexity in a system to allow interaction between parts of the system in response to the detection of a "difference" (1979, p. 102).[22] There must also be recursiveness (1977, p. 242) or circular chains of cause and effect that allow for the relaying, coding (1979, p. 235), and transforming of information as it is cycled and new information loops back into the system (pp. 102, 114–142). Information received from at least two levels allows comparison and contrast in two ways of looking at things and the formation of rules commenting on rules (metarules), metamessages (1979, p. 128), and logical typing (p. 235).[23] Such circuits and loops of information (1979, p. 141) show self-correcting properties (p. 117).

The potential implication of such a way of conceptualizing mind is the possibility of broadening the base of evolution to include the natural evolution of mind or consciousness in the universe. Such a hypothesis would follow then entirely from within the extension of a natural systems model, with no need to appeal to transcendental sources. The traditional emphasis on evolution versus creationism has often served to lock at least popularized science into a defense of a materialistic model of natural selection that already has shown ample signs of shortcomings. Despite the return to center stage of the appeal of genetic and evolutionary models in sociobiology (Wilson, 1978, 1980), the traditional basis of Darwinian models has received considerable criticism from within biological science itself. Central to these critiques have been alternative models of evolution based on "punctuated equilibrium" with periodic phases of rapid change, and renewed emphasis on clarifying the role of the environment in evolution.[24]

Other critiques involve an increasing appreciation for the role of purposiveness in the functioning of biological systems. Despite his position in favor of expanding but not basically challenging the modern evolutionary synthesis, Mayr (1988) nonetheless argues that philosophy of science, overly invested in physics as its norm, needs to catch up to the organismic assumptions of biology as a field. A new philosophy of biology would involve greater appreciation for the characteristics of living systems, among which purposiveness figures as a central issue. Mayr (pp. 45, 60) describes biological systems as teleonomic, defined as "goal-directed" by a "program" (e.g., DNA), although he contrasts this with a metaphysically teleological position. Allen and Starr (1982) go so far as to argue that purpose and anticipation are part of biological phenomena, foreshadowed at a more diffuse level in the abiotic world too (p. 65). They hold to the necessity of maintaining complementary scientific models of living systems which honor both chance and anticipation as explanatory principles (p. 61).

The classical Darwinian metaphor of "survival of the fittest" and competition is also being critiqued in favor of increasing emphasis on cooperation in nature (Augros & Stanciu, 1987). Likewise the possibility of conceptualizing both upward and downward causation through interactive hierarchical relationships between levels (Grene, 1987; Sperry, 1988) has broadened the basis for understanding evolutionary complexity, and by implication challenged traditional mechanistic assumptions of evolution as totally reducible to the dynamics of upward causation alone. Increasing emphasis also is being placed on the role of humans in consciously facilitating the evolution of transnational cooperative "supraorganisms" toward the interests of global peace and survival.[25] Yet rarely does the critique explicitly come, even from a religious perspective, that natural selection as a hypothesis does not go far enough in explaining evolution, rather than going too far. Usually the argument stops short of the radical possibility that evolution is a process involving not just physical systems, or even socioemotional instinctual systems à la sociobiology, but the evolution of mental systems or consciousness. It is this revolutionary possibility that modern systems theory by extension may open up as hypothesis to be explored.

This analysis brings closer the work of Teilhard de Chardin (1959) who writes of the movement toward increasing complexity, interiority (p. 87), and infolding of consciousness in the universe in rhythms of differentiation and unification. It consciousness exists, he argues, it has a history as part of the interrelated web of the universe. We might note also the work of Russell (1983) who argues that the planet itself will arrive at a level of complexity of consciousness and organization, ushering in a shift to a new level of organismic system which he articulates as the "global brain." Recall too, though, as we move perhaps uncomfortably close to metaphysical sounding phrases for those accustomed to the language of sensory data science, Laszlo's (1973, p. 191) reminder that the evolution of "reflexive consciousness" is not an issue of external teleology but of the inherent property of systems to move toward greater complexity. At no point is there need for appeal to external power or purpose to set free the importance and intrinsic quality of consciousness, thus conceived, as an inherent part of the universe.

A second radical shift in thinking and hypothesizing opened up by modern systems theory is the possible arbitrariness of the line drawn between organic and inorganic, or between animate and inanimate. Whereas philosophy of science and much of conventional biology had conceptualized life on the model of physics and inanimate matter, and it has been considered a breakthrough to conceptualize living organisms in their uniqueness, irreducible to inanimate systems, systems theory allows us to resee properties of systems in terms of their continuity across levels of complexity, in a sense extending our capacity to witness proto-properties of life "downwards" to lower hierarchical levels. In a similar way, Schrödinger (1969, pp. 81–91), despite noting the difference between disorder at the quantum level and increased order at the level of life, also points attention to possible parallels in physics to the "'order-from-order' features" of life (p. 89), and reconceptualizes similarities (pp. 62–65) between crystals (seen as repetitive configurations or periodic solids), molecules (or non-repetitive, aperiodic solids), and genes (aperiodic solids or crystals).[26] In a similar but even more speculative way, Watson (1979) suggests the possibility that the replicating pattern of DNA may have been modeled after the patterning of crystals, of clay. We are indeed in a different metaphorical realm in which clay teaches life how to be a pattern. It is interesting in this sense of "living clay" to note with Sagan (1980, 125–126), reporting on the Viking study of Martian soil, that the clay showed many properties of living matter such as the absorption and release of gases and the catalyzing of chemical reaction, not dissimilar to such processes as respiration and photosynthesis. Thus when he speaks of our being "made of starstuff" (p. 233), we might image a far more profound shift in thinking in this phraseology than commonly understood or perhaps even intended under non-systems models.

Finally we come to a philosophically profound shift in hypothesizing made possible by systems theory, a shift by which the traditional dichotomy of arguments for freedom versus determinism might be transcended. Thus Laszlo (1973) argues, much as he did above, that the same natural-cognitive system can be seen from two perspectives. Looked at externally, the total system can be said to be interdetermined by the whole nexus of interactions with the environment. Looked at from within the system, the experience is one of apparent freedom and self-determination. A very complex system increases choices and flexibility in responding, by increasing the autonomy of internal decision making and self-reorganizing systems, thus reducing determination from the outside environment. It is interesting to note also that with freedom comes the capacity for error, the "correlate of freedom" according to Laszlo (p. 275). Laszlo argues that this decision-making determination or how one handles information is where the increasing freedom lies, yet at the level of output or behavior we can see the total picture, the way in which even the flexible percepts one experiences when making choices are themselves shaped by learning within the total system.

Pattern and Interrelatedness

In tracking the hypotheses of systems theory models we have entered a metaphorical landscape of rich and diverse perspectives on wholeness and interrelatedness in the biological world. We are given a tool to explore the holism spoken of by Smuts (1926) in his groundbreaking work on organismic models. It is a world which dissolves thing and noun perhaps every bit as much as the world of experience opened up by modern physics. Bateson (1972) continually urges against the dangers of noun language, quoting Anatol Holt's desire for a bumper sticker reading "stamp out nouns" (p. 334).[27] "There are no 'things' in the mind," Bateson writes (p. 275), only relationships between information, contexts. He objects even to referring to the transmission of a neural impulse as if the message is a thing; instead it is "news of a difference," information about a difference that travels through the system (p. 454).

Despite his earlier grounding in cybernetics, Bateson seemed to make minimal use of such terms as input and feedback in his later writing, preferring concepts like form, order, and pattern that had to do with relationships and organization. He sought to replace substance-oriented materialistic concepts with concepts of pattern and communication.[28] Epistemological errors occur, he maintained, when we confuse the language for understanding events in terms of forces and energy with the language of communication in terms of patterns and relationships.[29] Ideas, relationships are not material; difference is not a quantity nor can it be localized (Bateson, 1977, pp. 240–241). "We are discussing a world of meaning," he maintains in *Mind and Nature* (1979, p. 110). Yet Bateson argues repeatedly against any dualism of mind and matter, insisting that epistemological focus on different levels of understanding or "universes of explanation" does not imply an ultimate dualism whereby mind and matter could be separated (M.C. Bateson, 1972, p. 236).

Bateson rejected the isolated computer model as adequate to describe mind (1972, p. 483). It is the more encompassing "dynamic unit" of human plus computer plus environment that can be seen to bear the characteristics of mind, not the computer by itself.[30] In the same way, Bateson argued that the "unit of evolutionary survival" is the organism plus the environment, not the organism acted upon by a separate environment. Thinking and evolving occur via total systems that include human and environment. Bateson went so far as to talk of the overarching "eco-mental system" (p. 484). The field of biology itself has evolved from a taxonomical interest in objects and Darwinian interest in species to a stress on ecology and the full continuum of life and complexly organized communities (Morowitz, 1972). The most far-reaching speculation and revisualization is toward seeing the planet itself as "the focus of aliveness," with "life . . . not so much a property of the individual as it is a property of the entire planetary surface" (p. 155). The Gaia hypothesis speaks directly to this view of the planet itself as a self-regulating organism (Lovelock, 1979).

Individuals cannot even exist apart from the ecosystem in which they are embedded. The essence of living systems is to be continually replenished, reconstituted by their exchanges with the environment (Morowitz, 1972). This is the characteristic of "dissipative structures" as studied by Ilya Prigogine, living systems stabilized by the flowing through of energy and matter which give them form and paradoxical stability, even though there is a constant change in the constituent parts as a result of the new food or energy consumed.[31] How close this is, argues Morowitz, to a sense of the Buddhist view of change and impermanence in which living forms become loci for a building up of order yet lose discrete and permanent identity to the flow which forms their being. Much as Capra (1975) turned to Eastern metaphors to capture a sense of the worldview he wanted to communicate via the concepts of quantum physics, it is not surprising that we would find the same tendencies here among those who seek to trace out the reverberations of a shift to holistic metaphors.

Those who write most beautifully of this vision of wholeness are the poets within the sciences, the storytellers of biology, such as Loren Eiseley and Lewis Thomas.[32] One is reminded of Heisenberg's (1974) sense that at the brink of wordlessness one turns to image, to poetry, perhaps even to religion. It is image that brings us the richness of the metaphors of life: pattern, order, complexity, organization. Again, like the legacy of modern physics and its concepts of probability, process, and dance of energy, the thing language has dissolved. Vocabularies are stretched to convey field, pattern, process. There are the spirals and curves of the shells, the opening of a fern, the paths of the seeds of the sunflower. The marvel of the biochemically diagrammed energy cycles in the human body, the spirals of DNA become a visual metaphor for complexity and pattern. Isolated structure gives way to total pattern; static function to continual process. The visual impact of books on pattern, symmetry, proportion, and geometry in nature and architecture celebrates and provides a critical complement to the world of words.[33]

The metaphor of biology then is pattern and design. And the emphasis on metaphor is singularly appropriate for biology, for according to Bateson, metaphor is the "language of nature" (Capra, 1988, p. 81), the language of relationships, of story (p. 78). Metaphor directs attention to similarity in structure or organization across realms or events; it is thus the logic of evolving organisms, the map of organization by which hierarchical levels evolve in levels of complexity, each level in a sense metaphoric for each other, creating the "pattern which connects" (p. 81).[34] In the expression of Needleman (1965, p. 10), the universe has become a "teaching," transparent again to old and new messages of unity across levels. The model of systems theory opens up new understandings of the old conception, "As above, so below," echoing worldviews as old as time or only recently recovered as in the medieval writing of Hildegard of Bingen of the cosmic spiral of creation (Fox, 1985), voices lost in the movement toward the mechanistic world models of our paradoxical enlightenment and endarkenment. Bateson goes so far as to argue that systems complexity in the universe gives rise to a naturalistic sense of the sacred in the encounter with pattern and order (Bateson & Bateson, 1987). Systems theory offers implications for philosophy and relational metaphysics which are beginning to be explored.[35] And more immediately, systems theory revolutionizes our understanding of the self and clinical psychology, to which we now turn.

Chapter Six

TOWARD A PROCESS PSYCHOLOGY: SYSTEMS METAPHORS OF SELF AND CHANGE

In personality theory and clinical psychology, systems models find roots in psychological approaches that challenge clinical reductionism in favor of holistic perspectives. Although often relegated to a minority viewpoint, these traditions constitute a kind of lifeline in a search for integrative models. At a time when Jungian thought was not even an academic option, a tradition stemming from Gestalt perceptual research, as well as from Smuts' (1926) emphasis on holism on a larger scale and Goldstein's (1939, 1963) at the more human level, stressed the importance of looking not only at perceptual processes but also human functioning in terms of ordered wholes. This challenge, joined by Maslow, Rogers, May, and other humanistic psychologists, was a significant attack on the analytic and elementaristic emphasis not only of structuralism and behaviorism but ironically of psychoanalysis too with its tripartite view of the psyche.[1] In fact, if there is any tendency toward a broad paradigm shift within the field of psychology, rather than the shift from miniparadigm to miniparadigm that has characterized the difference between schools, it lies in this growing tendency to move from a focus on individual events to the matrix, field, or relationship in which this individual datum is embedded.

The increasing importance of the whole context is seen at many levels: in research methodology, with a move to factor analysis and multifactorial design; and in therapy, with a move from an individual to group emphasis, particularly as represented by the intact system of the couple and family. Family therapy is only one of many forms in which systems theory is reflected in current psychological practice, but it is paradigmatic of the profound shift in assumptions that governs the treatment of symptoms in the context of complex interlocking events.[2]

As part of a move toward increased acknowledgement of the importance of systems, psychologists show signs of broadening the scope of their inquiry or intervention toward concern with the wider contexts in which they operate. This was especially noteworthy in the significant move toward preventive interventions in community mental health before an era of funding cutbacks.[3] To this concern for preventive intervention in the wider social community might be added a range of activities in social advocacy and change, the concern for the political/economic realities reflected in the discipline and practice of psychology, increased activism on behalf of such global issues as nuclear disarmament and peace,[4] and finally the long-overdue but significant trend toward increasing cross-cultural investigation and research within the field of psychology proper.

In current psychological metatheory, the need for an alternative understanding of persons that avoids positing the Western individual self and its epistemological problems as a basic paradigm is receiving increasing attention. For example, Gergen (1988, 1990b) moves psychology closer to the possibility of a systems perspective in affirming an alternative "relational" social science paradigm. Actions and communications are conceived in terms of "relational nuclei" in which two or more people interact, the individual conceptualized as the "intersection" of relational nuclei (1990b, pp. 584–585). Research examining emotions as components of relationship patterns and articulating the regularities in these interchanges, has followed from this approach. While not explicitly translating into a fully extended systems theory, Gergen's relational theory shares with systems theory the capacity to be both integrative and generative of transforming social understandings, some of the central criteria advocated by Gergen (1980) for theory evaluation.

Systems theory emerges in a cultural context of increasing concern for wholeness and speaks to that concern, providing a guiding theory by which to articulate our understandings of interrelatedness across domains. It reflects the need for a new, culturally relevant paradigm that can address these issues in ways that challenge traditional analytic or reductionistic models of understanding. Systems theory confronts especially the need for critiquing the singular reliance on a modern Western view of the individual self, and thus its theory of self emerges also against the context of the wider concern for articulating wholeness.

Systems views of the self in a sense participate in a constructivist perspective. As we have seen, that which is most real for Bateson lies in the relationships of things, in ideas of pattern. He repeatedly argued on behalf of the synthesizing nature of mind and insisted to his audience (1972, p. 478) that you don't "really" see "me," but rather you see pieces of information, information about differences, relationships, which you synthesize as "me." Thus by extension we construct the idea of the individual self. Yet Bateson's constructivism serves to unmask the self as an essence or identity.[5] If the new systems theory of the self is also a construction, it is not based ultimately on a denial of what could be called an ontology or of some sense of reality to be understood. His is not a claim of relativism.

Rather, Bateson's apparent "idealism," that redefines reality with reference to a "network of ideas," a concern for contexts, and an ecology of mind,[6] reaches out toward an understanding of the intrinsic patterned nature of the "eco-mental system."

Systems theory witnesses to a radical reconstruing of the relationship between knower and known. As we will see in this chapter, the impossibility of extracting a clearly bounded and separate self from the interrelationships and cycles of information exchange in which we are embedded is a hallmark of this approach. It suggests the inevitable interconnectedness or co-creation of knower and known, as that which we call mind comes into existence at the same time that the "objects" of our sensory and perceptual experience also come into view.[7] Bateson is interested in breaking down conventional dualisms of epistemology, and his claim to a monistic epistemology lies in this direction, joined also by Laszlo's (1973) emphasis on the monism of systems theory (p. 292).[8] We will see in this chapter that systems theory opens a view of the self that is potentially compatible with other theories of self ultimately grounded in ontological assumptions, particularly those drawn from Eastern insights. Like systems theory, these theories stand in tension with radical constructivist viewpoints, despite agreement with many constructivist insights about the ways the commonsense or apparent individual self is invented and construed.

Systems Metaphors for Self

Probably nowhere is the turn to systems assumptions more radical or fundamental than in the reconceptualization of the self made possible by Bateson's analysis. Historically, Bateson (1972) provides the most extensive and comprehensive metaphor for the interrelated self in modern psychology, drawing from the biological metaphors of systems theory and from information-processing theory or cybernetics. Who are we, then, according to Bateson?

It is critical to remember with Bateson that the fundamental unit of analysis, of understanding, of survival is the organism plus the environment. As we saw in the last chapter, systems are organized wholes interacting with respect to related environments (Laszlo, 1973); we are holons (Koestler, 1967), wholes relative to our smaller parts (organs, molecules, atoms) but parts relative to the larger wholes in which we are embedded (societies, ecospheres, planetary systems, etc.). Systems evolve in the direction of increased complexity and organizational hierarchy, and for Bateson and Laszlo mental properties are "immanent" (Bateson, 1972, pp. 316, 460) in certain levels of organization in all complex natural systems.

Mind has to do with interpreting information about differences gained from at least two levels (Bateson, 1972, 1979). Any system which is complex enough to fold back on itself, to offer these dual levels for creating information about differences, can be coded into levels of rule and metarule to structure and interpret the information available in the interests of adaptation.

At the human level, the process of receiving, interpreting and acting on information about the world is a complex interactive process and the term "mind" refers to the entire system. Thus, in the analogy used by Bateson (1972), when "I" chop down the tree, a whole stream of events ensues in which my eyes receive light wave impressions from the tree which in turn are processed by my cortex. Messages are sent to the muscles, which swing the axe, thus receiving further information regarding the stroke as it contacts the tree and sending renewed information to the retina and on to the brain and so forth in an interactive circuit. Where, asks Bateson, does mind begin and end? At what point in this chain of interacting events does "I" begin and end? Instead of continuing to hypothesize a "delimited agent" or "I" performing a specific goal-oriented act (p. 318), Bateson proposes that the term self refer to the entire system of interpreting and interacting with new information. In his broadening of the metaphor of self to refer to the entire interacting System, self no longer refers to an individual "me" with conscious identity only, a noun or a thing. Self becomes a perspective or metaphor for wholeness, interacting with a larger wholeness. Nothing less than a complete revolution in our metaphor for self is implied.

Bateson is doing what all theorists perhaps end up doing—using metaphor to break the hold of limiting metaphor, using a new metaphor to get beyond an older metaphor. Thus not only does he give us a new meaning for "self," but in a sense dissolves the self as metaphor. Self as "thing" (Bateson, 1972, p. 318), whether as expression of ego functions, identity, action process or wholeness, is to be left behind. As Bateson readily points out (p. 462), this shift requires a radical restructuring of thought. It requires a total shift in the locus of self from individual wholeness to total embeddedness and interrelatedness of all systems with each other. "Open systems" characteristics have typified a number of Western personality theories which oppose behavioral and psychoanalytic assumptions of human reactivity and homeostasis, but most retain an idea of the "integumented" personality contained within the skin (Allport, 1960, p. 306).[9] It is this idea that Bateson most centrally challenges. Bateson's use of the term "self" opens up a way of looking at the inherent interconnectedness of us all as humans and of human with inanimate matter/energy via information loops and the message of a difference; it recognizes the possibility of conceptualizing ways in which you and I are one Self, sharing one interacting system of potential cosmic consciousness (see also Campbell, 1972).

In effect, though Bateson distinguishes the language of physics and force/energy from the language of communication (without resorting to mind/matter dualism), the systems model/metaphor for the self seems metaphorically congruent with the view of the universe given in modern quantum physics, with its portrayal of the dynamic energy transformations of an interconnected universe and the translation of atom from thing into shifting concentrations of energy patterns having tendencies to exist. Likewise, the systems metaphor for the self moves in the direction of kinship with insights from Eastern religious thought which emphasize, as in the Hinduism of the *Upanishads*, the ultimate identity of individual essence and highest cosmic principle, or even more congruently, the experience of no-self of Buddhism.[10] For these traditions, realization and enlightenment involve the surrender of individual particulateness and ego-preoccupation to the experience of nonduality or interdependence. And surprisingly, if not ironically, the systems metaphor of self, in dissolving the individual concept of self to include the richness of interaction as the focus of attention, is not so far from the behavioral blueprint of response and environmental consequence, intertwined in a continual, never-ending sequence. This difference between behavioral and systems models is akin to that between Newtonian and Einsteinian models, between abstract skeletons and the complexity of models attempting a new level of detail, between mathematical formula and visualized image, between linear chains and complex loops or patterns.

Have we dissolved the metaphor of self, or do we have a new process metaphor for self? In this way of thinking, self is a viewpoint or a perspective, not a thing (Hillman, 1975). Self might mean a perspective by which attention is paid to wholeness, to interrelatedness. Perhaps one "selfs" or one "is selfing" when we perceive wholeness, we tune in to our connections, our participation in greater wholes. Self is channel to a way of receiving information in terms of its connections. Self means seeing from the center. We have the capacity to operate with other metaphors—to focus on conscious problem solving, on identity and uniqueness, and these qualities have valuable uses as tools in adapting and living, as well as showing developmental appropriateness at stages of life.[11] Yet, ego-based perspectives based on individual particularity are of lesser scope, involve fewer variables and complexities and therefore risk errors of judgment, compared to the wider perspective of the systems self.[12] Modern clinical psychology predominantly has used individual metaphors of self and left the larger perspectives to science and religion. It will be the task of a systems psychology to seek ways of helping people develop more inclusive metaphors for self, which also might facilitate the kinds of broader perspectives necessary for envisioning solutions to global dilemmas.

Self is a perspective from which I see "me" as only one level of hierarchy, connected to all. Yet my "me-ness," even in its partiality is genuinely and fully there, for that which is me can be seen as a kind of unique concentration of energy, a warp in the total field, a combination of unique though interacting parts. The systems view of self thus allows with Teilhard de Chardin (1959) a way to conceptually honor individual uniqueness in the system of total complexity to an extent not usually found in Eastern thought.[13] And yet there is no boundary or edge to "me." I am not something I own. "Me-ness" is not a possession, like an identity, but a perspective, one side of an ambiguous figure. I am embedded, inextricably connected with what is. As Lévi-Strauss (1978, pp. 3–4) writes, "I appear to myself as the place where something is going on, but there is no 'I', no 'me.' Each of us is a kind of crossroads where things happen." Self is more of a witnessing and a surrender, not the stock piling of self-knowledge or rehearsal of life history.

In light of this systems transformation of the self, one readily can see why revolutions have directed attention to purging language systems to facilitate new ways of seeing. Can one carry this wider vision of self without slipping into old habits? Would we be better off without the word self at all? How does a systems psychology, a process psychology keep consciousness focused on the whole rather than the part? How can a systems psychology help individuals reconceptualize themselves in keeping with concepts which radically change their perceptions?

Are there stages of evolution in the development or perception of the relevance of a systems view of self, akin to the transition Jung wrote of between ego and self and found recurrently in the world's religious traditions as a process of learning to surrender ego? Is the discipline of behaviorism ironically a possible training ground for detaching from ego-preoccupations (*my* feelings, *my* thoughts, *my* sensations, *my* emotions, *my* needs) and individual melodrama that fix attention on irrelevant aspects of ego metaphors and make the transition to larger perspectives so difficult? The spiritual teacher Gurdjieff (1975, p. 75) was not so far from Skinner in arguing that indeed most humans have no self, no "I," no center connected to a greater whole; we are "plural" beings, robots buffeted by pleasurable and painful consequences. From this angle, behaviorism is a kind of Protestant "cold turkey" approach to enlightenment that stripped away attachment to particularity and individual separatism but never sufficiently re-embedded the response-consequence bones it exposed in a medium capable of nurturing connection to the total universe and levels of being. It mistook laboratory cleanliness for cosmic reality, and line for texture. We will pursue these questions at greater length, examining implications of systems theory concepts for therapeutic intervention, including personal decision making and action, and for self-growth and transpersonal development.

Systems Approaches to Therapy

Systems models join other therapeutic perspectives that place central emphasis on the importance of surrender to the larger whole as a way of mediating and transcending internal conflicts. Looking specifically at some of the implications of systems consciousness for therapy, Bateson (1972, pp. 309–337) directed attention at the dilemma of the alcoholic who is locked typically in a symmetrical pattern or battle between the part of him/herself that wants to drink and the part that wants to stop. Seen from the perspective of a wider view of the self, attempts to help the alcoholic too often end up buttressing only one side of this conflict versus the other through appeals to developing more will power. The condition of being split between parts of oneself needs the remedy of wholeness, however, not an escalation of the splitness. Bateson argued that the only exit from this type of splitness came through a move to a complementary mode or surrender to a greater level of wholeness, by which the system could shift from an escalating polarity to responsive attention to the total set of needs.[14] Thus the conceptualized solution is for the alcoholic to surrender to the reality that all parts, including the desire to drink and to stop, are parts of the self and in fact part of the greater system in which the alcoholic is embedded. Only with surrender, a concept fully compatible and represented by the Alcoholics Anonymous' appeal to a higher power, can one bypass the escalating and deadlocked competition of part with part. Alcoholics Anonymous, in which persons acknowledge their own inability to solve their problems alone through self-will and learn to surrender to a larger perspective, provides a healing metaphor of wholeness which might become a more widely adopted model of therapy in our time. The essence of the model is not the structure or details of AA, however, but the shift from a technology of self-control to a reconceptualization and refeeling of the self as surrendered and in fact already inescapably part of a larger whole, not only the self as construed from my own perspective of growth, but the self as part of the larger universe.

Bateson's model of the central importance of surrender for therapeutic change and possible exit from the dialectic of battles of self-control might become then an important model for all therapeutic strategies wherein an individual is caught in a war against oneself for control and change. The goal is to surrender to a type of awareness which refocuses the point of tension, with unwanted behavior falling away by its own weight rather than as a result of a tug of war. Perhaps all therapeutic change must rely on a principle of surrender of parts to the experience of a total whole, whether conceived of metaphorically as a whole external to the person or inclusive and internal to the person.

The similarity is striking between Bateson's model and the Jungian emphasis on therapy as movement toward identification with the larger self, though for Jung, the process of psychological healing is often articulated explicitly in terms of recovering a numinous and spiritually understood relationship to the larger whole.[15] We see the model of surrender also at work within psychosynthesis and therapeutic models in which the multiplicity of our various subpersonalities needs recognition with respect to the interests of the whole of who we are. Therapy involves learning to give each subpersonality a "voice" from which the varying parts can negotiate a solution which honors them all in some kind of appropriate balance. The center of the person must expand to include the totality of all these and other potential voices. In the more radical holistic view, common also to transpersonal psychology, the center of personality is best seen as that wholeness which transcends any of the individual voices per se. By honoring completeness as in Jungian perspectives, systems models work against a goal of perfectionism in human personality that would exclude dimensions of our wholeness.[16] Thus ironically systems theory serves as a caution even in the therapeutic task, which only too often is a disguised version of perfectionism.

Another type of inner conflict aided by a systems analysis pertains to the splits between mind and body that are encouraged by our rationalistic valuing and Cartesian dualism. Systems emphases are seen in the decreasing tendency to treat the body in isolation from psychological dimensions, whether the point of intervention begins in medicine (Chopra, 1989) or psychological practice. The importance of dissolving a dualism of brain/mind or body/mind has been emphasized in many schools of therapy as well as in the new field of sports psychology and is reflected in a wide range of approaches to therapeutic body work from neo-Reichean, bioenergetics, and Feldenkreis to the retranslation of meditation techniques and yoga as therapeutic strategies in the West. Other approaches try to wrestle with the mind/spirit dualism that has accompanied much Western thought and seek to legitimize spiritual issues within the contexts of psychological intervention (see Welwood, 1983).

It is a view we recover sometimes only in the face of great pain, when suddenly, in the space of solitude, we are overwhelmed by the immensity of the beauty that is life—the loving, the partings, the interconnected lives woven through time and always. At those moments the view is so beautiful that the heart stretches past its limits with the intensity of the connection. In this moment, all is blessed and precious—the priceless moments of treasured choices, the uniqueness that will never be again, the coming and going of individual essence into light. Each unique life one has loved or known in some way stands like a jewel one may never see again quite that way, and yet it is all there, forever, a gift of sorrow into joy: to have seen anyone, whatever the connection, go through the moments of time, stretched as we are across eternity, to lose and yet to have it all. Is there room in the human soul or heart to witness this beauty, the fabric of shared being, the threads of lives that are woven even now in interconnection?

Couples Work: Systems Insights for Relationships

Imagine for a moment an interpersonal conflict with an intimate friend in which you are both stuck in anger over a perceived disagreement. Each person stands at one pole of a perceived difference, focusing on "my" thoughts, "my" feelings, "my" wishes, "my" regrets, and "my" preoccupations. Currently psychology offers tools for each individual to negotiate, compromise, set goals and evolve from each individual stance, and they are rich tools used often in couples therapy. Yet new alternatives open in shifting to a systems vision of ourselves as inextricably part of each other in the universe of interrelatedness. The potential implications of systems thinking, the dim awareness that in a sense you are me, I am you, might release us from the hurt and disappointment we demand and exact from each other as tribute to our own struggling and dawning individualities. If you and I are ultimately one, perhaps I can honor the differences you are expressing as another perspective from which the larger "us" is seeing momentarily, and lessen my need to have you be just like me to verify my own perspective. No matter what you do, in a sense you carry me forth. I can only wish you well as we explore the facets of our own evolution in wholeness. The need to control in human relationships which seems to follow the fear of separateness might be relinquished from this perspective. The stress is no longer on our separate rights and identities as the basis for negotiation, but on a realization of our connection. Therapy provides an increased awareness and responsiveness to this level of love and mutual concern rather than a rule book for individual allegiances to self-growth.

For Gregory Bateson, love as understood in systems perspectives is far different from love understood individualistically. Love is seen as "cutting across the person as the locus of consciousness, and focusing on complexities above and below" (M. C. Bateson, 1977, p. 64). Love is the "consciously experienced aspect of precise but unconscious computations about patterns of relationship" (p. 62). Love then corresponds to wisdom's understanding of interconnectedness, to "how the world is made" (p. 68), and at the same time, the world is such that this quality of love moving into consciousness is the most basic experience (pp. 68–69). Furthermore, Bateson draws attention to the way in which relationships, partnerships, and marriage need to be conceptualized and understood as patterns with a life of their own; they are not simply the sum of two people's individuality and must be cared for on their own level as systems (p. 64). The relationship itself needs nourishing, beyond the important work in self-growth or communication contributed by each of the partners.

The ultimate oneness of us all, the locus of our selfing within the interconnected web of all reality, leads to a whole new perspective on loss also. In a systems theory retranslation, rather than focusing microscopically on the particular severing we experience between us and the one we love and have lost, our viewpoint broadens. In this wider angle of vision, the movement together and apart between those we meet in life becomes part of a dance of connection. The sense of loss is real within the shorter vision, and not to be suppressed, but the wider eye that sees the loved one carried away, yet connected by subtle threads as the pattern recedes, keeps the sufferer from getting trapped in the experience of separation. The shift in focus allows a reseeing of the whole network in which we are immersed, surrounded by many who love us and are part of the closer, thicker pattern of care, rather than featuring only the one part of the pattern that is receding. It is crucial to understand this re-visioning not as a repression of emotion but a shift in perspective which of its own natural broadening gives respite from the fixation of pain. It is not that we try to cut ourselves off from loss, but that we reimplant the loss within the larger perspective within a universe composed in such a way that ultimate loss is a radical impossibility.

Letting go of the past becomes a reminder that we do not own people. We witness the drifting off in patterns of more distant connectedness, bubbles, threads of light that get more distant in the web of being. What saves this image from the casualness of the "Gestalt prayer" is the commitment to ultimate connection that marks this vision. This is not a "live and let live" defense of a sphere of me-ness, into which others may or may not drift, and toward whom I will make few efforts to follow once their energy passes by my own. Instead the systems perspective holds a sense of participation in the whole that insists on a re-immersing in the totality of who we are. It is thus a fallacy to focus in on the loss of one event and neglect the pattern that is still there in the total web of beginnings and endings. This is not "easy come, easy go," but in fact a wrenching sense of the flow and pattern of all life as beginnings and leave-takings. There is a process and life cycle to all events, not just literal birth and death. Part of you is always part of me, not only in a sense of reowned projections, but in the literal, concrete patterns we share, however distant.

The desires for permanence, for perfection, for control are born in the forgetting or perhaps even the fear of this vision. The task for us is to learn to witness the flow. We need to be able to be present at the whole array of feelings expressed by loved ones, including irritation and anger, without feeling responsible or guilty or even needing them to be different. It is as if a part of you is caught in that state, needing compassion for the humanness that grabs the attention of the moment, pulling the cosmic "us" off center and glued to the shorter focus. The practice so highly valued in Eastern thought of letting go of attachments to ego needs is predicated on a vision of the oneness we are, beyond the pull of isolated, personal preoccupations. Whether it is our own melodrama or that of another that we mistake for the total picture, the challenge is still to refind the point of wider vision which helps make the attachment fall from the tree under its own overripe weight and excess.

A complementary metaphor to systems emphases comes from Sheldrake's (1981) hypothesis of morphogenetic fields posited to underlie and provide the pattern and guide for living forms.[17] While this theory is highly speculative at this point, it offers an intriguing heuristic for the possibility of repatterning interpersonal relationships. Therapists already use the concept of reprogramming, of providing new cognitive assumptions or new imagery by which to anchor new response repertoires. Would it not be helpful to broaden or enhance this concept to include two-person or family level patterning, such that couples and families might be able to revision their relationship patterns and blueprints to allow for the regeneration of a stronger set of possibilities? The potential usefulness of this metaphor for helping couples and families to visualize new paths of interpersonal action joins other related metaphorical work being done in Neuro-Linguistic Programming and various approaches to family therapy. It highlights the extent to which a pattern in fact literally will replicate itself unless fundamental change occurs at the level of pattern, not simply of overt behavior.

Systems Ethics: Images of Interrelatedness

Systems implications for relationships open into models for relating to the world as relationship. They introduce an ethic of interrelatedness based on surrender to the perspective of the highest inclusiveness; decisions are best made from the perspective of the largest whole or most-encompassing system. Bateson (1972) suggests that our decisions be entrusted only to those whose highest loyalty is to the most integrative and comprehensive level of system (p. 463), and that this also serve as a basis for "personal" decision. In other words, the key to concrete action is in the extent to which all individual decisions can be made with awareness of more inclusive loyalties. This means political decisions, interpersonal decisions, all decision; and it is a task of monumental challenge. It is the challenge of constantly exercising awareness and loyalty to the greater whole, without losing appreciation for the parts of this whole. The danger comes, Bateson cautions (1972, p. 485), when we "separate mind from the structure in which it is immanent," and begin to make decisions decontextualized from relationship, society, or ecosystem.

Systems ethics have much in common with models of ethics arising from feminist perspectives,[18] yet without the gender loadings we see there. In particular, Gilligan's (1982) research on patterns of moral development is highly relevant.[19] Working in the tradition of psychological research on morality begun by Piaget and Kohlberg, yet challenging the universality and normative quality of their findings, Gilligan has found a dramatic contrast between two approaches to ethical decision making found more often in men versus women, although not exclusively. As an example of this approach to studying morality, a classic case is posed in which we are asked whether Heinz should or should not steal a drug that is exorbitantly priced from a druggist who refuses to make the drug accessible to Heinz at a price he can afford. Only this drug will save the life of Heinz's wife. The conventional definition of the highest ethical stage of morality was to argue that yes, he should steal the drug because appeal to an abstract principle of saving a life transcended allegiance to other social conventions. This was the type of answer prototypic for men, whereas Gilligan reported women repeatedly showing a "proclivity" to "reconstruct hypothetical dilemmas" (p. 100), having difficulty accepting the terms of the question as valid ethically. The question of rightness and wrongness and the crux of the ethical issues at stake seemed to have as much to do with the ethics of the druggist's choice as with Heinz's dilemma. Why were there not more alternatives that could be brought to bear to force or allow a different choice on the part of the druggist? By refusing to clearly answer in a straightforward alliance with the ultimate principle of a life to be saved, by challenging parts of the question, these women appeared to be less fully committed to an abstract principle and hence judged less ethically developed by these norms. Gilligan asks, however, if they do not in fact represent, not a lesser ethics, but another approach that carries wisdom neglected in the path we have been most taught to follow.

Essentially Gilligan (1982) contrasts two approaches to ethics: an ethics of principle and an ethics of relatedness. On the one hand is an ethic based in its highest ideal on an appeal to abstract universal principles of justice, beyond consideration even for what society has conventionally agreed is appropriate, and beyond allegiance to individual reward or instrumentality. It is an ethic that can be likened to a form of mathematical calculation, where certain parameters can be fed into a linear equation and a specific right action will emerge. This is an ethic of justice and law, of duty to principle, of the necessity for judgment. What ought I to do is a question that follows naturally from the belief in a right action, a possible perfection, a best choice.

In contrast to this view, Gilligan (1982) found an equally intense and poignant approach to the ethical task, but which seemed to reflect a different context and set of parameters. In this alternative vision, ethical decision making represents a process not of weighing abstract principles, but entering into a total context of potentially competing elements and finding a choice that pays honor to the widest circle of circumstances and nuances in the web in which each decision stands. Rather than a linear formula, the metaphor is more like a network of perspectives needing consideration and balancing. There is no lack of coming to terms with detail or hard choices, but rather a respect for decisions issuing forth from a total contextual exploration, with perhaps a focus on the uniqueness of each choice. The accent is not on duty, but on responsiveness to a totality. The abstract principle is only part of the total context of respect for the individuality and uniqueness of each choice.

While Gilligan observed this contrast in ethical decision making in the context of male-female differences, her concern is for broadening our base of ethical decision making to include both approaches. Her analysis provides further imagery then for constructing and feeling our way into a systems ethic, seeking clues for a new guide to living. One of the many strengths of systems theory as a guide to a new ethics is its power in offering a gender neutral conceptualization that also remains true to these insights.

In exploring systems metaphors that inform ethics and choices in living, the concern is to stretch into possibilities of new perspectives and actions congruent with a worldview of interconnectedness.[20] We are more familiar with the search for the "correct" solution through responsibility to a principle of rightness. We have not learned to trust an ethics of connection and responsiveness to that which is, where compassion or love is the deepest response to the truth of interrelatedness, and where caring for creation, for all levels of the total system, including ourselves, becomes the central impulse. We might speak more accurately of an ethics of being, of the outflow of caring and love, an ethics of response-ability, in the sense of ability to respond (Slater, 1974). Like an ethics of action and duty, it too involves surrender, but a surrender to the flow of experience and interconnected reality, not to abstract command or principle. Only as I become aware of the network of interconnectedness do I learn to guide myself in harmony with the whole and thus move through crisis points. Whether this means greater freedom or not is paradoxical and unclear, for movement in attunement with the threads of the universe, with the lines of natural consequence is a great responsibility and focusing point for action. I am grounded in a universe of which I am part, from which I cannot fragment off without great consequence. Life has already started; I am in motion already as part of the All; there is no neutral timeout spot from which to claim or seek the next best step.

In this vision there is an interesting connection to the concept of karma, a sense that choices are to be made according to their natural alignment with the way in which the universe seems to operate. If all is interconnected, then that which one gives out, one will get back. If one moves outward in force and antagonism, these forces push back. If one moves outward in love, the universe responds in kind. There is no need to be commanded to do so; this is the essence of the fabric, the ultimate reality of which we are a part.

Perhaps as we step through the metaphor of duty into an ethics of interrelatedness we cross also between the realm of action and being, one of the classical dichotomies or complementarities which have separated East and West and challenged personal efforts at integration.[21] Even the insistence on an ethical language of action and doing may lead us away from an awareness of times when being receptive and not-doing may in fact be greater wisdom. The Taoist concept of wu-wei, of active non-action, of learning to be receptive to the most fruitful time, and not push the gestation of possibility beyond its natural cycle are learnings not easily found in the West. The blessings of "moon consciousness" as Neumann (1973, p. 60) calls these qualities, the subtle trusting of the planted seed to grow in darkness and secrecy, the sustaining of the incubation of all creativity—these are tasks of undoing, of unlearning, so hard for a culture trained to measure worth in terms of output, action, and visible, tangible change. Systems ethics allow a kind of complementarity between action and receptivity, fostering decisions made in full awareness of our embeddedness in larger contexts of wholeness. Thus, although systems perspectives impel action, they are predicated on a surrender to the concerns of a larger, differentiated whole whose simultaneous, complex, competing needs all deserve consideration and balance.

Action and Surrender

In light of the importance of surrender in systems theory and ethics, it is possible that we must rethink the whole context of modern Western therapy as focused on active change. The Western versus Eastern contrast between an ethics of action versus being is a polarity also found within Western models. For example, cognitive-behaviorism emphasizes active intervention in concrete particulars of a person's life; in contrast, depth psychologies place central value on developing fuller awareness rather than change per se. It is precisely this contrast which first led behaviorists to critique psychoanalysis for its apparent lack of evidence or concern for demonstrating behavior changes in those seeking analysis. It would of course be an exaggeration to deny any interest in change by depth approaches, but their critical concern is with the shift in consciousness that premises such change, all else being secondary and under the full choice of individuals coming to know themselves with greater candor and subtlety, beyond even the locus of their initial complaints.

This contrast in perspective shows up in accentuated form in the differences between the cognitive-behaviorally compatible school of Neuro-Linguistic Programming (NLP) and Jungian analytical psychology. NLP shows its allegiances to an active, goal-oriented, agentic stress on excellence, personal power, clean crisp action, decisiveness, and a whole technology of tools for change. The risk in its extreme is of becoming a remarkably efficient but fast food approach to change, issuing from the latest technological advances and packaged in bitesize, learnable, interchangeable, and programmable chunks to facilitate assimilation and control. It is a new technology of control, more cognitive and sensitive to hidden dimensions of being human than its strict behavioral predecessors, but a therapy in service of an ethics of change nonetheless. If you are sad, there are tools to rid you of that. If you are anxious, you can chain yourself out of your conditioning into new resourceful states of action. Mulling around experiencing a negative feeling becomes taboo in the efficiency of becoming a fully actualized, competent human being.

In contrast to this picture is the Jungian perspective, seen from this angle as far closer to the ethic of surrender, of receptivity, of letting happen, even at the risk of miring down in an inner search or getting lost in archetypal paths of meaning. If NLP values too highly the concrete and the pragmatic, Jungian perspectives in their extreme carry a different danger of preoccupation with arcane wholeness or belittling the nexus of daily decision making. It is as if NLP and Jungian approaches are shadows to each other. Lest this description of these approaches ring too harshly or caricatured, note also the possibility (as with all shadow reciprocities) of tremendous learning available from the dialogue. Might not these therapies be ultimately compatible if each is conceived for different purposes or tasks of life?

To borrow the Jungian perspective that the challenge of midlife involves movement from identification with the ego or partial sense of who we are to the surrender of centeredness to the larger and more total self, might not NLP and Jungian analysis be complementary aids to this process? Thus NLP becomes a fit tool for the first half of life, a preparation for the process of ego detachment, cleaning up the person's "act," training one in the sensory acuity needed in gaining a fuller awareness of one's own states and environmental changes, helping the ego set goals or outcomes and achieve accordingly, unhooking addictions and knee-jerk conditionings in preparation for learning how to be. The Jungian path then might provide a deeper and more comprehensive sense of the wholeness we seek to enter and live from, a schooling in listening and surrender, a voice to explore the question that comes even with a life filled with successful outcomes: Is this all there is? When one tires of reprogramming one's negative feelings, when sadness seems a tender point of truth not an emotion to be cleverly obliterated or retrained for better "adjustment," then the Jungian voice is the one we may turn to for a longer nourishment. Both visions thus can help to inform a comprehensive systems model, if kept in relationship to the paradigmatic need for surrender to the larger whole.

Systems models offer a framework by which to more easily assimilate insights from Asian and Eastern psychological models. Bateson (1972, p. 487), in fact, specifically notes the relevance of "Oriental philosophy" to correct for the danger of "Occidental" epistemology and its implications for action in the world. The contrast we have seen between learning to change one's relationship with the world through active intervention, rather than through an increased awareness of what is, also corresponds to Western versus Eastern concepts of control, for example. Primary control, a process of gaining control by *manipulating* change in one's environment or personal behavior patterns is characteristically North American; secondary control, or the process of gaining control and its correlate of comfort through *adapting* to the realities of one's surroundings and living in harmony with that which is, characterizes Japanese modes (Weisz, Rothbaum, & Blackburn, 1984).

Therapeutic strategies parallel these differences in psychological perspective.[22] For the Westerner, therapy is aimed typically at the elimination of symptoms and toward a change in the key relationships in one's life through increased assertiveness, negotiation, and other means of intervention. Instead of stressing such change in behavior, many therapeutic approaches in Japan in contrast would be focused on developing a new perspective for a situation such that one might live with the problem situation with greater peace and freedom. In this perspective, the goal is not to solve the problem, but to shift one's perspective to allow one to live in a different way relative to the total situation.[23] Classical Morita therapy involves the virtual isolation of the individual from any source of reinforcement and only the very gradual reintroduction of activity in keeping with an emphasis on work for others, rather than a self-preoccupied stuckness that keeps attention recycling only on the narrow needs of the solitary ego. The emphasis is on learning to do what needs doing in response to the present moment, rather than trying to avoid or change what one is feeling. A complementary emphasis occurs in Naikan therapy, which aims through explicit training in a kind of structured meditation, to help a person shift from preoccupation with the illusions of ego and conflict that have characterized the problem situation to a reappreciation of the needs of others and the whole network of reciprocal obligation and loving connection in which one is ultimately connected.[24] Reynolds argues that emotions and feelings come and go like the weather; one must not be attached to trying to change them, but remain responsive to the concrete demands of the network of obligations and choices in which one lives. For Reynolds, Morita therapy with its Zen-like attention to acting in awareness of the present moment is held in natural balance with Naikan therapy, with its emphasis on the embeddedness of us all in inescapable interdependencies which when recognized lead to the experience of ongoing gratitude. One can see similar emphases to systems ideas in this counsel.

Though there is to be sure a long tradition of cultural valuing of duty and communal obligation in Asian nations, the emphasis on the self as intrinsically interpersonally embedded and defined (Roland, 1988) is only one way that systems theory overlaps with Asian perspectives on the self, particularly the Chinese (Hsu, 1985). Asian perspectives from India and Japan reflect even more fundamentally a worldview in which the temporarily grasped ego self with which we identify is a provisional and ultimately false concept. In this view, problems follow the misleading creation of an independent self, separated out by analytical thinking from the larger consciousness of which we are a part. It is a case of mistaking our small mind for "Big Mind" (Suzuki, 1970), instead of seeing their ultimate oneness. Western self-control models, in replacing external duty and connection to a larger social context with a kind of internal duty to one's own ego, often forget that this very commitment to the narrow self can perpetuate the problem. It is often only when we surrender even the need to try to solve our particular truncated problem, the melodrama of our ego identification, that real change is possible (Dass, 1974; Dass & Levine, 1977). It is an old wisdom common to Rogerian and Gestalt perspectives also, that only with acceptance of that which is does one gain the standpoint from which to move on to whatever else one is. We make room for the next step by reincorporating our disowned polarities to provide a neutral and enhanced field from which to grow.

The same challenge applies to therapists themselves. As long as we are preoccupied with the need to help, meaning that we are attached to the vision of helper, or the need to see change to feel we are helping, we will have difficulty learning to be with another as witness to their own possibilities.[25] If someone wants to change, and I as therapist hope for them the same changes they envision with attachment, I cannot be with them as they broaden their base for a new surrender and wider choice. Learning to let people be, whether in therapy or personal relationships, knowing how to refrain from the helpfulness of insightful feedback that overloads the very being of the one we "help," is a task more difficult than any save love, of which it is perhaps another voice.

When Wallach and Wallach (1983) critique psychology for its support of selfishness, they aptly critique the unfortunate side effects of much of the human potential movement in focusing on "my" needs, "my" feelings, and "my" conveniences. They muster evidence for perspectives within the field which move the accent away from the limited needs and interests of the ego. They note theories which stress the need to contribute to something beyond oneself, calling on Adler's sense of social interest, on Erikson's stress on generativity, and on Frankl's examples of ways to transcend suffering through existential commitments to the need of others. They turn also to the Eastern and Asian philosophies and practices in which service to others or concern beyond the self is critical to psychological recovery and health, and to Western strategies of therapeutic paradox, humor, and paradoxical intention, which engage the person in a new attitude where they can laugh at themselves and become less self-preoccupied. The Wallachs' critique of models of selfishness offers a strong parallel to issues emerging from the systems models we have been exploring, including the central shift in focus from "me" to the totality in which I am embedded, and the stress on interventions that do not chronically serve to reinforce "my" feelings, needs, thoughts, and distress as the paramount issue at stake. Yet it is important to note that from a systems perspective, the reason for such a shift is not an appeal to an ethics of duty in which one needs be reminded of moral responsibilities to others. Rather systems theory offers a worldview whose very reality of interrelatedness evokes a caring response in harmony with this awareness. Thus the use of the term "selfishness" may harken us back to a duty base of ethics in its tone, rather than helping us revision a universe in which ethics follows from awareness of interconnectedness.

Transpersonal Models of Wholeness

It would make sense in an understanding of systems theory that the whole variety of therapeutic traditions that we have surveyed might each have a useful place within the hierarchical levels of learning in a interrelated scheme. This is precisely the kind of organization offered by Wilber (1977, 1981) who from a different but profoundly integrative perspective seeks to provide a map for how we might learn to move in harmony with insights of wholeness in living.

In Wilber's scheme, the primary reality he calls "unity consciousness" (p. 13), or the experience of oneness with all that is. This type of consciousness transcends the duality of subject and object that characterizes most types of consciousness, and though one cannot know what reality is like by external study which necessarily preserves the subject-object split, through discipline one can put oneself into a position of openness to experience reality through one's own participation and interconnectedness with reality. The experience of reality from the inside is reported as one of unity and interconnectedness with all that is. There is no sense of differentiation between me and the world, self and other, but rather a sense of connected being. All is—without label or judgment. The perceptual state or set from which the world is experienced as whole, where there is a unity of self and all, may be entered via many different paths and disciplines, and we have seen that it resembles the perspective opened up by systems theory.

While Wilber argues that unity consciousness is the primal perception, it is one quickly lost sight of in the expansion of mind into more and more complex forms of consciousness. As consciousness evolves toward more and more complexity, it reflexively folds back on itself, creating dichotomies. The first major dichotomy to emerge is the distinction between self and other, self and environment. We begin to draw a line between our skin and all that is outside of us and hence different. We forget our embeddedness in the rest of the ecosystem with which we are interdependent. The second dichotomy to emerge is the distinction between body and mind, or body and ego. Our conscious rational ability to plan and problem-solve comes to see itself as the center of our personality and draws a line or duality between itself and our body. The body and its needs and apperceptions are forgotten and relegated to an inferior position in modern life. The third major duality to emerge in humans is created by the line which most of us learn to draw between those parts of us that are acceptable and desired and those parts of us which we would rather disown or ignore, the part of us which Jung calls the shadow. We begin to forget that we have a shadow side and instead are ready to project our own qualities onto others in forms we either hate or love.

Thus, for Wilber, what we call normal waking consciousness is characterized by at least three major dichotomies and divisions between our acceptable and unacceptable sides, between our minds (egos) and our bodies, and between our individual selves and the rest of the world. This means that ordinary consciousness is divided, fragmented, and very far from the type of unitive experience of the world which seems available as a primal human experience. Human development passes through stages of differentiation and boundary-making as our identity recedes from primal consciousness to progressive identifications with a body-ego, a mental-ego, and a social-ego, each stage demanding a disidentification with previous self-understandings and a transcendence to a new awareness (Wilber, 1980a, 1980b). Only gradually does the awareness emerge of potentialities for higher unities of experience and the possibility of disidentifying with the ego-self we have come to think we are, in order to continue transcending to new levels of unity and wholeness. It is this very hierarchy of splitness and developmental evolution of stages, governed by the need for increasing levels of wholeness, that provides a valuable framework for organizing the multitude of therapies that exist today (Wilber, 1977, 1981). Thus, we could argue that at the level of healing persona-shadow splits, Freud, Jung, Rogers, Kelly, and even Skinner have much to contribute in returning areas of skill or ownership of qualities to the person's own repertoire and awareness. At the level of the body-mind split, the various approaches to body work, Gestalt, neo-Reichian, Feldenkrais, and Sheldon's constitutional psychology have much to offer. Finally in moving to reincorporate the self-world split, the work of Jung, Lewin, Assagioli, systems theory and Eastern thought offer rich resources. Keutzer (1983a) suggests the principle of complementarity as a model or metaphor for approaching the task of integrating the major approaches of behaviorism, psychoanalysis, humanistic-existential, and transpersonal theory.

Using a different set of levels but a similar commitment to integration, Ajaya (1983) also seeks to demonstrate the appropriateness of various therapies to different levels of problem. Ajaya, however, uses his hierarchy to argue even for the limits of systems theory. To the extent that systems theory keeps levels intact and does not surrender to the implied oneness beyond and sustaining of this system of hierarchy, Wilber would potentially agree. For in Wilber's analysis (1977, 1981), the last split to be healed is the very split into subject and object that characterizes the rational inquiring mind, even we might add the mind intent on experiencing the intricacies of systems theory. To acknowledge the separation of theory from that which is, and to witness for oneself the dissolving of self in the All, requires the preparation best carried in our time by the vehicle of direct experience and spiritual discipline.[26]

We come then to a profound disjuncture. The very insights into an interconnected world, when carried by metaphor, remain remote from the direct and immediate sense of knowing. Systems theory speaks profoundly of a universe of interrelatedness, but as theory, cognitive structure and metaphor, cannot carry us into the very realm to which it points. Yet this is not really a new problem. It is the problem of all knowledge as approximation, of metaphor as a vehicle that must be tested, problems we have seen to characterize the legitimate use of metaphor in all fields. Why would it not be even more true in the realm of personal and ethical experience that we cannot bypass the testing?

Seen from a developmental perspective, the disjuncture might more accurately be conceived as an illustration of an organic process in cognitive development. Thus, Koplowitz (1984) argues that "general systems" thinking can be seen as a more flexible and inclusive mode or stage of cognition that supercedes formal operational or linear thought in Piaget's model, with "unitary" modes superceding in turn even systems thinking.

In either case, where are the clues as to how to test the limits of systems insights vis-à-vis unitary consciousness, or how do we discern any possible distinction between these modes? How do we carry out the testing of the limits of metaphor in this context? Wilber (1977, 1981, 1984b) points us to the Eastern traditions, and the value of meditation as a type of empirical tool for witnessing to the insights affirmed by spiritual traditions throughout the world. Yet how does the contemporary West prepare for such a practice, without using meditation out of context as a technique, as limiting as any technology unattached to a wider perspective? The growing field of transpersonal psychology may perhaps be a great help to this working out of a systems psychology, in calling on metaphors to help us move as Westerners beyond strict identification with our personalities, bodies, minds, feelings, or even we might say our highest "selves."

Transpersonal psychology teaches us to distinguish between the many identifications we have labeled as self and the broader center from which our greater identity is realized.[27] Similar to the self for Jung or Assagioli, this wider center is at one with the larger universe, such that acting from this center is to move in greater harmony with all that is. The challenge is to learn to move from attachment to the ego qualities we think are us to this wider center of acceptance. The fallacy of much of the West, argues Gurdjieff (1975), is to assume that this center of personality is ready made, whereas instead it is the product of immense effort to learn to disidentify with the ever-changing, almost random movements of our various thinking, feeling, and moving subcenters. There is a tremendous irony here, in Gurdjieff's similarity to Skinner in arguing for the robotlike quality of much of human existence without a self.

As we have seen, Skinner in his emphasis on the non-existence of self has much in common with non-Western traditions in this respect. Skinner may help provide, somewhat paradoxically and unintentionally, a critical first step in addressing the problem of moving beyond identification with partial facets of who we are. Rather than attacking Skinner from a transpersonal perspective, we might use his theory to free us from the attachment to the melodrama of our feelings and inner states, much as we might use NLP to clean up our conditionings in preparation for the same type of transition to a broader identification. For those aspects of ourselves in which we demonstrate our robotness, Skinner's work is entirely appropriate, and any spiritual seeker knows how far these robot traps extend. When Skinner (1983) says feelings are not important for understanding the human, we may protest, when in reality perhaps feelings indeed are not ultimately important except as clues to where our egos are trapped or stuck.

If Skinner becomes a surprising aid, Assagioli (1965, 1973) provides in psychosynthesis a more congruent practice for learning to disidentify with our various subpersonalities and act from a higher Self, expressing a Will subordinate to this Self rather than to an obstreperous superego. The heart of the relearning is actually a kind of "unlearning" of our attachments, seen throughout the array of transpersonal and Eastern approaches we have surveyed. It is the practice of learning to allow feelings to be, yet not create them into shrines by our identification; it is the practice of learning to be gentle with ourselves (Welwood, 1983). It is the initiation into the "tender heart" (Trungpa, 1984, p. 46) by which our center bears the eyes of sadness and joy in witnessing the reality of all that is. It is training in the witness, in presence, in acceptance, in a wider awareness. It is a discipline in which the soaring of mystical insight is only a beginning, not an end (Needleman, 1980). And finally it is a path that returns us to the Now, to life in the daily world of unexpected demands, the non-mountaintop reality of washing dishes, telephone calls, and teeth to be brushed. Chop wood, carry water, is the Zen attitude. Cultivate your garden. It is a quiet image, but no less precious or helpful for its simplicity. It offers a small metaphor for integration and an image of wholeness to help us in these most fragile and exciting of times.

In our exploration of metaphors for self, we have come a long way from the clean-lined language of behaviorism; but whether asceptic or full-bodied, metaphor is metaphor nonetheless, to be judged by its usefulness in opening up new terrain. While the language and tone of systems metaphor rings mystical to an ear accustomed to more linear language, the systems metaphor may actually more closely mirror the phenomenological complexity of the world captured by such forms of science as Chinese empiricism (Porkert, 1974), where abstraction and the "fallacy of misplaced concreteness" (Whitehead, 1925) have been less dominant than in Western science. Science works via a process of abstraction and re-immersion in concrete detail, a dance of hypothesis and testing, of theory and data collection. It is time for abstraction to be re-immersed in new complexity.

Metaphor is the language of approximation; it is a realm for fruitful borrowing and mutual enrichment; it is a level of abstraction where paths with separate content or type of analysis can interact. Systems theory began perhaps in the first movements toward higher understandings in all fields. While the closeness of some of its language to cybernetics and information-processing theory makes the tone sound new, systems theory offers metaphors for the self that are very old, yet congruent with modern physics and biology as well as world religious traditions, and complementary to other metaphors for self that anchor our particularity and uniqueness. If systems metaphors of the self are to be critiqued, it is not because they are metaphor per se but because they too may distort the reality we may come to know.

Part Three

INDRA'S NET

PROLOGUE

I had not been to the ocean all summer. As I walked with effort across the long stretch of dry sand that mounted on the edge of the shore and came finally within the muffled roar of the surf that autumn afternoon, it all began to fall into place. Yes, that was what was missing. Yes. The smell of the damp, ancient foam and seaweed, the rhythm of the ocean's incessant messengers to shore. I had forgotten her voice, the heartbeat of the earth. She who gives and takes away. The ocean, the living earth, the moving earth, surging, breathing, a feeling of home.

There is a horizontal god unknown to the mountain climber, whose vertical god meets one at the embrace of mountain peak and sky. The horizontal god is born of the water and shore, the meeting of a rhythmic pattern of embrace and retreat, of change and inconstancy, yet ever the same. She speaks a different voice, another voice—not of what to do, or which path to take or how to find the way up and out, but how to perceive, how to receive, how to be. The horizontal god teaches about waiting for treasures, about patience, and the right time, not about striving and climbing and success and achievement. Even walking on the sandy shores of the horizontal realm abounds in learning to handle patience, slogging through uneven sand, the whole body surprised at the inertia of a forward step, with nothing firm to resist and push against for balance. This is the language of learning to be, not figuring out what to do. The horizontal questions have to do with networking and living now, here, not how to get out, up, away.

The same threshold to the quieting of the heart is crossed in coming back down from the higher reaches of the mountain trail into the sun-dappled presence of a softer mystery. There too lives the horizontal god of connection, not soaring. The forest can be a cathedral, when the light crosses its path and the vertical god intersects the horizontal god in a new domain. But as the sunlight fades, or even as it graces the moments of the crossing, the light is a visitor to a silence or the sound of the wind's presence, and one enters a world which will be there even as the light fades. In this soft-needled home of an interconnected ecology of peace and beauty, the forest breathes in itself. Like the ocean, the forest exists just as it is, not through inspiration or transecting God's rays, but as realm of infinite variety, pattern, order, disorder, chaos, and design, precious because it is. And we too become a part, even in the brief time we share with the trail.

Chapter Seven

IMAGES OF WHOLENESS: TOWARD A UNIFYING SYSTEMS METAPHOR

The vitality of systems theory as an interdisciplinary metaphor and model, with considerable implications for constructing a worldview of wholeness, invites us to examine the potential role of this metaphor in the field of religion as well. The importance of metaphor in science and psychology is paralleled by its equally formative role in religion, and in none of these fields has this realization been entirely comfortable. Just as those committed to scientific thinking have had to stretch at times to acknowledge the essential role of models and metaphor in approximating knowledge, so too the person committed to a religious path of truth may fear an eclipse of meaning in acknowledging the partiality of human vision for expressing a sense of ultimate reality and concern. Yet religious language expresses a truth claim and affirms a cognitive value and meaning referent; it does not simply express human emotion or experience (Soskice, 1985). And any path to truth must ultimately grapple with issues of the limits of knowledge and objectivity, the necessity for approximating ultimate truths, and the role of metaphor and models in the approximation of these truths. However numinously they may be experienced, or deep the convictions of the realities to which they point, the concepts by which we attempt to express ultimate reality share many things in common with the uses of metaphor that we have seen in other fields.[1]

The power of metaphor and myth lies precisely in their capacity to suggest and attempt to grasp that which is essentially ungraspable in words and rational, linear logic. Metaphor and symbols, in their capacity to point beyond, provide a bridge to glimpse the fleeting insights we have into that which we hold to be most important, real, or significant about our experience of reality. It is the capacity of metaphor and myth to carry feeling as well as thought, to reach toward wholeness, to transcend polarity, to embody knowing in a tangible experiential language rather than pale abstraction, that gives this mode of expression its power in religion. As Eliade (1959, 1963) writes, myth reenacts the context of the real, the time of origins, bringing ultimate and sacred dimensions into present intersection with reality. For Geertz, metaphor is the mediating language central to religious conceptions, conveying a sense of meaning that is not overly theoretical or theologized (Van Herik, 1984). For Ricoeur, symbols carry the capacity of pointing beyond themselves in an open-ended way; the symbol in some sense "precedes meaning" (Bynum, 1986, p. 9).

The concern for the dangers of idolatry that has characterized the history of world religious traditions is in many ways an issue directly related to the role of metaphor. The concern to avoid idolatry is the concern that human images and concepts of ultimate reality or divine essence not be mistaken for the reality toward which our limited and partial human vision points. And whether idolatry is expressed in a golden calf, or a concept of God that has come to fall short of carrying full meaning in an age, the essential similarity is the mistaking of a vehicle of truth and worship with the ultimate referent of its meaning. Feminist critiques of patriarchal metaphors of God are contemporary expressions of this concern.[2] Eastern religious traditions have been especially insistent in acknowledging the inadequacy of all labels and concepts, names and images for ultimate reality. In this perspective, even the highest of spiritual metaphors must be surrendered as "neti neti," not this, not that. The profound proliferation of mythological imagery and the many gods and goddesses of Hinduism serve as a paradoxical reminder to the spiritual seeker of the many faces of divine reality, each of which may seem a valid window to the divine or only partial and relative, depending on one's perspective. Similarly the pantheon of Greek mythology offers a polytheistic metaphor for the infinite richness of ultimate reality (Miller, 1981). In all traditions, the tension between views of God as immanent within all reality, expressed in multifaceted ways, and the image of a transcendent God beyond and separate from all that can be conceptualized, is a tension riding on the crests of two metaphorical systems, perhaps ultimately complementary to each other as the two sides of God (Berger, 1981). As a correction for the dangers of idolatry and literalism, multiple models or metaphors are needed by religious symbol systems.[3]

A great obstacle to sensing the truth-carrying power of metaphor in religion lies in modern misconstruings of mythic forms of expression either as untruths or as fables to be "demythologized" (Rogerson, 1984). The portrayal of myth entirely in terms of a presumed prescientific causal explanation also rendered them vulnerable to erosion before the assault of science and reason, in the demythologizing periods of fifth-century B.C.E. Greece and post-Renaissance Enlightenment (Anton, 1983). However, myth may be understood as a more integrative and holistic way of knowing than that aimed at by science, as a vehicle for synthesis and for truth as experienced. Myths are metaphorical statements about an ultimate concern; they always hint at more than can be expressed in words, enriching truth and reality by that very capacity. Far from undermining the spiritual power of literal renderings, myth can add levels to the intensity and subtlety by which truth is understood (Campbell, 1972).

Myths contribute to cultural and social integrity, yet cannot be reduced to their social functions to provide a "storehouse of adjustive responses," "restore" individuals to "rapport" with society, foster social integration, "strengthen tradition," or even interpret and render culturally meaningful the primary problems of chaos, suffering, and evil. Nor are myths reducible to a psychological role as guide for living, providing a pattern to aid in a "second birth" for humans.[4] From the perspective of religion, the accent on the human as mythmaker needs always to be seen from a framework which stresses the ultimacy of the referent of the myth, not the power of human as creator of the myth. The human as religious is called to the limits of myth by the very complexity and paradoxical quality of that which confronts us and compels our attempt to understand.

Myth can be seen to reflect a "science of the concrete" (Lévi-Strauss, 1966, p. 16), rich in description and classification rather than abstract law, aiming at a total understanding and seeking resolutions of key polarities such as nature/culture. Myth is like the pattern of a musical fugue in which recurrent relationships form a texture that can be read like an orchestral score; the myth maker composes in meaning not sound.[5] Yet myth exceeds these cognitive, structuralist dimensions.

Myth is a way of speaking about the larger unknowns and totalities traditionally judged inappropriate for science and psychology to address, until more recent trends toward renewed attention to cosmology and "Theories of Everything" in science and "grand theory" in the social sciences.[6] Myth is essentially integrative and insists on the context of the wider picture (Greeley, 1972). Myth provides a way of being grounded in the universe (Eliade, 1958), revealing a "transparency" and translucence to meaning and significance. Myths have a logical pattern of their own, shaping our view of the world as "organs of reality" (Cassirer, 1946, p. 8). The language of myth is symbol, concrete image and metaphor, a "picture-language of the soul." Myths speak the language of ambiguity and paradox, the language of feeling truth, "emotionally experienced" reality.[7]

To enter the realm of myth is to search to see the whole of reality and ultimate connections that defy human perception. Myth, encountering the limits of all language, is a way of approximating truth that offers images and metaphors where fixed words fail. Myth suggests a reality more powerful than any literal allegiance.[8] To remythologize is not to destroy what we know but to add hermeneutical levels of nuance and meaning, mirroring inner and outer truth for the spiritual journey. For many, metaphor and myth have been the road back to a more living sense of their home religions, a revitalizing of the imagery, for example, in the Judaeo-Christian tradition of the Garden of Eden, the exodus to the Promised Land, the forty years in the wilderness; or in Christianity, the birth of the divine child, the inner trials and the Garden of Gethsemane, and the crucifixion and resurrection.[9] Ricoeur (1970) argues that it is possible or even necessary to take a second step toward innocence or the "second naïveté" of a "postcritical faith" (p. 28), to remythologize on the other side of demythologizing, to enter the possibility of finding new levels of meaning that enrich rather than betray our present understandings. For others, the passage to one's own mythic tradition has been opened by recovering the power and beauty of myths from other global traditions, an opportunity unprecedented in history (Campbell, 1972).

Metaphors of Ultimate Reality in our Time

The reappreciation of metaphor and myth is a challenge to recognize and recover the metaphorical quality of present views of ultimate reality and to continue the exploration and reconstruction of God language in our time. The search is for metaphors which can add and enrich, can return experience of ultimate reality to new depths. Feminist theology has played a central role in the search for a new language and naming (Daly, 1973) which can serve as harbinger to a new consciousness, challenging our assumptions and stretching us toward a new openness. Yet much feminist-inspired language of a mother/father God, of God as He and She with metaphorically feminine qualities as well as masculine, and of the recovery of the Goddess keeps us anchored too firmly in gendered imagery and an idolatry of personality. Even McFague (1987), in seeking models to reflect a contemporary ecological perspective of ultimate interrelatedness, ends with affirming primarily personal metaphors of relationship. Standing as a corrective to the dangers of literalizing metaphor, Tillich's (1952, p. 188) sense of the "God beyond God" reminds of the need to seek God the verb, not God the noun (Daly, 1973). If, then, we try to leave behind the dangers of idolatry of personality whatever the form, where do we find metaphors in our search for the divine? Are there images great enough for our time?

One cannot really reconstruct a religious perspective, however, but only "receive" it as "given" in experience and hope to find metaphors and models complex and rich enough to grasp and convey its mystery. Thus the search must be grounded in a return to the "data" of religion, to the phenomenology of religious experience (Gilkey, 1969). The importance of meditation in witnessing spiritual realities directly for oneself rather than relying on indirect belief, as stressed within Eastern traditions and increasingly as recovered in the West, expresses this concern. This emphasis is central to Wilber (1984b), for example, who argues that spiritual disciplines are a type of "scientific" process, an empirical methodology capable of yielding predictable, consistent findings or insights when followed with proper discipline and training. Weber (1986, p. 7) describes this type of process as "inner empiricism."[10]

And surprisingly, the return to experience is being facilitated for many today by the metaphors and models of wholeness found in physics and biology. Modern science is returning us to phenomenology. For in the experience and awareness of wholeness and unity, of oneness, connection, and a response of compassion or love, the essential insights and data of religion and science draw closer together. It is this insight into wholeness that reaches out for new models that can express this ancient understanding for our times.[11]

The imagery and power we confront in a view of the universe portrayed in recent science may carry us closer to a feeling-filled sense of awe and mystery than many of our contemporary associations to the God symbol. The world we enter is a world of energy transformations beyond time, a world which may familiarize us with a new way of surrender as we are forced to relinquish traditional views of matter and space to embrace larger mysteries. Are we so very far from the stretch required to witness the All, the Being and Becoming we call God? When we turn to the microlevel of physics, and the models and imagery that defy our commonsense experiences of thingness, we discover a universe inviting us to a dance of cosmic energy, where matter no longer exists as thing but dissolves into a play of subatomic particles coming in and out of existence. Atoms become a reification, an idea, a concept superimposed upon an interrelated spacetime continuum. Electrons show tendencies to exist; atoms reflect the constantly changing probabilities of bunchings of spacetime, the condensing of energy in the flow of experience rather than separate things in themselves. Interrelatedness and change characterize the modern universe (Capra, 1975)—a web of connection, of energy, movement in and out of being. Concepts previously held as incompatible, such as light as wave or particle, seem best understood through a theory of complementarity, in which the question we ask the universe affects the way in which we are given information about what is. Chaos seems to emerge even within apparently deterministic though nonlinear events, yet reveals an even deeper ordering (Gleick, 1987). The world we see around us may reflect the unfolding of an "implicate order" of wholeness (Bohm, 1980).

Systems theory portrays a world where all that exists can be seen as intricately interrelated through a nested holarchy of systems, each level a part of the next highest level. As we have seen (Laszlo, 1973), a system is an organic whole existing with respect to its relevant environment. The key term here is wholeness, reflecting the quality of synergy (Fuller, 1969) in which the whole is greater than the sum of its parts. This pattern of wholeness appears to operate in the direction of greater complexity and organization, reversing the tendency towards entropy and disorder, showing characteristics of adapting through homeostasis and the evolution of new forms of existence. In consequence, our focus of inquiry must turn from individual events, nouns, and things to relationships and process. We require a new way of seeing, a spatial shift away from traditional figure/ground. Pattern, order, complexity, interrelatedness—these are the bones of the universe. Design is basic to nature, biology is showing us. The universe can be a teaching as we live between dreams (Needleman, 1965). To enter these realms is to encounter mystery and awe, to confront majesty yet connectedness. We enter a realm that challenges all we know, yet calls out with a familiarity from some deeper place.

The search for a religious language of ultimate reality to reflect the experience of wholeness in our time, to lend the metaphors for a new dream, is also a search for an image adequate to the best of our knowledge across the domains, so that reality is not split between secular and sacred, scientific and religious. If we must demand of contemporary science that it take us to the edge of possibility, of the transformation of matter into energy that marks the insights of modern physics and the evolution of complexity reflected in modern biology, we must ask of religion that it too carry us to the edge of what is humanly perceived at the meeting ground of all perspectives or dimensions. The surrender of spiritual metaphor must come on the other side of exploring the most inclusive metaphors that we can know from this side of mystery. We must enter into a task of creating living myth, drawing even from the metaphors of modern science as in the past cultures drew from worldviews anchoring the insights of their times (Campbell, 1972).

To see God in terms of pattern, energy, light, process, totality, interconnectedness is not to make God wear familiar clothes but to do what all peoples have always done, to experience wholeness in our imagery for ultimate reality such that we inhabit one world, whether physically, psychologically, or spiritually. We are not reducing God to that which is known, but taking our furthest glimmers of what we can know as the scaffolding for stretching to the greatest mystery beyond. It is a crucial point, which makes an absolute difference from the perspective of faith. Modern science offers a new training of the eye which has perhaps the unintended impact of helping us move closer to the threshold of awe.

To turn in the same book from the domains of psychology and science and attempt to cross the threshold of religion is a step to be taken with caution and trepidation. This is tricky business, exploring the interface between models of reality drawn from different domains. The issue is not to attempt to prove the existence of a worldview of wholeness by virtue of its emergence in different fields. We are not in search of hypotheses from science to be used like proof-texting from religious sources in demonstrating the validity of any other worldview or schema. The vision of the world reflected in modern physics cannot and was in no way intended by the physicists themselves to constitute any kind of proof of metaphysical or spiritual worldviews (Wilber, 1984b). Physics can only give us its own perspective. So also with systems theory. If the vision of wholeness opened up by these developments makes certain types of religious or psychological perspectives more compatible, more congruent with these insights, then this is a gift of flexibility and openness, not proof. Yet if one believes that somehow spiritual insights and scientific glimpses of truths must be aimed at the same ultimate reality, that they explore the same moebius strip of reality, however different the language and perspective, such possibility of congruence seems promising for dialogue and vision.

Scientific discovery does have much to say to religion, but not by way of proving insights. The issue is more one of reminding and daring us to think big enough, cosmically enough. Surely the sense of supernatural must be at least as far-reaching as the best we can know of the natural. Perhaps in fact we might break through to a new understanding of the word supernatural as super natural, not beyond the natural but the celebration of the full awesome reality of the best we can know and even more. In this issue of celebration, extension, challenge, and transforming vision rather than of proof, metaphor becomes a key ally in reminding us of the shortness of whatever vision we do possess, of the tentativeness of any hypothesis and particularly of the images we draw from them to guide our way. It would be the greatest of ironies, and the easiest of possibilities, if the new wave of popular understandings of physics and biology were to become a dogma preventing openness to newer visions to come. It seems more hopeful to consider the growing rapprochement of science and religion, of cosmology and myth, as an invitation to a dialogue disrupted far too long ago rather than the gearing up for a formal debate in which one party will be judged the winner.[12] If systems theory emerges as a unifying metaphor for our time, opening up new understandings of divine process, it is but a reflection of what has already been experienced from within religious insights.

The hope is to join voices in dialogue, cacophony, and potential harmony in an effort to reach new insights in our time. The work is one of receptivity to new names, to new forms, to insights into old truths, and to exploring metaphors capable of carrying these meanings. These metaphors may carry us beyond classic polarities of immanence and transcendence, of God and World, God and Self. We seek metaphors distilled of the limitations of human imagery yet capable of inviting intense and personal response, metaphors that use all of our knowledge rather than requiring that we exclude and split ourselves into incompatible categories as the price of faith. The movement to express the experience of divine wholeness that carries us toward the metaphors of science, of modern quantum physics and systems theory in biology, is not a deification of science, but part of the process instead of turning beyond God the noun to God the Verb, from God the Father/Mother to God as Light, the Source, Energy, Power, Love. To speak of God as It, That, That which is—is not to turn God into a thing, but to try through human language to free God of partial attributes.

The transformations in worldview that follow from the struggle of science to expand its own metaphors, may reflect clues to an organic, existential experiencing of divine reality in our time. Religion and science have perhaps not in centuries come so close as to offer this complementary gift to each other. But let us beware, the search for integration must be done at the metaphorical level. We seek clues for an understanding of the power and immediacy of ultimate reality in our time. We seek to release mystery, not to contain it even in a modern cosmology.

Clues to a Systems Ontology

Toward the end of his life, Gregory Bateson turned increasing attention to a consideration of the most encompassing system that can be said to exist, embracing all possible subsystems. In a book published posthumously, he and his daughter Mary Catherine propose to enter "where angels fear to tread," from which their book, *Angels Fear* (1987), takes its title. Their quest is for an understanding of the largest level of wholeness as it relates to an experience of the sacred and religious insights. They identify their exploration as an epistemology of the sacred. Bateson argues for the necessity of the experience of the sacred as a way of apprehending the interrelatedness of all that is and the "pattern that exists." For Bateson, the sacred is a witnessing and recognition of relatedness and relationships as fundamental to an understanding of the universe, accompanied by an experience of awe, carrying an inevitable element of mystery, and preserved somehow as a necessary corrective to the human tendencies to divide up the world and experience into separate parts and dualities.

This perception and experience of pattern which mediates a sense of the sacred has much in common, claims Bateson, with the fundamental insights of religious perspectives. Bateson, however, does not wish to identify this insight as grounds for either an ontologically materialistic worldview or what he calls a supernaturalist worldview. In fact, systems theory for him offers an alternative to the historical cycling between these two poles "from one posture of discomfort to another" (p. 51). Systems theorists seem typically much committed to the premise that systems theory is grounded in an at least partially empirical and descriptive epistemology, rather than an ontology purporting to explain the world or the "real" as it is in itself (Seidler, 1979). However, Bateson himself acknowledges that "there can be no clear line between epistemology and ontology" (p. 19), and Laszlo (1973, p. 143) ventures to explore systems philosophy at least in part in terms of what he calls a "framework for an ontology." And certainly the potential metaphysical and spiritual implications of a systems perspective bear exploring (Oliver, 1981), at least to the extent that we inquire into what kind of worldview might be compatible or share an affinity with that opened up by systems theory.[13] For such a worldview would be founded on a revolutionary witnessing to the fundamental interrelatedness of all that is, a premise carried potentially as insight within many world religious traditions, but often in contradiction to strong dualities held equally central to these world cultures.

It is important to understand immediately that what Bateson is affirming as the sacred is a shift to a way of seeing in terms of the most inclusive system. It is a type of awareness that grounds a sense of awe and recognition of the beauty of the larger system (Bateson & Bateson, 1987, p. 181) of which all is a part. In a sense religion has been an essential corrective (p. 204) to "insufficient holism" in our understanding of the universe, particularly in our misunderstanding and dichotomizing of mind and matter (p. 179). Religion has the potential of standing as a model for thinking in terms of the metaphorical relationships between all of life and the totality (p. 195), including the necessary language of paradox and the inevitable sense of mystery that accompany all expressions of mind. This dance of metaphor, at sufficient levels of complexity to capture a sense of pattern and mystery, has been perhaps in some sense adaptive for humans (p. 198), but Bateson would argue that it follows too from an understanding of the "integration and complexity of the natural world" (p. 200). Thus the sacred emerges from the universe, and religions are a response to it. "You cannot *construct* something and designate it as sacred" (p. 149). Yet it is not necessary to postulate a supernatural explanation for this wholeness, nor need one revert to materialism.

How are we then to understand the worldview evidenced in this "groping towards a description of the largest mentally or ecologically organized systems that we can either perceive or imagine" (p. 160)? To do so we must recall the fundamental premises of systems theory. An epistemology or ontology of wholeness would be based first of all in an affirmation of the interrelatedness of all that is. Bateson insists throughout his writing on the dangers of thingifying reality. There can be no ultimate substance or thingness in the universe, no immutable essence. All is process. Yet underlying all change and process is pattern. Process is ordered, yet open to emerging novelty and creativity. Possible affinities are readily suggested between these affirmations and those of process philosophy and theology, Buddhism (Macy, 1976, 1991), and Chinese philosophy, as well as modern quantum theory and chaos theory.

Second, systems theory affirms that the basic model of the universe is organismic and telic. It witnesses to a universe of organized complexity, to ordered wholeness. All that exists tends toward increasing complexity, capable not only of self-sustaining maintenance but of organizing itself into ever more complex and regulatory suprasystems. The universe is holarchical, organized in terms of embedded "holons" (Koestler, 1978), each relating to a larger whole. "The cosmic matrix evolves in patterned flows" (Laszlo, 1973, p. 292). Purpose returns to the universe in terms of teleonomic increases toward complexity and organization, rather than in terms of a teleology directed from without (Oliver, 1981, p. 89).

Third, systems theory avoids most of the classical dualisms of philosophical and religious perspectives[14] and calls us to new understandings of mind and matter, subject-object, self and other. Laszlo (1973) in fact goes even further in this direction than Bateson in breaking down even a division between "inanimate" and "animate" matter in the evolution of natural systems and holarchies. Bateson too wishes to eliminate the mind/matter dichotomy of post-Enlightenment perspectives, and argues that his distinction between the physical world (the Pleroma) and the Creatura (or the mental processes that emerge immediately with life and biological events) is only one of logical type, of organizational level, and is essentially nondual. Creatura and Pleroma are in no way separable except as "levels of description" (Bateson & Bateson, 1987, p. 18). Deriving these concepts from Jung's use of these words (p. 16), Bateson argues that biological systems inevitably encompass a level of information exchange and increasingly active organization, and thus the phenomena of life are inherently characterized in terms of mental processes (Creatura).[15] In fact, the language of biology, he argues, is one of metaphor and pattern (p. 27). There can be no line between mind and matter that divides them as two substances.[16] As Laszlo writes (p. 293), "mind is but the internal aspect of the connectivity of systems within the matrix."

Mentality (Creatura) extends thoughout the evolution toward increasing complexity and more encompassing systems. Bateson specifically argues that this does not mean that a sufficient quantity of matter can give rise to mental phenomena as in the materialistic worldview (Bateson & Bateson, 1987, p. 117), but rather that the language of mind is pattern and relationship. Thus the language of evolution and even of genetics speaks of pattern not number; information in embryology must be patterned in codes of spatial and other relationships, not in such messages as "five fingers" (p. 204) or "ten appendages" (p. 115). The message "units" are not stem and leaf but the relationships between (p. 27). In addition there are gaps (pp. 39, 96), uncommunicated messages in life's processes (pp. 80, 86), information which must be withheld from consciousness perhaps to allow for smoother functioning (p. 96), information that works more effectively to guide behavior in a kind of subliminal calibration rather than an active, ego-directed trial and error correction method (p. 43). Knowledge about the whole wider system may show the same kind of necessity for "faith" (p. 96) that bridges the smaller gaps or "secrets" which occur between our actions, perceptions, and our conscious knowledge of them. At all levels, more exists than can be known in description (p. 164).

Just as mind/matter dichotomies are transcended in systems theory, we have also seen a radical challenge to the possibility of self-other dichotomies, and ultimately, to the distinction of subject and object (Laszlo, 1973, p. 293). The latter point has not been so widely underscored in systems thinking, but exists as possibility, and is particularly relevant to philosophical and religious perspectives (Macy, 1976, 1991).[17] The former point we have encountered in systems views of personality, in which the concept of self is dissolved and categorical distinctions between self and the rest of the environment, including other persons, cannot be maintained. Freedom and determinism is another polarity which can be reframed in systems thinking as an issue of level and perspective. Recall Laszlo's biperspectivalism regarding natural-cognitive systems, from which mental and physical dimensions of the system reflect differences in perspective. Likewise, freedom and determinism reflect the viewpoint from inside versus outside, of part versus whole.

A fourth major implication of systems theory is a challenge to linear notions of causality and a recentering of the locus of causation within a network of interrelated events and process. Intercausality thus pertains to all events, and linear claims of cause and effect cannot be made. This claim is one of the most subtle and powerful in systems perspectives. Here systems perspectives are profoundly in harmony with Buddhist (Macy, 1991)[18] and Chinese perspectives. Thus systems thinkers can speak of the importance of "downward causation" (Sperry, 1988) as complement to more scientifically conventional upward causation implied in a materialistic view of evolution.[19] Organized complexity exerts a downward influence to match the upwardly evolving systems. Though not ascribed to supernatural causation, this complex intercausality does not rule out in principle the influence of the largest suprasystem on all that exists.

Finally, systems theory grounds an ethics which we have seen to follow from an appeal to the context of the highest suprasystem, to the widest perspective on wholeness, and to the profound interconnectedness of all that exists such that all is precious and of value, without respect to level of hierarchy. Context and care mediate an ethics contrasting to one of rule and principle.[20]

In affirming the sacred, Bateson ends surprisingly far from where he may seem to begin in his repudiation of supernatural authority as normative. In the end, sheer materialism is left farthest behind. And this is part of the power and intriguing quality of systems theory as a basis for reflective metaphysics, for it offers an avenue out of conventional scientific materialism yet without forcing categories from beyond experience. Systems thinking offers the possibility of moving closer to the insights that have grounded religious traditions, yet without necessitating appeal to a supernatural understanding of divine energy. Nor does it of necessity exclude such an understanding, though Bateson would choose to have it so. Boulding's (1968, p. 8) reference to "transcendental systems" as the highest level of systems opens another way to ongoing dialogue.[21]

It may still come as a surprise, though, that when Bateson speaks of the sacred as the "pattern that connects" (Bateson & Bateson, 1987, p. 145) or as the "integrative dimension of experience" (p. 2), he means to define something that may be "recognizable as sharing many of the attributes of what [humans] call God" (p. 160). Or again, he seeks the "interwoven regularities in a system so pervasive and so determinant that we may even apply the word 'god' to it" (p. 142), or "Eco." The sacred is the "integrated fabric of mental process that envelops all our lives" (p. 200), the "unity in which we make our home" (p. 142). His is an immanental ultimacy; "transcendent deity is an impossibility" (p. 6). Bateson seeks a monism (p. 7), a unified wordview in which scientific and religious questions do not need to occupy different spaces nor be answered from different terrains.[22] Yet his basic metaphors, models, and stance come from science, albeit a science open to the profound implications of a nondualistic worldview, and the extent to which this perspective can ever be felt to be fully compatible or informative of spiritual traditions will continue to be a point of tension for the present discussion.

Metaphors of Interrelatedness: Compatibilities and Affinities with Systems Ontology

Systems ontology stands in considerable contrast to ontologies of transcendence and hierarchy, in which divine reality is construed to be incommensurate with human reality, time, and change. Such hierarchical ontologies which underlie much of the Western religious heritage, and encompass many worldwide traditions as well, tend to give rise to dualities between body and spirit, mind and matter, human and God, as well as vertical spiritual metaphors of spiritual ascent, aspiration, striving, and search. Though powerful metaphors for the transcendent aspects of ultimate reality (H. Smith, 1976), they tend to portray the immanence of divine reality as derivative, experienced in moments of mystical insight when God appears as permeating all the world.[23] Systems metaphors join feminist perspectives not only in a critique of vertical ontology as gendered, but in a powerful concern for introducing alternative metaphors for embodied spirituality, for healing the mind/matter split and related dichotomies, and for founding an ethics of interrelatedness and responsiveness.[24] Yet in seeking alternatives to gendered metaphor and seeking to create a significant dialogue between scientific and religious insights, systems theory offers clues to an ontology particularly apt to speak to our time in ways that can build on the work done by feminist theologians in drawing attention to these critical concerns.

Affinities between systems perspectives and world religious traditions emerge in several places, particularly as we have seen in mystical expressions within world spirituality, but also in Christian and Hindu evolutionary perspectives held by Teilhard de Chardin (1959) and Sri Aurobindo (1956). Yet the most compelling parallels come from process philosophy and theology,[25] and even more congruently from Buddhism, particularly in the Chinese form of Hua-yen, and Chinese philosophy and religion (Olds, 1991). Thus as we continue to explore systems perspectives on God, world, and self, central foci to be engaged by the "analogical imagination" (Tracy, 1981, p. 423), we can draw in part on insights and metaphors from these traditions which offer points for further dialogue in articulating an ontology of interrelatedness. My intent here is not to develop such an ontology explicitly, but to suggest avenues for further exploration and the wealth of traditions from which such clues might come.

While a nondual understanding of ultimate reality has been conveyed in terms of "ground of being" (Tillich, 1952, p. 157), cosmic consciousness, or in the Buddhist tradition as Suchness, it is Whitehead (1925, 1978) and process theology which provide the transition in the West to a metaphysics of organism and a new way of seeing. It is the basis for what Griffin (1989) calls a constructive "postmodern theology."[26] Process theology in a sense foreshadowed the relevance of modern science to contemporary theology, and seems in many ways highly compatible with systems insights.

Process, not substance, is the essential characteristic of the universe for Whitehead (1978), who describes the world in terms of a philosophy of organism. To do justice to the world in its concreteness is to convey the complexity of its interrelating fields. All reality is interrelatedness, and concrete fact is process, not isolated events. To focus on any one part as real is to commit the fallacy of misplaced concreteness,[27] for it is process and connection that are most real, most concrete. Nature is extended in durations, actual occasions by which what we know as reality comes into and out of being and value. Through the concrescence or gathering of its range of apperceptions and experience into one unity, an actual occasion comes into being, informed also by the realm of potentiality or eternal objects.

In this kind of universe, God becomes the name given that principle or process by which the total interrelated web of possibility is capable of becoming actuality. God is that interrelatedness by means of which all actual occasions emerge from potentiality into actuality. God is the ground of concrete actuality, the ground of all alternatives, the condition for the structuring and limitation of actual being, the condition by which things realize themselves (Whitehead, 1954, 1978).

Yet process theology, as elaborated also by Hartshorne (1948, 1967, 1984), stops short of a full vision of interrelatedness. In postulating a linear time dimension to process (see Odin, 1982), process theology tends to set limits on intercausality and underestimates the possibility of genuine creativity within an ontology of total interrelatedness.[28] In keeping the dimension of God's primordial nature as encompasser of eternal objects separate from God's consequent nature by which all reality is preserved as part of God, process philosophy also has gaps in the reciprocal interrelatedness of all that is.[29] To correct for some of these dangers, Oliver (1981), drawing from both process and systems insights, tries to recast a philosophy of relatedness in totally relational terms. Concepts or "bi-perspects" (p. 157) in his schema are inherently relational or bipolar, and he attempts to represent an understanding of God and the world as inward versus outward perspectives on his most central ontological relational concept, the "Totality of Relations" (pp. 166, 168–175).

Such apparently abstract conceptions of ultimate reality as offered by process and systems metaphors have been criticized for lacking in intimacy. Yet it is possible to have a passionate, feeling-filled connection to the more abstractly articulated, but richly concrete experience of that which is, of Isness, a kind of surrender before the awesomeness of that which goes beyond concepts. Personal and impersonal views of the divine are illustrations of a polarity better understood by the principle of complementarity, in which each image holds truth depending on how we ask our question (Barbour, 1974).[30] While being afraid of the idolatry of nature worship or paganism, we have clung instead to an idolatry of personality, unable to see divine energy animating the universe in this immediate experience of connection, to experience presence without person-mediated constructs.

Other points of profound complementarity between systems thinking and religious and spiritual perspectives come from nondual perspectives on the universe (Loy, 1988). We are not so very far from the type of description of reality offered by Eastern traditions and meditation practices which also help to release a new way of seeing.

In the Hinduism of the *Upanishads*, divine reality is represented as Brahman, that which is beyond all form and division, yet nondual essence is veiled by an appearance of duality. The world of incarnate reality comes into existence as a dance of form, the illusion of maya and separateness (H. Smith, 1958). In this movement of polarity between two great forces or levels of being in the universe, as seen in another path within Hinduism, the one pure essence (Puruṣa) beyond all form gains material existence through the medium of the dynamic, changing, multiple forms of Prakṛti (Brown, 1974). Yet ultimately the meaning of liberation lies in a way of seeing this duality as only relatively real, a perspective which returns one to an awareness of the one wholeness beyond, in and through all reality, from which we are never separated except through the illusion of clinging to thought, image, and separate ego. Throughout Hindu tradition, despite its elaborate and extensive mythology of divine form, there is a profound emphasis on the ultimate inadequacy of any concept or image in grasping a sense of that whole.

In Buddhism, these concepts are dissolved even further as the universe is experienced as a flow of change and interconnection. Ontology gives way to epistemology, as what we can know is seen as a flow of interrelated events, dependently co-arising with mental differentiations from the field of larger consciousness. As Macy (1991) convincingly argues, Buddhism offers a relational understanding of reality based on the experience of mutual causality and the dependent co-arising of knower and known, and thus perhaps the closest hermeneutic for elucidating concepts in general systems theory. Nothing exists separately; no "thing" exists.[31] There is no self, nor separate agent to stand against as subject to object; no divine reality or first cause to differentiate from that which is. Even expressions such as consciousness, Buddha-nature, Mind are far too ontologically laden to be accurate. Buddhism is essentially an encounter, a witness to nothingness, to no-thingness, in its identity with ultimate reality.

Chinese forms of Buddhism, particularly Hua-yen, turn this witnessing and understanding of nothingness and the dependent co-arising of all things into a positive understanding of the interconnectedness of all that is.[32] Thus Hua-yen affirms as its central image of reality the metaphor of Indra's net, a living web extended infinitely, bearing at each intersection of time, space, and thread glistening droplets or jewels, each reflecting all others in the universe. A similar metaphor is found in Tibetan Buddhist Lama Govinda's description of the worlds of inner and outer reality as "two sides of the same fabric in which threads of all forces and all events, of all forms of consciousness and of their objects are woven into an inseparable net of endless mutually conditioning relation."[33] Related images of the interconnectedness and unity of all reality are found throughout Chinese writing, as in neo-Confucian Chu Hsi's (1130–1200 C.E.) image of the moon which is reflected holographically in all reflecting surfaces (Chan, 1963, p. 638) though remaining undivided, yet even here the image may be borrowed indirectly from Hua-yen. Hua-yen offers the cardinal teaching metaphors of Fa-tsang (643–712 C.E.) where he suggests that ultimate reality is like a room filled on all sides, top and bottom with mirrors, in which sits a Buddha and a lighted candle, with the image of the light reflected in all directions infinitely and simultaneously (Chang, 1971).

Chinese traditions of Taoism and Confucianism, particularly in its neo-Confucian form, portray a world of process, flow, harmony, and organism. The "embodied unity of all things" and its moral significance are central to this tradition.[34] Ethics arises as a mode of alignment with the total pattern (tao), in a harmonious relationship between individual excellence (te) and patterned wholeness (Hall & Ames, 1987). Te and tao are complementary, polar concepts, like yin and yang, holding together the integrity of a nondualistic universe as it moves through change and process in a dance of expression. As in systems perspectives, mind and matter are inseparable, just as li (pattern) and ch'i (matter/energy) inextricably pervade the cosmos.[35] Chaos is not conceived in Chinese ontology as antithetical to cosmic order, to be divided into rule-bound structuring principles (Girardot, 1983), but rather has a harmonious order of its own, suggesting again links of compatibility with insights from dynamical systems theory.

An affirmation of unity through process, differentiatedness, and immanence echoes also in Teilhard de Chardin (1959), who speaks of the unfolding of complexity and consciousness in the universe, with movement toward unification yet differentiated parts, each reflecting the universe uniquely. The metaphor of cosmic consciousness images God in terms of the totality of that which is, Isness, the interrelated transformations of energy and consciousness, with matter and energy interconverting, evolving in complexity and awareness, and connection-love.

The systems vision of wholeness, of an interrelated and ever-changing universe in process of transformation, is a critical and far from trivial generalization, as Wilber (1984b) fears is the fate of most of the popular translations offered us of modern physics. What saves these images of wholeness from triviality is their transformative character, their capacity to excite and challenge vision, to push us through the eye of paradox into a surrender of preconceptions. If Wilber (1984b) is right that we also need a direct and non-secondhand encounter with the empirical reality of an interconnected universe, rather than a verbally digested free lunch from the annals of popular science, then this still does not deny the power and importance of practicing new models and modes of thinking. If ultimate insights are beyond words and reality itself exceeds all concepts, a training in a worldview that moves us closer to a nondual universe still seems a powerful aid to spiritual centering in this chaotic time of shifting metaphors. Systems metaphors may offer that "ontological flash" that opens up new vision.[36] It is the power of a new model to encourage new thinking and experimentation that is its test, not the question of its apparent banality when reduced to a cosmic one-liner. The old one-liners die with difficulty, and opportunities to practice new ones should not be dismissed as simple proselytizing or redundancy. They are carriers, vehicles, metaphors for the passage.

Yet Eastern thought cautions us on the limits of systems imagery or related metaphors in conceptualizing the divine. Can we avoid what Wilber (1984b) calls the danger of claiming a simple identity between ultimate reality and an affirmation of all that is? Wilber's concern is to remind us of the difference in levels of awareness between seeing an ultimate reality of oneness beyond all duality and actually experiencing oneness with that reality. Compared to this point of experienced oneness, a point approximated in mystical experience and through meditation, to speak of the essence of all that is still implies a dualistic consciousness which acknowledges the world of interrelated form, rather than the sheer experience of a formless, nameless unity. Wilber (1977, 1981, 1984b) points recurrently to a hierarchy of experienced reality, with ultimate unity undergirding the whole, but as long as one focuses on this hierarchy with its underlying essence, one is still in the partial vision of duality. The world is still separate from essence. He, and Ajaya (1983) even more explicitly, are concerned that to embrace the whole as seen perhaps in systems views is to stay attached to divisions and forms, even as a total system of form, rather than the wholeness beneath or beyond the all.

In summarizing this important concern for the difference between dualistic and nondual perspectives, the difficulty and challenge of finding words to get at experiences beyond words is also apparent. A great deal depends on what we mean by the All that we are affirming. Can we affirm the All as divine if what we mean is not a cataloguing of reality as we see it, even including the concepts or experience of universe and ultimate oneness, but some higher unity by which all is one, beyond any awareness or division between universe and essence? Surely this is not so foreign an affirmation in light of the ways we have seen Eastern traditions cross paths of familiarity with a systems view of the world as totally and supremely interrelated.[37] In the process of reaching higher realizations of ultimate reality, can we not move closer to an experience of Oneness by dissolving the world of form from the inside, discovering its boundarylessness through immersion in this imagery of thinglessness and interrelatedness, rather than trying to transcend to an ultimate or foundational Oneness as in perennial philosophy or Wilber's perspective. In other words, a systems, process view of divine reality may be a path in and through to Oneness, prepared for through the richness of imagery and training in seeing, rather than a path that goes beyond, beneath, and above any such associations, though the ultimate arrival point beyond all conception and separation may be the same.[38]

Conceptions of God and Self

Against the backdrop of systems understandings of divine reality, a systems view of self has a renewed level of significance, raising new questions for the relationship between divine reality and selfing. How are we to understand our part in an interrelated world whereby God is understood as that by and through which all is? In the process of stretching the concept of self in systems theory to include the larger interrelated context in which we are each embedded, the dimension of selfing meets the expanded sense of God we have been tracing in this chapter. If God can be seen as that totality of all that is, that principle by which all comes and goes into being and becoming, and if we as selves are inextricably embedded in this matrix, how are we to understand the relationship between the constructs of God and Self? This vision of interconnectedness allows new ways of seeing some of the classic paradoxical questions as issues of possible complementarity, in which depending on our perspective we see a different insight into the whole. God and Self emerge perhaps as complementary concepts like wave and particle in nuclear physics, or part/whole, energy/matter, determinism/indeterminism, animate/inanimate, being/doing, void/meaning, personal God/abstractness, ego/Self.

In systems thinking, the word "I" becomes a linguistic metalevel name for a part of the universe that seems to be pinched into reality or concentration here. The self is a template placed on those parts of reality in our vicinity, dangerously confused by us as separate, yet inextricably embedded in totality. We become parts of an interrelated universe. We become parts of cosmic consciousness, a "subsystem" of the "larger Mind" immanent in the broader ecology of the universe, a Mind that even Bateson (1972, p. 461) notes may be what "some people mean by 'God'." Fundamental to systems theory is the affirmation that interrelatedness is basic to the universe, and this concept taken to its most profound implications may mirror and reflect equally profound shifts in thinking about the nature of the self and the nature of divine reality. It is for each to experience how far this metaphor can unfold the clarity, power, and mystery worthy of the highest we may know.

New visions of the relationship of divine and human open up with this further metaphor. We are challenged to consider reconceptualizing the separate soul or ego in terms of its ultimate identity with the unity beyond. The absolute split between God as Other and individual self is radically shaken, or rendered into an issue of complementarity reflected in the kinds of questions and implications addressed by Eastern and Western traditions. The ultimate separation of God and human, the concept of a vertical power hierarchy of higher versus lower existence, concepts challenged also by feminist theologians such as Mollencott (1983)—all are further shaken in this view of world as matrix of divine energy and human intersection. In a view whereby God is interconnection, the love or "metaphysical gravity" (Fuller, 1979) which holds the universe in connection, prayer becomes less petitionary than a honing in to oneness with totality, a kind of centering or alignment. Perhaps God is a name for my personal relationship with the universe when I am in the perspective of alignment, when spontaneity, joy, forgiveness, and love issue from a calm sense of immediate connection with all process.

The potential identity of God and ultimate self, the self beyond the level of narrow ego identification, has not been a problem within Eastern traditions where this affirmation is central to these worldviews. In Hinduism, ultimate awareness witnesses to the identification of Brahman, underlying essence of the universe, and Atman, or the highest realization of the Self. And not only are our separate selves ultimately of one essence with God-energy, but you and I are also ultimately one at this level. Buddhism again takes this portrayal even a step further, in dissolving the concept of Atman altogether. For Buddhism, the existence of a separate self is an illusion. The highest meaning of life is found in a surrendering of attachment to a separate ego identity and a realization that we are one with the flow of the universe.[39]

The modern West, however, poised in counterpart to the East, with reciprocal strengths and weaknesses in addressing these issues, inherits a strong sense of the separate ego and individuality. Thus, the potential ultimate oneness of divine and human seems perhaps threatening, blasphemous, or in fact conceptually impossible within many Western traditions. The East, with greater steeping throughout its cultures in the legacy of connection and communal embeddedness, with its parallel danger of neglect of the individual, has stronger social and religious underpinnings to support this mode of conceptualizing. In the West, it is the mystical traditions which have come closest to this path of oneness found so often in Eastern thought, and these traditions have always been a minority, though constant accompaniment, to the Western path. Within mysticism, the ultimate identity of divine and human is a frequent affirmation. As Huston Smith offers in a subtle yet powerful retranslation of an Indian image, the slipping of the dewdrop of individuality into the sea of ultimate reality can be understood not in terms of loss, but through the image of the dewdrop "opening to receive the entire sea,"[40] an image surprisingly compatible with the intent of many of the systems metaphors we are exploring.

In approaching these issues from within Western perspectives, it is critical to recall that the self which is experienced as one with God is not the self of everyday ego identity. Instead it is a self much closer to Bateson's redefined and extended self or the self described by Jung as the totality of all that one is, including conscious and unconscious aspects, of which the ego remains a small fraction of the whole. In fact, in trying to understand this larger self in the context of religious and spiritual questions, thinkers wrestling with this issue have often moved to a conscious recognition of the importance of symbol, metaphor, and archetype in exploring this terrain. Just as we must enter a world of paradox in which the principle of complementarity may provide clues for partial questions, we also enter an explicitly symbolic level in which we search for clues for what it means essentially to be a spiritual human being. Eliade (1958), for example, speaks of the way the human being itself "becomes a symbol" through myth, thereby entering into a new relationship with a "living cosmos" (p. 455). So too, when Jung explores issues of self and God, he refers continually to the self-archetype and the God-archetype, reminding us that we can only experience and speak of the symbolic forms and resonances these archetypes evoke in us, pointing but never arriving by this process at the referents in themselves.[41]

For Jung, self and God archetypes mirror each other as the reflections of wholeness within and without, lending the realm of inner psyche and outer universe a relationship of reciprocity and identity in one psychoid reality as he called it.[42] In a sense we look with Kant (1949, p. 258) at the parallel awesomeness of the inward directed glance at the "moral law within," and the outer glimpse of the "starry heavens above." Outer reality and inner psyche join in a fundamental relationship of reciprocal energy, from which part and whole reverberate as two perspectives on one reality. As the God image comes to reflect the totality and ground of the universe, the self or soul is born in the movement toward a perspective or experience of wholeness. The spiritual dimension of human life comes to refer not to a belief system, but a state of awareness by which one perceives, experiences unity, oneness, isness without judgment. Atonement becomes retranslated as at-onement. We become at this level of perception part of God, part of Isness, witness to the awesome interrelatedness of all that is. The self becomes a centering perspective on a wholistic reality, part of divine or cosmic consciousness.

There is also a sense among those who direct their attention to these questions, that the wholeness witnessed in the power of self and God images, as inner and outer reflections of one totality, is also an evolving wholeness in a changing universe of energy and form. We can hear the insights of Jung (1969a) into the experience of an evolving God so dramatically portrayed in his *Answer to Job*. Or we can turn again to Teilhard de Chardin (1959) and his parallel sense of an evolving cosmic consciousness which retains, as with systems theory, a sense of the infinite importance of each individual unique nuance as a developing part of an evolving whole. What then is the role of self in this potential evolution not only of God-image, but of God itself in a universe moving toward higher consciousness or playing out the potentiality of cosmic energy and consciousness? As concentrations of consciousness, we become the eyes of the universe, Campbell (1972) reflects and summarizes, serving as points of consciousness bearing the divine back to itself. This thought also echoes Teilhard de Chardin's conviction that the "noosphere," the evolving totality of a conscious universe, needs to "find its eyes" (1959, p. 280). As Bateson believed, "human consciousness is potentially the organ of self-knowledge for the entire ecosystem" (M. C. Bateson, 1977, p. 70). If these metaphors retain a duality still to be transcended in a more Eastern metaphor of ultimate oneness, we are reminded once again of the limits of metaphor in the face of paradox and the possible relevance of a principle of complementarity in these great spiritual traditions.

We live in a powerful time of new awarenesses. The universe is revealed in new metaphors of organicity and complexity, dynamic process and purpose that open channels of accessibility to the spiritual in our time. The connection is wholeness, the heartbeat of the divine, the echo by which we seem to recognize and feel the presence of God. These metaphors, when owned and experienced from the inside out, impel us to a new type of action, a new ethics, a new way of helping and healing pain in ourselves and others.

It is to the metaphors and models of science, and systems theory in particular, that we have returned throughout this book in search of a unifying metaphor for our time. While one could argue that ours is a scientific age, in which only views certified by scientific rationality will pass the aegis of authority, I do not turn to these images for this reason, nor with any attempt to offer "proof" for a worldview of wholeness. It is because the images of wholeness find echoes in the work of science and psychology and the insights and heritage of religion that systems theory becomes noteworthy as part of a scaffolding to support a dialogue by which fields so long separate might connect. Intrinsic in this exploration has been the assumption that psychology cannot afford to be very far from the highest visions of reality offered by science, nor can psychology and science remain out of dialogue with the highest visions of psychological experience and metaphysical insight offered by the world's great spiritual traditions. The moebius strip metaphor comes once more to mind as we note the rapprochement and points of potential dialogue for scientific and religious models and speculations opened up by the heuristic of systems theory in psychology. Though often understood as opposing traditions, the metaphors of scientific and religious searches for truth bring us perhaps unexpectedly to a common surface and continuum of questions in the process of approximating truth, offering each other fruitful hypotheses not proof, vista for movement not documents for crystalization.

It must be remembered that any metaphysics of wholeness that seeks to represent the insight of "undivided wholeness," falls short in its task if it conveys this wholeness as something accomplished or constructed (Schumacher, 1981, p. 452) or even in some sense discovered or witnessed, rather than as "always present" (p. 443) and, as Wilber (1977, p. 298) voices, "always already" there. Thus to convey a sense of wholeness we must move beyond a description of part and even "whole" (Schumacher, p. 443), as if the whole could be conceived of separately from that which is. It is this paradox that haunts systems theory in its translation into ontology, just as it haunts all ontologies.

Metaphor and image, however invaluable their role and whatever the field, must always fall short of the reality they seek to suggest or model. But it is the questing we seek here, the invitation to dialogue. The finding perhaps lies beyond, in a personal space and time, when one puts down the pen or eye of scholarship and pays homage to that which is. If the world we seek to enter is enriched by metaphor, it is still a verbal world from which the veil of words must fall to loose the seeing. Even as I write to explore the voice and riches of metaphor in psychology, science, and religion, something remains ever uncaptured, glimpsed yet always to be surrendered. For metaphor is only an offering, an attempt to meet the rational mind halfway, but then it is time to be silent again.

NOTES

Chapter 1

1. Gergen (1982, Chaps. 1, 5 especially) offers an extended look at these issues in philosophy of science, including sources for a critique of traditional "logical empiricist metatheory" (p. 115), in both its logical positivist and critical rationalist forms (p. 113). He argues instead on behalf of what he terms "sociorationalist metatheory" for the social sciences (p. 207), with emphases on knowledge as socially constructed and historically embedded (pp. 201–206) among other central assumptions. See also K. J. Gergen (1987a). O'Donohue (1989) provides a very clear summary of critiques of logical positivism by Popper, related concerns by Lakatos and others, and the relevance of metaphysics to psychology in light of these critiques. Note also Barbour's (1990) contrast of the views of Popper, Kuhn, and Lakatos in philosophy of science (pp. 32–34, 58–60).

Criticizing logical positivism's claim that scentific knowledge can be derived solely from sense impressions (p. 152) and empirical fact, Popper (1985) defended the "conjectural character" of knowledge (p. 104). In this view science follows rules by which hypotheses derived from theory can be falsified (but not verified) by observation and experiment (p. 102). Popper's critical rationalism has received considerable criticism in turn by Feyerabend (1978, 1987), who argues more radically that science is historically embedded and affected by a variety of factors beyond this method, and that science does not and should not proceed solely by rules of empiricism and criteria of falsifiability. Feyerabend (1978) defends instead the necessity of methodological pluralism (p. 47) or "epistemological anarchism" (p. 181), in which knowledge is best generated in a context of multiple, diverse alternative theories from a variety of domains (pp. 39–45).

Another major source of criticism of positivist empiricism has come from hermeneutical traditions which opposed the normative claim of empiricism as an adjudicator of understanding and construed primary data in terms of meanings rather than sense impressions. Hermeneutical traditions also emphasized the contextual embeddedness of knowledge and the inevitable role of interpretation. For a diverse array of essays, with critiques, exploring the relevance of hermeneutics for psychology, see Messer, Sass, and Woolfolk (1988).

The "cognitive revolution" and rising importance of internal mental constructs and processes in cognitive behaviorism represents another way in which positivist or radical behaviorism has been challenged. Meichenbaum (1988) suggests that the "cognitive revolution" has led to incorporating hermeneutical insights into empirical psychology. Others are less optimistic that the cognitive revolution, as it has been operationalized in experimental procedures, can incorporate the insights of the "contextual revolution" or a full appreciation of an "interpretivist, constructivist" view of human experience (Bruner, 1990, pp. 4–9, 106, 108; see also the critique of Meichenbaum's argument by J. Wakefield in Messer, Sass, & Woolfolk, 1988, pp. 131–148). Bruner urges the remaining need for a psychology based on the "concept of meaning" and the ways meanings are constructed and "negotiated within a community" (p. 11).

The social impact of theory as praxis and social critique, and the cultural embeddedness of inquiry and psychological constructs, are other recurring themes of constructivist and hermeneutical inquiry (see Gergen, 1982, pp. 192–207; Messer, Sass, & Woolfolk, 1988, pp. 21–25). See also an overview of critiques of positivism and a summary of the return of "grand theory" to the social sciences (Skinner, Q., 1985, Chap. 1). For a critique in turn of contemporary constructivist epistemologies, see Rothberg (1990).

2. Leary (1990a) builds on the base provided by Ortony (1979) and others in bringing the literature on metaphor into the history of psychology.

3. Eldredge and Gould (1972) argue this point via an elaboration of the way classical evolutionary theory of "phyletic gradualism" served to delay alternative readings of gaps in fossil records and the conceptualization of new models for evolution based on uneven periods of rapid change (pp. 83–86).

4. Note also Keller and Grontkowski (1983) on the epistemological consequences of "reliance on the visual metaphor" (p. 208), as seen in the "radical" separation of subject and object (p. 220) and related issues.

5. See Polanyi (1946, 1959, 1962, 1966); see also on involvement in discovery (Polanyi & Prosch, 1975, p. 63; Sanders, 1986).

6. Kuhn's work on paradigms remains highly influential, despite critiques from Lakatos and Laudan on issues affecting changes in research programs that they feel Kuhn and followers ignored. See Gholson and Barker (1985) for a summary of these critiques. For a related discussion of the role of metaphor in scientific change, see also Farrell (1986); Gholson and Barker (1986).

7. The stories that introduce subsections of these chapters are often derived and adapted from the fund of folk wisdom which appears in a variety of forms and sources. Those adapted from the tales of Nasrudin are noted, due to their easy accessibility in the collections by Shah (e.g., 1972, p. 26, for a variation on this tale).

8. Jung (1971) articulated these concerns in terms of differences in psychological "type" among theorists.

9. Considerable research attention has been devoted to exploring the implications of Rosenthal and Jacobson's (1968) prototypic study of teacher expectations and student performance, where teachers were given false information about the

likelihood of intellectual growth in a randomly chosen subsample of students. According to Rosenthal and Jacobson's study, students for whom rapid increases in intellectual level were predicted showed at the end of the school year significantly higher IQ gains than those students for whom no growth had been predicted, despite the fact that teachers were not consciously aware of treating the two groups of children any differently. Harris and Rosenthal (1985) used meta-analyses involving 180 studies to identify processes by which such effects might be mediated.

Despite its heuristic value over two decades, the Rosenthal and Jacobson (1968) study also has been met with increased criticism. Issues relevant to such a critique are summarized by Wineburg (1987a), who also directs critical attention to the misuses and overgeneralizations in which the study has been enlisted as evidence. See also Rosenthal's reply (1987) and Wineburg's rejoinder (1987b). In longitudinal data from sixth-grade math classes, Jussim (1989) found support for the influence of "modest" self-fulfilling prophecy and biasing effects, but primarily for the role of accuracy in accounting for the relationships between teacher expectation and student performance. Harris and Rosenthal's meta-analyses also have been critiqued by Chow (1987).

See also Henshel (1982) who examines the limits of the self-fulfilling prophecy and the methodological dilemmas for social prediction which it poses.

10. See Sibicky and Dovidio (1986) for an investigation of self-fulfilling prophecy relevant to counseling settings: the discovery of negative stereotypes about people seeking counseling and the impact of these preconceptions on social interaction.

11. Note Boulding's (1985, pp. 138–139) application of the "Heisenberg Principle" to the social sciences: "When the communication is part of the system we are communicating about, then communicating about it will change the system itself" (p. 138).

12. Gergen (1990a, p. 293) argues that systems metaphors are particularly strong in challenging such conventional epistemological assumptions of positivist empiricism.

13. On the emerging field of "metapsychology" (Stam, Rogers, & Gergen, 1987; Gergen, 1982); on the impossibility of objective verifiability or grounding of psychological language in objectifiable event (Gergen, 1982; K. J. Gergen, 1987b); on the dependency of meaning on sociohistorical context and construction (Gergen, 1973, 1982, 1985; Gergen & Davis, 1985; Gergen & Gergen, 1984).

14. See Kuhn (1970) on the "community structure of science" (pp. 176–187). For an even more radical critique of the hidden power issues in the dominant role of science in modern culture, see Feyerabend (1978, pp. 296, 299–301). On hidden power issues in social psychology, see Parker and Shotter (1990). For an analysis of the "socially constructed nature" (p. 2) of psychological research, see also Danziger (1990a) who adds, however, a concluding qualifier that "to say that psychological knowledge bears the mark of the social conditions under which it was produced is

not the same as saying that it is *nothing but* a reflection of these conditions" (p. 195).

15. On "generativity" (Gergen, 1978) and the "value-sustaining function" of theory (Gergen, 1980, pp. 278–279); also K. J. Gergen (1987a, pp. 17–18). On generativity and the capacity for opening up "alternative metaphors" (Gergen, 1982, pp. 143–145); on the role of metaphors in reconstructing culture and social change (Gergen, 1990a, pp. 273–274, 295).

16. See H. Smith (1989, p. 217); Griffin (1988, p. 9); see also Foster (1987, p. 108) regarding logical inconsistencies of relativism. See Rosemont (1988) for a critique of Quine's (1969, pp. 26–68; 1960, pp. 26–79) "ontological relativity" and other conceptual and linguistic relativisms in the context of issues in comparative philosophy and translation. Rosemont proposes the potentially more heuristic (p. 67) concept of "homoversal principles" (pp. 52–53), which contrast with universals and are seen as true "relative" to Homo sapiens (p. 70).

17. On critical realism see Barbour (1974, pp. 37–38, 41–42, 47); also Barbour (1990, pp. 35, 43).

18. For a discussion of the "quantum logic" of Birkhoff and von Neumann, as extended by Finkelstein, see Zukav (1979, pp. 263, 276). See also Herbert (1987, pp. 177–185).

Chapter 2

1. For functions of theory, see Rychlak (1968) and Hjelle and Ziegler (1981); Hall and Lindzey (1978, p. 14) on theories as blinders; Heisenberg (1974) on theories needed for new levels and domains.

2. See Hall and Lindzey (1978, p. 14) on distorting preferences for parsimony; a model must be "adequate. . . ." (Rychlak, 1968, p. 67); "not *how* the phenomenon. . . ." (Schelling in Kerényi, 1963, p. 155).

3. See Rychlak (1968) on parsimony and abstraction, even in stimulus-response models.

4. See Northrop (1946, pp. 163, 448) on contrasting "theoretic" and "aesthetic component[s]" West and East; Holbrook (1981) and Porkert (1974) on contrasting Western and Chinese science.

5. See Maslow (1966, p. 49) on the twofold task of psychology and the capacity for awe in science (p. 21). See Blackburn (1971) for the articulation of a "sensuous-intellectual complementarity" in science. See also Siu (1957) on Taoist science.

6. See Maslow (1966, p. 72) on the importance of comprehensiveness: "Before all else science must be comprehensive and all-inclusive. It must accept within its jurisdiction even that which it cannot understand or explain, that for which no theory exists, that which cannot be measured, predicted, controlled or ordered."

7. See Rothenberg (1979) on "Janusian thinking," the role of image in "imagination" and generating metaphor (pp. 66, 69–71); on the role of intuition and insight in relation to psychology and science, see Ornstein (1972); Judson (1980); on the relationship of imagery and technology, see Ferguson (1977).

8. Note that Feyerabend (1978, pp. 165–169) radically challenges the possibility of separating the contexts of "discovery" and "justification" or privileging the latter.

9. Adapted from the Sufi story of Nasrudin (Shah, 1972, p. 22).

10. On "semantic positivism" see Wheelwright (1982, p. 57); also see Turner (1974, p. 28) on the "thought technicians who clear intellectual jungles."

11. On metaphor in discourse, see also Lakoff and Turner (1989); Ricoeur (1977, p. 287); in daily thinking, see McFague (1982, p. 15). On "root metaphors" as related to four "world hypotheses" (formism, mechanism, contextualism, and organicism), see Pepper (1942). For discussion of root metaphors in science and religion, see MacCormac (1976, pp. 93–101). For an argument proposing narrative as a useful root metaphor for psychology, with ties to Pepper's root metaphor of contextualism, see Sarbin (1986a). For an example of social critique which appeals to the need for new root metaphors, see Winter (1984, pp. 1–28). In light of the emphasis in this book on systems theory, it is noteworthy that Pepper later added a fifth world hypothesis based on the "root metaphor" of a "purposive, self-regulating system" (Laszlo, 1973, p. 15).

MacCormac (1985, pp. 19, 47–49) proposes the term "basic metaphor" as an extension of Pepper's concept to any "fundamental presuppositions underlying a theory or even an entire discipline" (p. 47), not just Pepper's world hypotheses (p. 49). Theories of metaphor also "presume a basic metaphor" (p. 188). To refer to less encompassing metaphors, MacCormac proposes the term "conveyance metaphors" (p. 48).

In a sense, all language may begin as metaphoric, and as it gains wide use, may collapse into a kind of literal status as part of ordinary language (see Leary, 1990b, pp. 6–7). "Metaphors serve as catalysts for linguistic change," argues MacCormac (1985, p. 16), although he does not go so far as to argue that all language is metaphorical (pp. 69–70).

12. On metaphor in the sciences and humanities, see Black (1962); Hesse (1966); Ferré (1968); Barbour (1974); MacCormac (1976); Ortony (1979); Gerhart and Russell (1984); Soskice (1985). On metaphor and issues of truth, see Vaught (1987). Gerhart and Russell (1984) also place primary value on the "epistemological function" (p. 107) of metaphor as intrinsic to "knowledge-in-process" in science and religion, and locate the importance of metaphor not in its linguistic expressive function (p. 108) but in its constructive role in the processing of meaning (pp. 93–94) and in facilitating an "ontological flash" (p. 120).

13. On the two poles of metaphor (McFague, 1982, 1987; Black, 1962); on the tension of "is" and "is not" and importance of negations in "analogical imagina-

tion" (Tracy, 1981). On metaphor as "tensive symbol" (Wheelwright, 1962, p. 93; 1982); on metaphor as "semantic impertinence" or "innovation" (Ricoeur, 1977, p. 291).

14. On imagery and affect in metaphor (Ricoeur, 1979); on the way metaphor "carries us" and the role of subsidiary meanings (Polanyi & Prosch, 1975, p. 79); on "semantic resonance" (Metzner, 1987).

15. See also Gergen (1982, p. 143–145) on the importance of new metaphors as a source of "generative theorizing" (p. 139). See also Danziger's (1990b, pp. 332–334) stress on the usefulness of a shared "metaphoric network" (from Ricoeur, 1977, pp. 243–244) for psychological research. Such networks allow a common basis for discourse in the history of psychology, yet also structure opportunities for theorists and researchers to pursue novel differences in emphasis within the ruling metaphorical network. Danziger also emphasizes the way ruling metaphors are culturally embedded (pp. 348–349) and programmatic (p. 351), playing a directive role in psychological practice.

16. On models and metaphor in science, see Hesse (1966); Barbour (1974); Leary (1990b). See Leary (1990a) for an excellent summary of metaphors in the history of psychology.

17. As cited by Judson (1980, p. 169).

18. See Heisenberg (1974) for a discussion of these issues of translation into ordinary language.

19. See Zukav (1979) on atom as idea (pp. 107–108), "massless particles" (p. 205), and a discussion of Max Born's articulation of the paradox of "spin" (p. 208). Also on the challenge of finding adequate language in modern physics (Capra, 1975). On issues of paradox in the language of physics and a more constructivist account of the language of physics (Gregory, 1990).

20. On two modes of knowing, see Royce's (1964) discussion; also Bruner (1986); as reflected in psychology (Kimble, 1984). Royce (1970a) also construes this polarity in terms of preferences on the one hand for the combined epistemological positions of "rationalism" and "empiricism," and on the other, for the epistemological position he calls "metaphorism," with its valuation of symbol and intuition (pp. 11–13, 27). Royce argues that all three "available ways of knowing" are needed and involved at some level in each of the three disciplines of science, art, and religion, for example (p. 13).

21. On signs and symbols (Royce, 1964); on a continuum of language modes (Wheelwright, 1982, p. 73).

22. On circumambulation of symbols (Singer, 1973); also on distinctions of sign and symbol from a Jungian perspective (Roloff, 1980).

23. See Royce (1965b, pp. 16–23). Note also Mair's (1989) call for a new "psychology in an intermediary mode" (pp. 42–48), a psychology that evokes, enlivens, and mediates a "poetics of experience" (p. 59). Such a "conversational psy-

chology" (p. xii) would seek to reflect the quality of the therapeutic relationship, extended as a vehicle of psychological inquiry" (p. 3).

24. On "one-to-many" symbols in science (Havens, 1968, p. 48) and symbolization in biology (Royce, 1965b).

25. See Gergen (1990a, pp. 292–293) on the "polysemic" aspect of systems metaphors which draw from a wide variety of domains and contexts beyond its history and connection with the natural sciences and biology, including computer language, cybernetics, holistic theories of organism and open systems models, economics, mathematics, and family theory, among others.

26. On the relationship between degree of involvement and precision of language (Barbour, 1974); see also Polanyi (1962, 1966) on "indwelling" and symbolic modes.

27. See discussion of Pauli's views on two poles for understanding reality in Heisenberg (1974, p. 227).

28. On existential criteria that "enhance" experience (Royce, 1959, p. 521), that convey a sense of the "unmanifest" (Havens, 1968, pp. 127–129). See Polanyi (1962) on criteria of "heuristic passion" (p. 143), "elegance" (p. 145), "beauty . . . and . . . profundity" (p. 15) and the distinction of "validation" versus "verification" (p. 202). See also the emphasis on the guiding principle of beauty in the "discovery of the true" (Heisenberg, 1974, p. 174) and Dirac, as cited by Judson (1980): "It is more important to have beauty in one's equations than to have them fit experiment (p. 11) . . . it's most important to have a *beautiful* theory. And if the observations don't support it, don't be too distressed, but wait a bit and see if some error in the observations doesn't show up" (p. 198). See also Platt (1961) on the informational and affective significance of a fundamental human response to pattern and by extension beauty.

29. See H. Smith (1958, pp. 136–139) on applying Heinrich Zimmer's metaphor of the river crossing in an understanding of Buddhism.

30. See Korzybski (1958, pp. 58–61) for a discussion of the observation that the "map *is not* the territory" (p. 58). On the relevance of Korzybski's premise for therapy and psychology, and the danger of static models, see Bandler and Grinder (1975, especially pp. 7–19, 43–44, 74–80). Bateson (1979, p. 122), too, makes use of Korzybski's famous map metaphor.

31. See Hoffman, Cochran, and Nead (1990) for a discussion of the way metaphor informs and in turn is altered and shaped by empirical research, with an important role for metaphor even in terms of theory disconfirmation.

Chapter 3

1. On the renewed valuing of theory, see Royce (1965a, 1982). See also Royce (1970a) for an overview of theoretical psychology. Also see Strong (1991) on the

need for theory-driven science in counseling psychology, and related debate concerning discovery-oriented research and appropriate timing and scale for theory testing (Gelso, 1991).

2. See Gluck and Patai (1991); Christ and Plaskow (1979); Olsen (1979). Note also the "intensive interview/case study approach" (p. 11) of Belenky, Clinchy, Goldberger, and Tarule (1986).

3. See M. Gergen (1987) for a challenge to the concept of "independent" variables in "synchronic" perspectives. On theory and research on life narratives, see M. Gergen (1987); on narrative in psychological contexts (Sarbin, 1986b). See also Gergen and Gergen (1986) who explore the role played by narrative form in psychological theory, and contrast learning theory, Piagetian theory, and Freudian theory as representing different narrative structures. On the social embeddedness of the self, see Verhave and van Hoorn (1984); on methods of historiography, Morawski (1984). For a comprehensive overview of alternate research methods focusing on ethnographic, phenomenological, and cybernetic paradigms, see Hoshmand (1989).

4. On Watson's influence on the neglect of mental imagery, see Kosslyn (1980); see Tolman (1967) for a critique of S-R learning theory; on "cognitive maps," see Tolman (1948); Chaplain and Krawiec (1968); on mental maps of cities (Milgram, Greenwald, Kessler, McKenna, & Waters, 1977).

5. On propositional versus imagery modes of "thinking" (Bugelski, 1977). See also Paivio (1970). On caution against any implication of internal pictures in the head (Block, 1981; Yuille & Catchpole, 1977).

6. Potential parallels between imagery and perceptual processes have also been suggested by other research (Marks, 1983; Kosslyn, 1975, 1980).

7. For example, verbal descriptive coding will be chosen more likely over visual coding to retrieve information regarding an overlearned item, such as whether a fish has leaves. A retrieval strategy based on imagery will be more useful to retrieve the less frequently noticed properties of an object or in evaluating subtle differences in size (e.g., whether a hamster or mouse is larger). For an overview of research findings, see Kosslyn (1980, 1983).

8. When given explicit instructions to solve certain identification problems with visual imagery, children and adults resembled each other in the time needed for the task, but with nonexplicit instructions, adults seemed to need less time than children, suggesting they have available to them a wider range of verbal propositional skills they can turn to when this offers a more streamlined alternative to problem solving (Kosslyn, 1980, 1983).

9. On imagery in therapeutic change (Sheikh & Jordan, 1983; Shorr, Sobel, Robin, & Connella, 1980) and in implosive therapy (Stampfl & Levis, 1967). See also J. L. Singer (1974) for an historical overview of imagery use in psychotherapy and behavior modification. On imagery in the human potential movement (Houston, 1982), in body work (Feldenkrais, 1972), and in sports psychology

(Suinn, 1983). On visualization and healing (Oyle, 1975), particularly in cancer treatment (Simonton, Matthews-Simonton, & Creighton, 1978). On eidetic imagery and the importance of an "experimental psychology of phenomenology" (p. 594), see Haber (1979) and accompanying peer commentaries.

10. In early work (e.g., Gardner & Winner, 1982), stress was typically placed on metaphor use as the ability to perceive and linguistically express a similarity between two factors from two different realms of experience. Vosniadou (1987, p. 871) considers metaphors as communicating meaning about a concept by "comparing it or juxtaposing it to a similar concept from a different conventional category." See Ortony, Reynolds, and Arter (1978) for contrasts between comparison and interaction theories of metaphor. Note also Glucksberg and Keysar (1990) who propose that metaphors be understood as "class-inclusion statements" (p. 17) rather than as comparisons. The emphasis here is on categorization and the central role of metaphor in communicating a "complex, patterned set of properties in a shorthand" (p. 16).

11. See Gardner and Winner (1978); Ortony, Reynolds, and Arter (1978); Leary (1990b).

12. For metaphors in these specific domains of psychology, see McReynolds (1990) on motivation; Averill (1990) on emotion; Hoffman, Cochran, and Nead (1990) on cognition; and Sarbin (1990) on abnormal behavior. See also Sternberg (1990) on metaphors underlying theories of intelligence.

13. On metaphoric capacities and deficits associated with brain damage (Gardner & Winner, 1978) or with schizophrenic and borderline states (Billow, Rossman, Lewis, Goldman, Kraemer, & Ross, 1987).

14. Developmental research has expanded to address such issues as: the ability to comprehend metaphors describing psychological or emotional phenomena (Waggoner & Palermo, 1989), visual metaphors (Dent & Rosenberg, 1990), a developmental shift from attributional metaphors based on appearance to those showing a relational emphasis (Gentner, 1988), factors or sources of difficulty moderating metaphoric competence (Vosniadou, Ortony, Reynolds, & Wilson, 1984), and further refinement of issues regarding metaphoric comprehension as similar in kind to comprehension of literal language (Waggoner, Messe, & Palermo, 1985). Vosniadou (1987) reviews the literature on the development of metaphor abilities in children, addressing such issues as refining the criteria for identifying metaphorical usage in young children and the relationship between metaphoric competence and conceptual development. Ortony, Reynolds, and Arter (1978) also provide an earlier review.

Two areas where previous research findings have been questioned increasingly concern the hypothesis of a U-shaped curve for metaphor use across the lifespan and the presence of cross-model matching as a precursor to metaphor. The suggestion of a U-shaped curve for metaphor development across the lifespan was based on research by Gardner and Winner. They found that very young children were able to give only predominantly concrete interpretations to metaphors. Preschoolers, however, accounted for the highest productivity of spontaneous and created metaphors, including well-formed metaphor production, although their metaphors were largely based on physical resemblances rather than more subtle parallels (1982). Three- and four-year-olds created more appropriate metaphors than seven- and eleven-year-olds who appeared to actively reject metaphorical modes and rely instead on literal modes (1978). Only as children approach adolescence did this willingness to return to metaphor reappear, with more consciousness of the tension implied by metaphorical construction as opposed to a literal one. The finding that the amount of metaphor formation in preschoolers exceeded even that for college students (1978, p. 133) has been particularly provocative, raising questions regarding possible mediating variables affecting the decline in metaphorical proclivities, such as training in formal logic and abstract thought, particularly in a culture which does not typically value mythic and metaphorical modes in mainstream society. Vosniadou (1987) suggests, however, that this U-shaped relationship may result from an overestimation of the extent to which the preschooler expressions were full metaphors (pp. 874–875), and further research is needed. Vosniadou, Ortony, Reynolds, and Wilson (1984) also differ from Gardner and Winner in arguing against the idea that a literal stage necessarily precedes metaphoric use.

Support for the early inception of metaphorical proclivities has been found in cross-sensory matching, observed even among infants who preferred looking at dotted lines while listening to pulsing tones, and observing continuous lines when listening to continuous tones, rather than opposite combinations (Winner, Wapner, Cicone, & Gardner, 1979). Such cross-sensory matches or synesthetic metaphors are found in adults and children, and may reflect basic tendencies fundamental to the capacity to perceive other metaphor (Marks, Hammeal, & Bornstein (1987). Here, too, Vosniadou (1987, pp. 872–874) questions whether these matches by similarity actually reflect the capacity to "override habitual forms of categorization," needed to qualify fully as a metaphor (p. 874).

15. See Dilts, Grinder, Bandler, Bandler, and DeLozier (1980).

16. For an example of empirical research on metaphor use in counseling, see Suit and Paradise (1985).

17. See also Merten and Schwartz (1982), who reflect on the conflicts occasioned in a community mental health center through different types of metaphoric emphases regarding "community" and "mental health."

18. On imagery, creativity, and the arts (Samuels & Samuels, 1975); on visual thinking in the arts (Arnheim, 1969). On visual thinking skills (McKim, 1980); on their relevance to breaking through creative blocks (Adams, 1979) or facilitating problem solving (Kaufmann, 1979). On the relationship between enhanced memory for imagery and creativity (G. A. Shaw, 1987). On analogical skills (Pellegrino, 1985) and computer facilitation of imagery and imagination (Dennett, 1982; Pagels, 1988).

19. Note also Bateson's views on play and fantasy in terms of metacommunication (1972, pp. 177–193).

20. On fantasy and imaginative aspects of children's play, perhaps accentuated in the current move toward privatized and internal play as opposed to external physical play, see Sutton-Smith (1971, 1985). Note, however, Sutton-Smith's (1986, pp. 154–156, 227) concern that we tend to conflate imagination and play through overextending the word "play." Not all imaginative activity is play; much infant "play" is actually the "work" of problem solving and mastery (pp. 129–147). Sutton-Smith (1979, pp. 296–298) also underscores the social embeddedness of play which is often neglected in approaches emphasizing play as increasing "mastery" or "creativity" (p. 296).

For research and theory suggesting relationships between imaginative tendencies in play and creativity and healthy psychological functioning, see J. L. Singer (1973); also Singer and Singer (1979). See also their research suggesting boys low in tendencies toward imaginative, fantasizing play are more overtly aggressive than high fantasizers (summarized in J. L. Singer, 1975, p. 136 and Pulaski, 1974, pp. 71–72).

21. Though Schachter and Singer's (1962) classic research study has received considerable criticism and elaboration over the years (e.g., Marshall & Zimbardo, 1979; Cotton, 1981; Reisenzein, 1983), it has been profoundly heuristic in engendering research and a wide variety of theories conceptualizing the relationship between cognition and emotion.

22. Parallels between left and right hemisphere functioning were also suggested by polarities between propositional-linguistic and appositional, nonverbal, visual-spatial modes (Bogen, 1973), between lineal and nonlineal orientations (Lee, 1973) and between right-handed versus left-handed metaphors in cultures around the world (Domhoff, 1973).

23. See Gazzaniga (1983a, 1983b); Levy (1983); Zaidel (1983).

24. See Pribram (1980) and a variation thereon (1990). See also Pribram (1986) on epistemological and ontological issues regarding mind/brain relationship.

25. On computer models and brain/mind issues, see Gregory (1981); Hofstadter (1979); Hofstadter and Dennett (1981). See also Pagels (1988) on heuristic and philosophical implications of a variety of contrasting computer models from the "sciences of complexity," e.g., serial processing versus parallel neural net models of the brain (pp. 114–141). Note also Penrose's (1989) critique of computer models as inadequate to explaining conscious judgments and his argument on behalf of a "non-algorithmic" or nonprocedural element to consciousness (pp. 392–449). Bateson (1972, p. 483) also had reservations regarding the adequacy of computer models to represent thinking if they neglected their embeddedness in the larger environment (see also chap. 5).

26. On the holographic model, see Pribram (1971, 1980, pp. 27–34, 1990, pp. 88–97). See also Ferguson (1978); Goleman (1979); Hampden-Turner (1981, pp. 94–97).

27. On the "implicate order" (Bohm, 1980; Briggs & Peat, 1984).

28. See Natsoulas (1981) for an extensive inventory of the types of problems of consciousness deserving attention in psychology; also Osborne (1981). See also Bruner and Feldman (1990) for an intriguing contrast of the "riotously luxuriant" metaphors of consciousness compared to the "more sedate" and "cultivated garden of metaphors" referring to cognition (p. 230). See also Valle and von Eckartsberg (1981).

29. Bruner (1990) in fact suggests that the computer models of cognition, despite early hopes to the contrary, are reimporting a "new antimentalism" (pp. 8–9), as the "processing of information" replaces the "construction of meaning" (p. 4).

30. On states of consciousness (Goleman, 1974; Green & Green, 1971; Tart, 1975a, 1975b, 1990; Deikman, 1982; Gebser, 1985; Wilber, 1977, 1980a, 1981; Grof, 1988).

31. For research on meditation (Bloomfield, 1976; Kornfield, 1979; Walsh, 1979). In a particularly unusual and elaborate study, Brown and Engler (1980) found support from Rorschach measures for the validation of stages in the process of meditation. Note, however, critiques such as that of Holmes (1984), who claims that the association of meditation and lowering of "somatic arousal" has not been supported by research. Likewise, the effort to extract critical elements from traditional meditative practices has suggested that other factors besides those judged central by traditional practicers may be associated with any positive changes observed (J. C. Smith, 1976). This latter critique, however, still leaves room for hypotheses regarding possible correlates in consciousness to whatever observed changes do take place.

32. Petrie (1979) has defended the cognitive value of metaphor in learning, although the extent to which metaphor is epistemologically necessary is debated by Green (1979).

33. On the importance of visual analogies in enhancing learning in chemistry (Rigney & Lutz, 1976), the value of higher imagery words in textbooks for enhancing comprehension and interest (Wharton, 1980), and the advantages of imagery strategies of problem solving for enhancing originality and internal control in students (Richardson & Wylie, 1984).

34. On organizing lecture notes graphically (Day, 1980); on using diagrams in teaching (Toth, 1980) or explicit models and analogies (Norman, 1980).

Chapter 4

1. On metaphor in personality theory, see M. B. Smith (1985); Browning (1987). For a discussion of the need for changing metaphors in psychoanalytic theory from scientific and detective models to a hermeneutical metaphor of con-

versation or case-oriented law, see Spence (1987). Surprisingly, a chapter on metaphors of personality is missing from the noteworthy Leary (1990a) collection on metaphors in the history of psychology, although Leary (1990b) does reflect on metaphor use by Freud, and Sarbin (1990) briefly looks at self and related concepts in the context of metaphors of therapeutic intervention (pp. 323–324).

Personality theory and global metaphors of the self have remained somewhat outside the dominant paradigm of research psychology for some time (see Margolis, 1987; Gergen, 1971, pp. 9–11), although selected constructs from personality theorists, e.g., the self-concept in Rogers' theory (1959), have received experimental attention (e.g., Gergen, 1971). However, there are increasing signs of a renewed interest in theory and the construct of self per se (see such works as Young-Eisendrath & Hall, 1987; Hewitt, 1989), and the concept of the self has remained relevant in cross-cultural investigations of culture and self (see Marsella, DeVos, & Hsu, 1985; Joan G. Miller, 1988; Heelas & Lock, 1981).

2. See L. D. Smith (1990) for an account of metaphor use in the behavioral tradition, especially the use by Skinner of selection metaphors from Darwinian evolutionary theory (pp. 255–258).

3. The hermeneutical emphasis from Ricoeur on "persons as texts" (Woolfolk, Sass, & Messer, 1988, p. 9), and on the increased attention to the self as story and constructed narrative in developmental psychology, psychoanalytic theory, and related areas of psychology (Bruner, 1990, chap. 4; Sarbin, 1986b; Howard, 1991), are central illustrations of the heightened awareness of self as construct. In a sense, the understanding of the self as constructed was also latent within transactional analysis of scripts (Steiner, 1974), and reemerges with more fundamental ontological moorings, in the notion of discovering and choosing one's personal mythology (Feinstein & Krippner, 1988).

Note that a constructivist assumption of the creation or shaping of the self within culture does not necessarily imply a lack of ontological referents to the nature of the self. See C. Taylor (1988, elaborated extensively in 1989) for a view that traces the shifting nature of understandings of the self to perceived changes of "moral topography" in relationship to new understandings of ontological referents. Only a strict constructivist interpretation insists on the total malleability of the self construct, and even vocal constructivists are often concerned to find some alternatives to complete relativism.

4. See in particular such cross-cultural understandings of the self as reviewed in Joan G. Miller (1988). Also see Joan G. Miller (1984) for an example of empirical research on differences between children and adults in the United States and India in their tendencies to attribute causes of human actions to internal versus contextual factors. For a critique of psychoanalytic constructs in the context of India and Japan and an effort to articulate a wider basis for cross-cultural psychoanalytic theory, see Roland (1988). See also Doi (1990) on the low tolerance of the Western psychoanalytic tradition for the type of dependent relationships based on *amae* and valued in Japan. See also chapter 6 for a discussion of Eastern psychological traditions and their relevance to understandings of the self in systems theory.

5. For further discussion of ego or conscious functions, see Erikson (1963) on the role of ego in his theory; Hartmann (1958, pp. 8–9) and Browning (1973, pp. 90–96) on the conflict-free ego sphere; Allport (1955) on the importance of conscious functions; Kelly (1963) on a cognitive theory of personality.

6. On the importance of emphasizing both autonomy and interdependence, see Tomm (1987). See also Franz and White (1985) for an intriguing critique and augmentation of Erikson's theory to include developmental pathways for both "individuation" and "attachment." Gardiner (1987) argues that Kohut's self theory with its "interdependent model of maturity" (p. 225) potentially incorporates aspects of both the classical psychoanalytic emphasis on autonomy and feminist emphasis on female bonding (p. 240).

7. On self-constructs and ideal self (Rogers, 1959, p. 200) and their role in reducing identity (Rogers, 1951, pp. 501–503); on the importance of unconditional positive regard (Rogers, 1959, pp. 223–224).

8. Another applied approach to identifying and embracing the "disowned selves" within us is articulated by Stone and Winkelman (1989, p. 27). They too represent personality as a "system of subpersonalities (selves)" (p. 15), stressing the role of the "aware ego" in witnessing and honoring the variety of voices (pp. 21–26).

9. On the independence of the self concept from empirical grounding (K. J. Gergen, 1987b); on the ongoing negotiation of self-conceptions in different social contexts (Gergen, 1981), the lifelong elaboration of self-not self boundaries (L'Ecuyer, 1981), the self as historically situated (Cushman, 1990) and socially constructed (Gergen & Davis, 1985; Shotter & Gergen, 1989). See Zurcher (1977) on the "Mutable Self"; see also Gergen (1991) on postmodern challenges to the conception of self amidst the social "saturation" accelerated by modern communications technology.

10. See Bruner (1990, pp. 99–138) on autobiographical construction of the self. For a critique of humanistic psychology's tendency toward an ahistorical understanding of the individual self-actualizing self, see Sass (1988). On more general issues in hermeneutical understanding of personality, see Messer, Sass, and Woolfolk (1988).

Note that Sampson (1989, pp. 1–2) includes systems theory among the major challenges to the notion of the bounded individual self, along with cross-cultural and feminist influences, social constructionism, critical theory, and deconstructionism. Gergen (1991, especially chaps. 6 through 8) explores postmodern potential for redefining the self from individual essence to a "relational self" constructed in terms of "immersed interdependence" (p. 147).

11. See Kalupahana (1987) for a discussion of central psychological principles of Buddhism. On Buddhist understandings of the self as construct of the mind (Ross, 1966; H. Smith, 1958), especially as interrupting awareness of our identity with the flow of experience (Watts, 1951, 1966). See also chapter 6, note 10.

12. See particularly Macy (1991) for an excellent treatment of Buddhism and General Systems Theory as hermeneutical resources for mutually clarifying central understandings regarding interrelatedness, mutual causality, and the nature of the self.

13. On the organism and its openness to the phenomenal field, see Rogers (1951, pp. 483–487); on the self construct or self-structure (pp. 497–507, especially 501, 503); for a diagram of the "total personality" (pp. 525–527). On the actualizing tendency, see Rogers (1959, p. 196); on increasing congruence between self and organism (pp. 203, 218). On increasing trust and openness to experience, see Rogers (1961, p. 189).

14. On the greater wisdom of the organism, see Rogers' essay "Do We Need 'A' Reality?" (1980, p. 106). On the formative tendency in the universe that Rogers contrasts with the emphasis on entropy and closed systems (p. 124), see his essay "The Foundations of a Person-Centered Approach" (1980, p. 133). On the importance of the experience and role of the total organism in the process of science, see Rogers on "Some Thoughts Regarding the Current Presuppositions of the Behavioral Sciences" in Kirschenbaum and Henderson (1989, p. 269).

15. See Lowen (1982) for a developmental model of ego functions which aims at integrating Jungian concepts and some systems concepts.

16. On the transcendent function, see Jung's essay by that title (1969c, pp. 67–91); see also Jung (1966, pp. 80, 110; 1971, p. 115). On individuation, see Jung (1966, pp. 110–111, 173–178), especially as tied to the tasks of the second half of life (Jung, 1969c, pp. 387–403; 1966, pp. 74–75). On the shadow, see Jung (1968b, pp. 8–10; 1966, pp. 26, 53–61).

17. On the self, see Jung (1968b, pp. 23, 31); on the self as circle, as wider personality and center of gravity, see Jung (1968b, pp. 190, 224). Jaffé (1971) and Singer (1973) also offer excellent portrayals of Jung's central concepts of self in the context of individuation.

18. For a helpful graphic illustration of the relationship of ego and self, see Samuels and Samuels (1975, p. 72).

19. See Lewin (1936) on the concepts of person, environment and lifespace (introduced pp. 12, 14) and an understanding of personality in terms of concepts of topology. See also Lewin (1935) on personality dynamics conceptualized in terms of fields, forces, vectors, and valences. See Lewin (1951, pp. 170–187) on the relationship between psychological and nonpsychological factors in "psychological ecology" and the problem of addressing the "multitude of forces" in a field (p. 173), problems of complexity in systems which systems theory will address from a somewhat different angle.

20. On the "psychoid" nature of reality, see Jung (1969c, pp. 176–177); also Jaffé (1971, p. 23).

Chapter 5

1. The works of Capra (1975, 1982), Zukav (1979), and Pagels (1982) are among the best known books of this nature, although preceded by the writing of Barnett (1957); Azimov (1966); Gamow (1961, 1965); Murchie (1967). See also Herbert (1987); Malville (1981); Postle (1976); March (1978); Wolf (1981); Gregory (1990). Note especially the work of Hawking (1988) on understanding time and related issues. See also Penrose (1989) who hypothesizes the need for radically revising quantum theory (pp. 348–349) and subsequent implications for more fully understanding the phenomenon of consciousness (p. 431).

2. "Through the looking glass" is the apt metaphor chosen by Briggs and Peat (1984) for the title of their book exploring models of wholeness in science. See also Morrison, Morrison, Eames, and Eames (1982), also available in film versions, for a photographic journey via the "powers of ten" to the world of the infinitesimally small and great.

3. See especially Zukav (1979) for a clear introduction to these issues. On the atom as "idea-like" rather than "matter-like" (Zukav, 1979, p. 81); on not existing in the classical sense (p. 108). See also Capra (1975) on the matrix of probable reaction channels.

4. On the bootstrap hypothesis and "interpenetration," see especially Capra (1975, pp. 292–293); also on web or network metaphors replacing fundamental building blocks, see Capra (1988, p. 66).

5. See especially Capra (1975, p. 186) on implications of quantum theory for reconceptualizing time and linear causality.

6. On the relationship of chaos models to "punctuated equilibrium" (May & Groder, 1989) and evolution (Laszlo, 1987); social change (Eisler, 1987); archetypal psychology (Abraham, 1989; May & Groder, 1989).

7. Also on Bohm's theory of "implicate order," see Bohm and Peat (1987); for an interpretation of Bell's theorem from this perspective, see Briggs and Peat (1984).

8. On models characterizing the "reenchantment of science" (Griffin, 1988; Weber, 1986; Sheldrake, 1981); on the emerging ecological paradigm (Dunlap, 1980) and the Deep Ecology movement (Devall & Sessions, 1985; Tobias, 1984). See Briggs and Peat (1984) who organize their book around the "emerging science of wholeness." Note the emergence also of ecological concerns voiced from both an "ecofeminist" (Diamond & Orenstein, 1990) and "transpersonal" (Fox, 1990) perspective.

9. On Sheldrake's argument that mechanistic models are secondary accretions to more fundamentally organic processes, see Griffin (1988, p. 16); also in Weber (1986, p. 85).

10. For a biography of von Bertalanffy and discussion of general systems theory, see Davidson (1983). See also James G. Miller (1978) for an extensive analysis

of "living systems" across levels of complexity, and Buckley (1968) for key sources in early systems theorizing. See also Boulding (1985) for a comprehensive look at the world construed as system across physical, biological, social, economic, political, communication, and evaluative domains. For a summary of the relevance of a "general systems perspective" for enhancing sociological models, see Buckley (1967, pp. 36–80). Particularly stressed are notions of organization (pp. 42–45), information rather than energy exchange (pp. 46–47), information as a relationship not a substance (p. 47), open systems (pp. 50–51), feedback and models of purposefulness (pp. 52–58), morphostasis and morphogenesis (pp. 58–66), and the need for more complex models of causality (pp. 66–80). See also Hampden-Turner's (1981) summary and portrayal of cybernetic models (pp. 158–159, 162–181).

Note work by Robbins and Oliva on identifying core concepts in general systems theory (1982, p. 382) used across disciplines (1984). See also Sirgy's (1988, pp. 25–26) classification of types of general systems theories in terms of contributions to philosophy of science, knowledge of behavioral phenomena across domains, and methodology. On various aspects of the "systems movement," and contrasts between von Bertalanffy's work and industrial/systems-engineering approaches or what Davidson calls "systems technocracy," see Davidson (1983, chap. 8, especially pp. 191–194, 205–206).

11. In what Frank (1970, p. 227) claims is the original use of this term, Weaver (1948) contrasts scientific problems of "organized complexity," involving "a sizable number of factors which are interrelated into an organic whole" (p. 539), with limited variable problems of simplicity or, at the other extreme, problems of "disorganized complexity" (pp. 536–538). Note also Rapoport and Horvath's (1959, pp. 89–90) similar contrast of "organized complexity" with "organized simplicity" and "chaotic complexity."

12. On epistemological issues critiqued by systems theory, isomorphic analogies, and related dimensions of systems theory, see Sutherland (1973) and Buckley (1968). On systems theory as an epistemological critique of positivism, atomism, reductionism, and linear causality, see A. Taylor (1977, pp. 21–27). Taylor summarizes systems theory as a monistic, holistic approach involving isomorphism across domains and argues for its special relevance for education in an age of information proliferation and critical needs for synthesis. Note, too, the inclusion of articles by von Bertalanffy (pp. 219–223) and Frank (pp. 225–233), with comments and rebuttal (pp. 234–244), in Royce's (1970b) collection on issues of unification in theoretical psychology. The authors consider respectively the relevance of systems theory and concepts of "organized complexities" in terms of a critique of reductionism (von Bertalanffy, 1970, p. 221) and promise for a more unified framework for psychology (Frank, 1970, p. 227).

On von Bertalanffy's epistemological position of "perspectivism" (p. 211), the "truth of many perspectives" (p. 212), the "interaction between knower and known" (p. 213), and the avoidance of total relativism (p. 215), see Davidson (1983, chap. 9). On von Bertalanffy's consideration of systems concepts as representing a new "paradigm" in the Kuhnian sense, see Davidson (1983, pp. 100, 189). See also Sirgy (1988) for a discussion of general systems theories as "paradigms" (p. 29) and an exploration of strategies for enhancing their unifying contributions, isomorphism, and heuristic power.

Note also Phillips' (1976) contrasting critique directed at Hegelian-derived organicism ("Holism 1") whose assumptions he argues were adopted by General Systems Theory (pp. 46–67). Phillips believes these assumptions are not antithetical to an analytic, mechanical method and critiques systems theory in terms of one of Popper's criteria for scientific theorizing (pp. 65–66). Phillips acknowledges, however, the importance of new concepts in science for relating to the study of organic wholes, a concern which he calls "Holism 3" (pp. 35, 123). Phillips' critique is particularly revealing of the extent to which the truly radical implications of systems theory—for conveying the inextricable interrelatedness of all that is—go beyond the dominant mindset and are subsequently misunderstood or critiqued as making knowledge of anything (or we might say any "thing") ultimately impossible. We will return to these issues and their implications for construing a radically interconnected world in chapter 7.

13. On holons, see also Koestler (1978).

14. On the way systems higher in the hierarchy constitute the environment for those at lower levels, see Allen and Starr (1982, p. 13); Salthe (1985, p. 83).

15. Note that von Bertalanffy (1968) considers cybernetics, which had developed separately (pp. 15–16), to be "but a part of a general theory of systems" (p. 17).

16. See also Maruyama (1963) in which adaptive self-reorganization or "morphogenesis" is related to "deviation-amplifying" control processes using positive feedback, in contrast to the "deviation-counteracting" aspects of "morphostasis" (see also Buckley, 1967, 58–62).

17. See A. Taylor (1977, pp. 32–42) for a model elaborating on Laszlo's concepts of self-stabilization versus self-organization as applied to the evolution of sociocultural systems, and the role of technology particularly in the latter self-organizing process. See also Laszlo (1977, pp. 6–13) for a summary of these "pattern conserving" (Cybernetics I) versus "pattern transforming" (Cybernetics II) processes in society (p. 7).

18. On the Second Law of Thermodynamics and entropy, see Gamow (1961); Rifkin and Howard (1980). On the entropy concept and general systems theory applied to complex society and "macrosociological" analysis (p. 2) in social entropy theory (SET), see Bailey (1990, especially chaps. 2, 3). On the concept of "negentropic" borrowed from Schrödinger's terminology, see Laszlo (1973, p. 44).

19. See also Laszlo (1981) on biperspectivism. Note also Tyson's (1982) suggestion of a "nondichotomous, dynamic approach to consciousness" (p. 496) suggested by von Bertalanffy's work, including an interpretation of meditation in terms of systems and hierarchies. See also LeGare (1987) on general systems the-

ory as a metatheory offering guidelines for neuroscience research, especially with respect to the concepts of hierarchical organization, open systems, and equifinality, where "the same final state may be realized from a number of different initial conditions" (pp. 113–114).

20. On consciousness conceptualized as emerging from more basic levels of "subjectivity," see Laszlo (1972, p. 87).

21. Also see G. Bateson (1979, pp. 102–142, 234–235) on criteria of "mind." See Maxwell (1983) for articles discussing and critiquing Bateson's *Mind and Nature: A Necessary Unity* (1979) from a symposium on that topic (pp. 253–283).

22. Note also according to G. Bateson (1977, p. 243), "message events are activated by difference," and differences are what gets mapped as mind (p. 240). Difference triggers the "interaction between parts of mind" (1979, p. 102). Differences are "not material," nor can they be "localized" or "placed in time" (1977, p. 240). "Mind contains no time and no space" (1979, p. 146).

To produce information "there must be two entities (real or imagined)" that "generate" news of a difference (1979, p. 76), yet each alone is a "non-entity," an "unknowable," a Kantian "Ding an sich" (p. 77). A change in a part between two different times might also "activate" a "receiver" (p. 106), the process supported by "collateral energy" such as metabolism (p. 235).

A difference is not a thing or a noun, yet it can be causal. Bateson used the hypothetical example of not writing to someone and getting an angry letter back from that person. The "cause" of the angry letter is understood as the difference between the "letter which I might have written and the letter which I didn't write" (M. C. Bateson, 1972, p. 90). Both are "fictitious" and "the difference is not a real object" either (p. 90).

23. On logical types and metamessages, see also Lipset (1980, pp. 189–191); on their relationship to understanding play (pp. 191–196; see also G. Bateson, 1972, pp. 177–193) and schizophrenia (Lipset, pp. 199–231). Note also the dual levels involved in understanding interaction: the level of the "participating entities" and the level of the "larger entity which is brought into being" through the interaction (Hoffman, 1971, p. 293).

24. The critique of the modern evolutionary synthesis, which combined Darwinian assumptions with genetics, was given popular impetus by Eldredge and Gould's (1972) reiteration of biologist Mayr's argument (Stanley, 1981, p. 108). According to Mayr, classical evolutionary theory neglected the origin of diversity and speciation, emphasizing mostly issues of adaptation (1988, pp. 163, 361). In an early article on the topic, Mayr (1954) suggested that speciation appeared to occur in small isolated communities over a relatively rapid span of time compared to the mainstream assumptions of slow, random accumulations of change in large population gene pools. The more popular accounts of Gould (1977, 1980) and Rifkin (1983) focus on this theory of "punctuated equilibria," emphasizing the possibility that evolution reflects periodic phases of rapid change rather than the proverbial

slow and steady process of selection. Such arguments have been compatible with fossil evidence (Stanley, 1981) that has begun to be taken more seriously by the dominant paradigm.

There has also been increased appreciation for the importance of environmental considerations in evolution, such as the "epigenetic landscape" articulated by Waddington (1942, 1957) by which environmental factors might interact, "canalize," and affect the sheer influence of genetic factors in the classical account of natural selection (see also J. M. Smith, 1958).

Mayr (1988) argues that Gould (and Eldredge) have overstated the extent to which recent critiques of evolutionary mechanisms represent a paradigm change in biology. Mayr argues that the "punctuated equilibria" view of speciation is compatible with pluralistic models within the modern evolutionary synthesis, some of which might argue for simultaneous slow steady evolutionary changes too (pp. 463–464).

25. On the evolution of transnational "supraorganisms," see Laszlo (1987). For hierarchical diagrams illustrating this process, see also Laszlo (1977, p. 12) and A. Taylor (1977, p. 33). See also Taylor's concept of "Copernican internationalism" (p. 39) and "multilevel transactionality" (pp. 39–41) whereby we come to live at several tiers of sociopolitical organization, with increasing "supra-national" (p. 33) levels present.

26. See Penrose (1989) for a fascinating hypothesis regarding a possible role for non-local quantum involvements in the growth of dendritic spines at neural synapses, in analogy with similar processes potentially at work in the growth of crystals or quasicrystals (pp. 434–439).

27. For Holt's proposal of the "Help Stamp Out Nouns" sticker (p. 63) and a discussion of the issue (p. 236), see M. C. Bateson (1972).

28. See May's (1976) discussion of Bateson's preference for concepts of form, order, and pattern (pp. 40–45) which Bateson contrasted with concepts of force, energy, and substance. May also discusses Bateson's critique of humanistic psychology for retaining its "third force" metaphor and ironically revealing an attachment to materialistic conceptions of reality (e.g., via forces, energy), despite an intent to offer a significant alternative to behaviorism (pp. 47–48). May's essay also appears in Brockman's collection (1977, pp. 77–102). Also see Lipset (1980, pp. 160–183) on Bateson's background and involvement with cybernetics, which preceded his work as "communications theorist" (pp. 184–238) and ecologist of mind (pp. 256–278).

Note the discussion in Maxwell (1983) by Kobayashi (1983, p. 282) of the way Bateson's "universe of discourse," although sharing many ideas with cybernetics, differs considerably from the mathematical cybernetics approach of a critic of Bateson (i.e., Gregson, 1983). Kobayashi (1983) locates Bateson's "premises" within a "nonmaterialistic, idealistic philosophical tradition" attempting "to bridge the gap between positivism and the realm of the arts and humanities" (p. 282).

29. G. Bateson (1972, pp. 480–481) discusses these errors in his essay "Pathologies of Epistemology" where he distinguishes, in terms derived from Jung (1963, pp. 379–380), between the world of pleroma (understood in terms of forces, energy) and the world of creatura (understood in terms of communication, relationships, pattern). See also Lipset (1980, pp. 272–273) for another discussion of this issue of levels of explanation. Though it is often difficult to hold this tension in level of understanding without collapsing it into a duality of matter and mind, such was precisely Bateson's intention. He insists that his epistemology is monistic (1977, pp. 239, 243), despite his earlier tendency to use dualistic language in some of his "language of report" (p. 239). He wants to find a way to "merge" approaches "seeking simplification" with those "acknowledging complexity" in such a way that we bring our metaphors from the complex to the simple, rather than only the reverse as in traditional science (M. C. Bateson, 1972, pp. 234–236). We will return to these issues in chapter 7 where we explore his concerns to bridge the sense of secular and sacred, to "move toward a pervasive sense of the sacred, applied to the whole of the Creatura and to the whole physical universe as it is made meaningful in human experience" (M. C. Bateson, 1972, pp. 236–237). Bateson's (1979, pp. 233–237) intention to more explicitly address issues of consciousness in a book called "Where Angels Fear to Tread" is discussed by Maas (1983, pp. 271–274) in Maxwell (1983).

30. See also Lipset (1980, pp. 273–274) on this theme.

31. See Briggs and Peat (1984, p. 169) on Prigogine's concept of dissipative structures.

32. See Loren Eiseley (1957, 1969, 1971) and Lewis Thomas (1974, 1979, 1983).

33. See Arguelles (1984); Cook (1979); Doczi (1981); Lawlor (1982); Stevens (1974); Weyl (1980).

34. Note also G. Bateson's central emphasis on "the pattern which connects" in *Mind and Nature* (1979, p. 8).

35. On implications of systems theory for philosophy and metaphysics, see Macy (1976); Seidler (1979); Oliver (1981).

Chapter 6

1. Note that von Bertalanffy (1970, p. 222) specifically underscores the relevance of systems theory to a critique of S-R behaviorism and summarizes other "systems-oriented" developments in psychology as reflected in the growing trends to critique mechanism. He also directs attention to the way psychology is challenging the "reactive" models of Skinner and Freud (1975, pp. 111–112) and moving toward more proactive, future-oriented models (p. 113). Von Bertalanffy (1962, pp. 13–15) defines his viewpoint as "Beyond the Homeostasis Principle" (p. 14). See also Davidson (1983, chaps. 4, 5). Von Bertalanffy (1970, p. 222; also 1968, p. 7)

notes Roy Grinker's (1967) observation that if there were another revolution (Grinker, p. ix) in psychiatry, it would be in the tendency toward a "unified" or "general systems" theory of behavior (p. v). See Frank (1970), too, who calls for a psychology that can focus on "organized complexities." See also June Singer (1990, chap. 9) on contemporary psychology's critique of positivism and reductionism and the beginnings of a new transpersonal paradigm.

Note also that despite the holistic, organismic, and integrative nature of general systems theory, systems concepts are not to be confused with other uses of the term "holism" in the social sciences and philosophy, such as used to emphasize the linguistic and cultural boundedness of thought or the embeddedness of meaning in social context. Ironically, the notion of social/linguistic "holism" has come to denote a self-containing language community of discourse and conveys a sense of an intact whole unto itself, thus implying almost the opposite of the kind of open systems emphasis on interconnectedness in systems theory. See H. Smith (1989, chap. 6) for both a discussion of social holism and a critique from another perspective.

2. See Watzlawick, Beavin, and Jackson (1967, chaps. 4, also 1 through 3) on the application of General System Theory to understanding "interactional systems" (p. 119), especially families and couples (see also chap. 5); also see Schultz (1984, chap. 3). On family therapy and understandings of families as dynamic systems, see Haley (1971); also Haley (1976) and Becvar and Becvar (1988), who raise issues regarding the larger social contexts within which family problems get defined. On the need to broaden the context and reframe the process of family "therapy" to a systems consultation model, see Wynne, McDaniel, and Weber (1986). See also the work of such pathbreakers in family therapy as Satir (1983) and Whitaker (e.g., Napier & Whitaker, 1978).

With reference to Bateson's views on family systems, see G. Bateson (1972, pp. 201–278), particularly with reference to the "double bind" hypothesis and schizophrenia, and the classic paper "Toward a Theory of Schizophrenia" by G. Bateson, D. D. Jackson, J. Haley, and J. Weakland (1956; reprinted in G. Bateson, 1972, pp. 201–227). See also the essay by his daughter Mary Catherine Bateson (1977, p. 66); also see Lipset (1980, pp. 184–238). See Hoffman (1971) for an application of Maruyama's (1963) stress on "deviation-amplifying," positive feedback processes (the "second cybernetics") to families and social systems.

3. Note that Sarbin (1990, p. 324) includes a discussion of "social systems therapy" as a metaphor of intervention placing the person in a "social context" and references chiefly work in community psychology. By using the operative metaphor of "the historical act" to define the meaning of social systems, however, he locates them within a narrower understanding of context and embeddedness than that potentially carried by a systems emphasis.

4. Note, for example, the application of systems insights and psychological tools for helping raise consciousness regarding nuclear threat, destruction of the environment, and global hunger, disease, and impoverishment, while at the same time empowering people to be able to feel and work through the "darkness" and

despair to "experience the power of interconnectedness" (Macy, 1983, p. 37; see especially pp. 24–37; also pp. 128–130 for an exercise on imaging the web of life).

5. Note thus that Bateson both "deconstructs" the individual self and offers a radical new understanding. Note parallels to Sampson (1990) who acknowledges his intent to deconstruct the "self-contained" individual "in order to constitute a differently structured kind of identity" which he calls "embedded individuality" (p. 124). In an even more radical parallel, note the way that aspects of Eastern and Western mysticism and meditation serve to deconstruct the nature of "normal consciousness" in order, however, to witness reality in another way (Rothberg, 1990).

6. On Bateson's "idealism," see May's discussion (1976, p. 36); on Bateson as redefining reality as a "network of ideas" and the importance of contexts, see Matson (1977, p. 76).

7. For an excellent treatment of the "co-arising of knower and known," in its parallels to Buddhism, see Macy (1991, chap. 7, pp. 120–123). In both systems theory and Buddhism, neither subject nor object is independent; they are mutually conditioned (p. 122). This understanding that the "true includes us, as knowers," that the knower is inextricably involved in the known, is the kind of relativism that systems thinking acknowledges, not a relativism that denies the possiblity of a truth that can be known or would make all claims to accuracy equal (p. 196). In fact, systems thinking profoundly argues that the fabric of moral value is built in to the universe through its interconnectedness, and witnessing to this evokes a characteristic moral response of reverence (see Laszlo, 1973, pp. 282–290), appreciation, or care. See also von Bertalanffy's epistemological position (chap. 5, note 12) and his advocacy of a morality based on "interdependence" (Davidson, 1983, p. 40).

8. G. Bateson (1977) claims to have a monistic epistemology (p. 239), with the relationship between reality and perception bridged by information about a difference (p. 240). Somewhere between the extremes of realism and solipsism lies a region where "you are partly blown by the winds of reality and partly an artist creating a composite out of the inner and outer events" (p. 245). See also Laszlo (1973, p. 292) who argues that in systems theory, one can "conceive of no radical separation between forming and formed."

9. Note that despite these observations and general support for the promise of open systems models, Allport (1960) suggests he takes a "conservative" position relative to radically challenging the integumented personality (p. 306). He voices concerns about whether general systems theory applied to personality can avoid the influx "from below" of concepts from physical and biological sciences, and about the ambiguity of a research position in which any observers are necessarily a part of the system they observe (p. 307), a dilemma shared however by theories of personality in general. Note that his concern of possible reductionism seems to reflect a misunderstanding of the nature of systems concepts, which are intended to be isomorphic across domains but not reductive.

10. For an important clarification of Buddhist concepts of mutual causality and no-self, as illuminated and discussed through a reciprocal hermeneutic derived

from general systems theory, see Macy (1991, chap. 6). Both perspectives challenge the idea of the separate self, and re-embed selfing in the context of ultimate interrelatedness. For helpful descriptions of Buddhist understandings of no-self and the implications of giving up attachment to the self-preoccupied ego as definition of who we are, see Rao (1988); Rinzler and Gordon (1980). See also Kalupahana (1987, pp. 38–43) for a discussion of the "middle path" (p. 40) between absolute self-negation or "annihilation" (p. 38) of the phenomenal self on the one hand, and the positing of an "eternal substance" or "metaphysical self" on the other (p. 39). On the Buddhist understanding of emptiness and the principle of "dependent origination" in terms of the interdependence of all concepts and things, see Crook and Rabgyas (1988) and Cook (1977). See also Crook and Fontana (1990) and Katz (1983). See Paranjpe (1988) on personality theory according to Vedanta, with reference to the "transcognitive basis of selfhood" (p. 209).

11. See Wilber (1980a, 1980b) for an articulation of a transpersonal developmental model in which the human evolves through various stages of differentiation from primordial unity and identification with a body-ego, a mental-ego or language-embedded self, a socially constructed rule-following self, and gradually higher levels of integration. Each subsequent level of self-identification, including those which contribute to finally releasing one from the sense of individual ego or self, occurs via a process of disidentification with the lower level and transcendence to a higher level of identification.

12. Note Mary Catherine Bateson (1972, p. 288) suggests that "consciousness" gives us "incomplete access to the complexity that we are." Poetry facilitates the mapping of a "set of relationships . . . onto a level of diversity in us that we don't ordinarily have access to." Gregory Bateson contrasted the "primary-process thinking" of the unconscious and its analogical metaphors with the conscious level capable of digital processes and negation (M. C. Bateson, pp. 297–298), though not in such a way as to imply a dualism, for the "entire body can be said to think" (p. 297). See also Lipset (1980, pp. 258–259) on G. Bateson's views of the relationship between unconscious and conscious processes. Bateson often quoted Pascal's "Le coeur a ses raisons que la raison ne connaît point" ("The heart has reasons of which the reason knows nothing") (Lipset, p. 258; also M. C. Bateson, p. 297). Bateson defined wisdom as the "knowledge of the total interacting system" (Lipset, p. 259).

13. This subtle issue of the "participatory" yet distinctive or "particular" nature of the phenomenological self as understood in both Buddhism and general systems theory is articulated with great skill by Macy (1991, pp. 183–185). Though profoundly interconnected and "inseparable" (p. 183) from the larger matrix in which it is embedded, the process self nonetheless is not immersed in an "undifferentiated whole" (p. 184). To release one's attachment to the construct of separate self opens out the self to the universe in its "suchness," not "sameness" (p. 185).

14. For a discussion of symmetrical versus complementary relationship styles in the context of alcoholism, see G. Bateson (1972, pp. 323–337). Escalating sym-

metrical relationships in couples or nations are witnessed, for example, where increases of aggression or withdrawal provoke similar behavior in others, with partners mirroring each other's behavior. Symmetrical styles are contrasted with complementary styles, where partners tend toward opposites of behavior such as activity and receptivity, patterns which can also change in directions of excess (p. 324), however. Although he argued that human relationships might benefit from a complex mix of symmetrical and complementary styles (p. 337) which might mitigate against excesses (p. 324), Bateson also maintained that the relation between a person and the larger system of which one is a part must "necessarily" be complementary (p. 337). The dynamics of symmetrical and complementary patterns and ways of intervening to change these patterns receive considerable attention in the family systems and therapy resources mentioned in note 2 above (see particularly Watzlawick, Beavin, & Jackson, 1967, pp. 67–70, 107–117). Note also clarifications by Schultz (1984, pp. 62–64).

15. See Jung (1933, pp. 123, 225, 229, 237); see also Jung (1966, p. 70).

16. For other approaches to work with subpersonalities, see also the Voice Dialogue method of Stone and Winkelman (1989), discussed in chapter 4, note 8. On the Jungian goal of wholeness, not perfection, see Jung (1968b, pp. 68–69) and the discussion of Jung in chapter 4.

17. See also Briggs and Peat (1984) for a summary of Sheldrake's views.

18. On ethical models deriving from feminist theology, for example, see Christ (1987); Daly (1978); Ochs (1977); Ruether (1979).

19. See Kittay and Meyers (1987) for discussions of the relevance of Gilligan's work for rethinking moral theory. See Auerbach, Blum, Smith, and Williams (1985) for a feminist critique of Gilligan's neglect of social class and other variables that might contribute to ethical decision making styles.

20. See Macy (1991) for insights into systems theory and Buddhist understandings of ethics and action (karma) in the context of radical interrelatedness (chaps. 9 through 12); also Macy (1990). On constructive implications of postmodern sensitivity to interconnectedness, see Griffin (1990).

21. On the contrast of emphases on Doing and Being, see M. C. Shaw's (1988) articulation of the "paradox of intention" in world spiritual and psychological traditions, whereby one reaches one's goal not by striving (doing) but by a kind of surrender to being. See also Sullivan (1989) for a contrast of doing and being (p. 21) in terms of metaphors of "masculine" and "feminine" principles or modes applied to therapy.

22. On therapeutic strategies deriving from Eastern perspectives, see Epstein (1980); Claxton (1986). On related Asian perspectives on "personality" and psychology, see Paranjpe, Ho, and Rieber (1988).

23. See Pedersen (1977); Weisz, Rothbaum, and Blackburn (1984); Reynolds (1980, 1984a, 1984b, 1986, 1987, 1989a, 1989b, 1990).

24. On Morita therapy, see Reynolds (1976). On Naikan therapy, see Reynolds (1983). See also briefer summaries in Wallach and Wallach (1983); Pedersen (1977). Note also Reynolds' development of a therapeutic and educational approach to "constructive living" which draws from both Morita and Naikan and makes these more accessible to the West (1980, 1984a, 1984b, 1986, 1987, 1989a, 1989b, 1990).

25. On the dilemmas of helping without attachment, see Brandon (1976); Dass and Gorman (1985). See also the way the attempt of beginning therapists to "do" or "help" backfires until they learn to simply "be present" (Shainberg, 1980; and a variation thereon, reprinted 1983).

26. Note that Macy (1991) offers a note of hope in resolving this dilemma through her interpretation of Buddhist and systems understandings of interrelatedness as they relate also to the experience of "objectless knowing" (pp. 131–134). We have seen that both systems theory and Buddhism articulate the interconnectedness or co-arising of knower and known. Macy argues, following systems theorists, that there is no reason why higher and higher nonreducible (p. 131) levels of awareness cannot ultimately lead to the mentality of the system as a whole, experienced at this metalevel as "knowing the knowing of knowing," betokening a kind of immanental consciousness that "would be always present, without beginnings or ending" (p. 134).

27. On transpersonal models, see Keutzer (1983b); Tart (1975b); Vaughan (1986); Walsh and Vaughan (1980); on identifications and disidentifications in transpersonal understandings of human development, see Wilber (1980a, 1980b). See also June Singer (1990) on transpersonal perspectives as a new "gnosis" (pp. 149–150). Note also Jung's use of the term "transpersonal unconscious" (1966, p. 66). See Grof's (1988) concept of a "holotropic mode of consciousness," defined as "aiming toward wholeness and totality of existence" (pp. 38–39) and manifesting in a wide range of transpersonal experiences, which he organizes in a "transpersonal taxonomy" or "cartography" (pp. 40–44).

Chapter 7

1. On metaphor in religion and science, see Barbour (1974); Gerhart and Russell (1984); MacCormac (1976); Ferré (1968); on the analogical imagination, see Tracy (1981). Also see Barbour (1990, chap. 2) for a further discussion of related issues on models and paradigms in science and religion.

2. See Christ and Plaskow (1979); Daly (1973, 1978, 1984); Goldenberg (1979); Ochs (1977); Ruether (1972, 1979). See also O'Flaherty (1980); Olds (1981, 1986).

3. On multiple metaphors, see Tracy (1981); McFague (1982, 1987).

4. See Kluckhohn (1972) on the social function of myths to provide a "storehouse of adjustive responses" (p. 102) and to "restore" individuals to "rapport" with society (p. 104); on the function of myth to "strengthen tradition," see Malinowski

(1948, p. 146). See Geertz (1973) on religious myth and symbol in connection with religion's role in interpreting and rendering meaningful the problems of chaos, suffering, and evil. For a consideration of myths in a psychological role to aid in a "second birth," see Campbell (1972, p. 46).

5. On myth in its role of seeking resolutions of central polarities, see Lévi-Strauss (1963, 1969); on analogies of myth and musical patterns, see Lévi-Strauss (1978).

6. For example, see Davies and Brown (1988) in science and Q. Skinner (1985) in the social sciences.

7. See Eliade (1959, p. 117) on myth as revealing "transparency"; on the translucence to meaning and significance, see McGlashan (1967). On myth as the "picture-language of the soul," see Campbell (1969, p. 37). See Watts (1963) on the language of ambiguity and paradox in myth. On the language of feeling truth and myth as conveying "emotionally experienced" reality (Campbell, 1969, p. 32); see also Fromm (1951); Langer (1957).

8. Note Kakar's (1990) clarification that in India, traditional myths are "vibrantly alive" as a "cultural idiom" to aid in reconstructing and integrating one's life in the psychoanalytic process (p. 439).

9. On ways mythic appreciation helps deepen understandings of the Garden of Eden, see Campbell (1972, pp. 25–28); on the Promised Land, see Campbell (1986, pp. 32–34, 61); on central events and images in Christianity, see Edinger (1972).

10. See also Paranjpe (1988) for a version of this argument as derived from Vedanta (p. 202).

11. Also see Albanese's (1990) work on nature religion in the American context, where she explores spiritual metaphors relating to the encounter with nature and such twentieth-century phenomena as quantum physics and increasing environmental concerns (pp. 151–152; also chap. 5). See also transpersonal perspectives on ecology (Fox, 1990) based on Arne Naess's ecophilosophical articulation of the need for "identification" (p. 231) with the wider "expansive self" (p. 217) which opens up to include the world.

12. See in particular Griffin's optimism for what he is willing to call a "new alliance" between a postmodern theology and a postmodern science (Griffin & Smith, 1989, pp. 48–49, 135–142; Griffin, 1989, pp. 76–82). See also June Singer's (1990, chaps. 4 through 6) look at the relationship between the frontier of science and the gnostic spiritual tradition in approaching mystery and the "invisible world."

13. See also A. M. Taylor (1977) who reminds that a systems approach, "for those who wish to pursue the quest" (p. 27), ultimately leads to considerations of a monistic ontology, with the universe as an "organized meta-system" or "cosmos" (p. 26).

14. On systems theory as transcending traditional dualisms, see Seidler (1979); Macy (1976, 1991).

15. See also a discussion of Creatura and Pleroma in chap. 5, note 29.

16. See also Macy (1991, chap. 8) on the "co-arising" of body and mind with respect to Buddhism and general systems theory.

17. See also chapter 6 for a discussion of the radical inseparability of knower and known; also chap. 6, note 7.

18. Macy (1991, chaps. 1 through 5) is an excellent resource here in examining the central Buddhist teaching of dependent co-arising and general systems theory as mutual hermeneutics to "illuminate" (p. 20) the nature of mutual causality and the ways it contrasts with one-way causality in Western and Hindu thought (chap. 1).

19. See also Grene's (1987) articulation of the relevance in biological explanation of control hierarchies where "information flows between levels in both directions" (p. 505).

20. See also Macy (1991) for a rich discussion of a "Dharma of Natural Systems" (pp. xii, 1), as articulated through the resources of Buddhism and general systems theory, with respect to such issues as the "co-arising of doer and deed" (chap. 9); of "self and society" (chap. 10), and a grounding of social ethics in a reality "structured" in terms of interrelatedness (p. 193, chaps. 11 and 12). Note also Laszlo's (1973, pp. 282–290) emphasis on "reverence for natural systems." See also, though with a different emphasis, Kohak's (1984) inquiry on a "moral sense of nature" with its sensitivity to natural imagery and its concern for a "moral order" encountered in nature (p. 72).

21. See also Boulding (1985, pp. 29–30) on "transcendental systems."

22. See also chapter 6 on G. Bateson's and Laszlo's emphasis on monism; note also chap. 6, note 8.

23. Note also Wilber's expression of "transcendence into the world" (1980b, p. 269) and his differentiation of a hierarchy of mysticism, following Zaehner's terminology, from panenhenic or "nature cosmic consciousness" (Wilber, 1984a, p. 29) to theistic to monistic forms of mystical experience (pp. 32–33).

24. On gendered issues in vertical ontology, see Ruether (1983); Olds (1989, 1990). On concerns for embodied spirituality, see Christ (1987); for an ethics of relationship and care, see Gilligan (1982).

25. See Olds (1990) for an overview of ontological affinities to metaphors of interrelatedness as found in feminist theology, Teilhard de Chardin, Sri Aurobindo, process philosophy, Chinese perspectives, and systems theory.

26. See also Griffin and Smith (1989).

27. See Whitehead (1925) on the "fallacy of misplaced concreteness," also discussed in chapter 2 with reference to issues in theory-building.

28. Note that process theology tends to affirm a single forward-moving sense of time, which Odin (1982), for example, sees as critical for the emergence of

creativity, and thus is likely to underestimate the possibilities for creativity in radical immanental systems. Griffin does stress the importance of multidirectional causality (p. 49) in a clearer way, yet retains a unidirectional sense of time (Griffin & Smith, 1989).

29. Note also Laszlo's (1973) concern for Whitehead's postulation of a "one-way causal connection" between a "Platonic realm of God and eternal objects" and actuality, whereby "eternal objects can ingress in actuality and thus qualify its course, but actuality does not affect them" (p. 245). Laszlo does note the "consequent nature of God" as an exception to this, and thus closer to the interconnectedness inherent in systems thinking.

30. See Barbour (1974, pp. 71–91; also 1990, pp. 48–49). Note also Loy (1988, pp. 288–291) on issues regarding a personal and impersonal Absolute and the concern for "overcoming the duality between God and the universe," a parallel to "overcoming mind-body dualism" (p. 288). He summarizes Spinoza's argument that to understand God as "not other than the universe . . . does not diminish God but rather elevates the universe" (p. 289).

31. See Hayward (1987) on open systems theories (chap. 18, also pp. 183–185) as a "conceptual framework" which, though in itself not ultimate, offers an alternative to "thing-thinking" (p. 237) and mind/body dualism, and thus constitutes "a way of thinking that is more in keeping" with certain Buddhist principles (p. 237). See also Macy (1976; 1991, chaps. 6, 7).

32. Note also that Macy (1991) underscores this type of interpretation in reference to the Pali Canon of "early Buddhist teachings" (p. 2). Note that it is precisely these types of insights into radical interrelatedness, also implied in systems theory, that most confound Phillips' (1976) understanding of holism and guides his critique (pp. 11, 54–55), leading him to dismiss holism as implying the impossibility of any knowing of part except in relationship ultimately to everything else, a premise he cannot maintain.

33. See Ross (1980, p. 54) for a description of this living web and the fabric metaphor from Lama Govinda (p. 118). On Indra's net, see especially Cook (1977); also Chang (1971); Capra (1975, p. 296). Note also the use of the image of "nature's jeweled net" as a model of "ecological Buddhism" for informing a new paradigm for the West (Ingram, 1990). See also Campbell's (1986, chap. 7, pp. 111–113) interpretation of the "net of gems."

34. See Leder (1990) on the transpersonal dimension of the "lived body" (p. 172) as a "jewel in Indra's net" (p. 173), and neo-Confucian insights (pp. 156–173) of living by the "ideal of forming one body *with all things*" (p. 167).

35. On translations and understandings of li and ch'i, see Needham (1956); Thompson (1988). Note Boulding's (1985, p. 16) term "mattergy" to convey a similar kind of relationship between energy and matter as ch'i, though in a different context.

36. See Gerhart and Russell (1984, p. 120), also discussed in chapter 2, note 12. See also Harding's (1986) emphasis on the role of "seeing" in arriving at an

understanding of a nondual universe via the vision of an interconnected reality in which there is no evidence for a separate "I." See also Crook's (1990) typology for representing states of experience in which the disciplined cultivation of outer-oriented attention and awareness is associated with dissolving boundaries "between self and situation" (p. 108).

37. See also Macy's (1991) reflections on these issues (pp. 131–134), also discussed in chapter 6, note 26.

38. This distinction of entry point, though ultimately a false dichotomy, may speak to some of the characteristics of typical Western versus Eastern starting places. Note also the relevance here of Harding's (1979) hierarchical cosmology which bears many similarities to systems perspectives on embedded wholes. Harding, too, conveys a striking sense of the complexity and interconnectedness of a nondual reality, witnessed via and through a number of levels or viewpoints, rather than through an effort to transcend.

39. On these insights from Buddhism, see H. Smith (1958); Watts (1957, 1961). See also Macy (1991, chap. 6). Macy suggests that in Buddhism, the process self is nonpermanent, nonseparate, and profoundly interconnected, yet characterized by distinctive experience (p. 184), in contrast to an immersion of the self in an "undifferentiated whole," more characteristic of Hinduism (pp. 184–185). In Buddhist views of the self, diversity and unity both receive emphasis (p. 185).

40. For a discussion of this reversal in interpreting the dewdrop image, see H. Smith (pp. 66–67) in Griffin and Smith (1989).

41. See Jung (1969b, pp. 58–59) on the "archetypal God-image."

42. On the relationship between the self-archetype and the God-archetype, see Jung (1968b, pp. 40, 63, 109; also 1969b, pp. 156–157, 160). Also see Jung (1968b) on the self-archetype and religious symbols of the self. On psychoid reality, see the discussion on Jungian theory in chapter 4 and a good overview in Jaffé (1971).

BIBLIOGRAPHY

Abraham, F. D. (1989). Toward a dynamical theory of the psyche. *Psychological Perspectives, 20*(1), 156–167.

Adams, J. L. (1979). *Conceptual blockbusting.* New York: Norton.

Adler, A. (1937). *What life should mean to you.* Boston: Little, Brown.

Adler, A. (1956). *The individual psychology of Alfred Adler* (H. L. Ansbacher & R. R. Ansbacher, Eds.). New York: Basic Books.

Ajaya, S. (1983). *Psychotherapy east and west: A unifying paradigm*. Honesdale, PA: The Himalayan International Institute of Yoga Science and Philosophy of the U.S.A.

Albanese, C. L. (1990). *Nature religion in America: From the Algonkian Indians to the new age.* Chicago: University of Chicago Press.

Allen, T. F. H., & Starr, T. B. (1982). *Hierarchy: Perspectives for ecological complexity.* Chicago: University of Chicago Press.

Allport, G. W. (1955). *Becoming: Basic considerations for a psychology of personality.* New Haven: Yale University Press.

Allport, G. W. (1960). The open system in personality theory. *Journal of Abnormal and Social Psychology, 61,* 301–310.

Allport, G. W. (Ed.). (1965). *Letters from Jenny.* New York: Harcourt, Brace & World.

Anton, J. (1983, March). Culture and creative transformation of myth—(1) From myth to tragedy: The classical tradition; (2) Alienation of the demythologizing of culture: The contemporary predicament. Two lectures delivered as part of the Thirteenth Annual Linfield College Philosophy Lectures, McMinnville, OR.

Arguelles, J. (1984). *Earth ascending: An illustrated treatise on the law governing whole systems.* Boulder, CO: Shambhala.

Arnheim, R. (1969). *Visual thinking.* Berkeley: University of California Press.

Asimov, I. (1966). *Understanding physics* (Vols. 1–3). New York: New American Library.

Assagioli, R. (1965). *Psychosynthesis: A manual of principles and techniques.* New York: Hobbs, Dorman.

Assagioli, R. (1973). *The act of will.* New York: Penguin.

Auerbach, J., Blum, L., Smith, V., & Williams, C. (1985). Commentary on Gilligan's *In a different voice*. *Feminist Studies, 11*(1), 149–161.

Augros, R., & Stanciu, G. (1987). *The new biology: Discovering the wisdom in nature.* Boston: Shambhala/New Science.

Aurobindo, *Sri*. (1956). *The future evolution of man.* Pondicherry, India: Sri Aurobindo Ashram/All India Press.

Averill, J. R. (1990). Inner feelings, works on the flesh, the beast within, diseases of the mind, driving force, and putting on the show: six metaphors of emotion and their theoretical extensions. In D. E. Leary (Ed.), *Metaphors in the history of psychology* (pp. 104–132). Cambridge: Cambridge University Press.

Bailey, K. D. (1990). *Social entropy theory.* Albany: State University of New York Press.

Bakan, D. (1972, March). Stimulus/Response: Psychology can now kick the science habit. *Psychology Today*, pp. 26, 28, 86–88.

Bakan, D. (1973). *On Method*. San Francisco: Jossey-Bass.

Bandler, R., & Grinder, J. (1975). *The structure of magic I: A book about language and therapy*. Palo Alto, CA: Science and Behavior Books.

Barbour, I. G. (1974). *Myths, models, and paradigms*. New York: Harper & Row.

Barbour, I. G. (1990). *Religion in an age of science* (Vol. 1). San Francisco: Harper & Row.

Barker, P. (1985). *Using metaphors in psychotherapy*. New York: Brunner/Mazel.

Barnett, L. (1957). *The universe and Dr. Einstein.* New York: William Morrow.

Barrow, J. D. (1988). *The world within the world.* Oxford: Clarendon Press.

Bateson, G. (1972). *Steps to an ecology of mind.* New York: Ballantine Books.

Bateson, G. (1977). Afterword. In J. Brockman (Ed.), *About Bateson* (pp. 235–247). New York: E. P. Dutton.

Bateson, G. (1979). *Mind and nature: A necessary unity.* New York: Bantam Books.

Bateson, G., & Bateson, M. C. (1987). *Angels fear: Towards an epistemology of the sacred*. New York: Macmillan.

Bateson, G., Jackson, D. D., Haley, J., & Weakland, J. (1956). Toward a theory of schizophrenia. *Behavioral Science, 1*, 251–264.

Bateson, M. C. (1972). *Our own metaphor.* New York: Knopf.

Bateson, M. C. (1977). Daddy, can a scientist be wise? In J. Brockman (Ed.), *About Bateson* (pp. 57–74). New York: E. P. Dutton.

Becvar, D. S., & Becvar, R. J. (1988). *Family therapy: A systemic integration.* Boston: Allyn and Bacon.

Belenky, M. F., Clinchy, B., Goldberger, N. R., & Tarule, J. M. (1986). *Women's ways of knowing: The development of self, voice, and mind.* New York: Basic Books.

Berger, P. L. (Ed.). (1981). *The other side of god: A polarity in world religions.* Garden City, NY: Anchor Press/Doubleday.

Berman, M. (1984). *The reenchantment of the world.* New York: Bantam Books.

Berman, M. (1989). *Coming to our senses: Body and spirit in the hidden history of the West.* New York: Simon and Schuster.

Bertalanffy, L. von. (1955). General system theory. *Main Currents in Modern Thought, 11,* 75–83.

Bertalanffy, L. von. (1962). General system theory—A critical review. *General Systems* (Yearbook of the Society for General Systems Research), *7,* 1–20.

Bertalanffy, L. von. (1968). *General system theory.* New York: George Braziller.

Bertalanffy, L. von. (1970). General system theory and psychology. In J. R. Royce (Ed.), *Toward unification in psychology* (pp. 219–223). Toronto: University of Toronto Press.

Bertalanffy, L. von. (1975). *Perspectives on general system theory* (E. Taschdjian, Ed.). New York: George Braziller.

Billow, R. M., Rossman, J., Lewis, N., Goldman, D., Kraemer, S., & Ross, P. (1987). Metaphoric communication and miscommunication in schizophrenic and borderline states. In R. E. Haskell (Ed.), *Cognition and symbolic structures: The psychology of metaphoric transformation* (pp. 141–162). Norwood, NJ: Ablex.

Black, M. (1962). *Models and metaphors.* Ithaca, NY: Cornell University Press.

Blackburn, T. R. (1971). Sensuous-intellectual complementarity in science. *Science, 172,* 1003–1007.

Block, N. (Ed.). (1981). *Imagery.* Cambridge: MIT Press.

Bloomfield, H. H. (1976). Applications of the transcendental meditation program to psychiatry. In V. Binder, A. Binder, & B. Rimland (Eds.), *Modern therapies* (pp. 95–117). Englewood Cliffs, NJ: Prentice Hall/Spectrum.

Bogen, J. E. (1973). The other side of the brain: An appositional mind. In R. E. Ornstein (Ed.), *The nature of human consciousness: A book of readings* (pp. 101–125). San Francisco: Freeman.

Bohm, D. (1980). *Wholeness and the implicate order.* London: Routledge & Kegan Paul/Ark Paperbacks.

Bohm, D. (1985). *Unfolding meaning.* London: Routledge & Kegan Paul/Ark Paperbacks.

Bohm, D., & Peat, F. D. (1987). *Science, order, and creativity.* New York: Bantam Books.

Boulding, K. E. (1968). General systems theory—The skeleton of science. In W. Buckley (Ed.), *Modern systems research for the behavioral scientist* (pp. 3–10). Chicago: Aldine.

Boulding, K. E. (1985). *The world as a total system.* Beverly Hills, CA: Sage.

Brandon, D. (1976). *Zen in the art of helping.* New York: Dell/Delta/Seymour Laurence Edition.

Briggs, J. P., & Peat, F. D. (1984). *Looking glass universe: The emerging science of wholeness.* New York: Simon & Schuster/Cornerstone.

Brockman, J. (Ed.). (1977). *About Bateson.* New York: E. P. Dutton.

Bronowski, J. (1965). *Science and human values.* New York: Harper & Row.

Bronowski, J. (1978). *The visionary eye: Essays in the arts, literature, and science* (P. E. Ariotti, Ed., in collaboration with R. Bronowski). Cambridge: MIT Press.

Brown, C. M. (1974). *God as mother: A feminine theology in India.* Hartford, VT: Claude Stark.

Brown, D. P., & Engler, J. (1980). The stages of mindfulness meditation: A validation study. *The Journal of Transpersonal Psychology, 12,* 143–192.

Browning, D. S. (1973). *Generative man: Psychoanalytic perspectives.* New York: Dell/Delta.

Browning, D. S. (1987). *Religious thought and the modern psychologies.* Philadelphia: Fortress Press.

Bruner, J. S. (1966). *On knowing: Essays for the left hand.* New York: Atheneum.

Bruner, J. (1986). *Actual minds, possible worlds.* Cambridge: Harvard University Press.

Bruner, J. (1990). *Acts of meaning.* Cambridge: Harvard University Press.

Bruner, J., & Feldman, C. F. (1990). Metaphors of consciousness and cognition in the history of psychology. In D. E. Leary (Ed.), *Metaphors in the history of psychology* (pp. 230–238). Cambridge: Cambridge University Press.

Bruner, J. S., Jolly, A., & Sylva, K. (Eds.). (1976). *Play—Its role in development and evolution.* New York: Basic Books.

Bruner, J. S., & Postman, L. (1949). On the perception of incongruity: A paradigm. *Journal of Personality, 18,* 206–223.

Buckley, W. (1967). *Sociology and modern systems theory.* Englewood Cliffs, NJ: Prentice-Hall.

Buckley, W. (Ed.). (1968). *Modern systems research for the behavioral scientist: A sourcebook.* Chicago: Aldine.

Bugelski, B.R. (1977). Imagery and verbal behavior. *Journal of Mental Imagery, 1*(1), 39–52.

Bynum, C. W. (1986). Introduction: The complexity of symbols. In C. W. Bynum, S. Harrell, & P. Richman (Eds.), *Gender and religion: On the complexity of symbols* (pp. 1–20). Boston: Beacon Press.

Campbell, J. (1969). *The flight of the wild gander: Explorations in the mythological dimension.* Chicago: Henry Regnery/Gateway.

Campbell, J. (1972). *Myths to live by.* New York: Bantam Books.

Campbell, J. (1986). *The inner reaches of outer space: Metaphor as myth and as religion.* New York: Alfred van der Marck.

Capra, F. (1975). *The tao of physics.* Berkeley: Shambhala.

Capra, F. (1982). *The turning point: Science, society, and the rising culture.* New York: Simon and Schuster.

Capra, F. (1988). *Uncommon wisdom.* New York: Simon and Schuster.

Carlson, R. (1972). Understanding Women: Implications for Personality Theory and Research, *Journal of Social Issues, 28,* 17–32.

Cartwright, R. D. (1978). *A primer on sleep and dreaming.* Reading, MA: Addison-Wesley.

Cassirer, E. (1946). *Language and myth.* New York: Dover.

Chan, W-T. (Trans. and Ed.). (1963). *A source book in Chinese philosophy.* Princeton: Princeton University Press.

Chang, G. C. C. (1971). *The Buddhist teaching of totality.* University Park, PA: Pennsylvania State University Press.

Chaplin, J. P., & Krawiec, T. S. (1968). *Systems and Theories of Psychology.* New York: Holt, Rinehart and Winston.

Chodorow, N. (1978). *The reproduction of mothering: Psychoanalysis and the sociology of gender.* Berkeley and Los Angeles: University of California Press.

Chopra, D. (1989). *Quantum healing: Exploring the frontiers of mind/body medicine.* New York: Bantam Books.

Chow, S. L. (1987). Some reflections on Harris and Rosenthal's 31 meta-analyses. *The Journal of Psychology, 121,* 95–100.

Christ, C. P. (1987). *Laughter of Aphrodite.* San Francisco: Harper & Row.

Christ, C.P., & Plaskow, J. (Eds.). (1979). *Womanspirit rising: A feminist reader in religion.* San Francisco: Harper & Row.

Claxton, G. (Ed.). (1986). *Beyond therapy: The impact of Eastern religions on psychological theory and practice.* London: Wisdom Publications.

Cook, F. (1977). *Hua-yen Buddhism: The jewel net of Indra.* University Park, PA: Pennsylvania State University Press.

Cook, T. A. (1979). *The curves of life.* New York: Dover.

Cooper, L. A., & Shepard, R. N. (1973). Chronometric studies of the rotation of mental images. In W. G. Chase (Ed.), *Visual information processing* (pp. 75–176). New York: Academic Press.

Corballis, M. C. (1980). Laterality and myth. *American Psychologist, 35,* 284–295.

Cotton, J. L. (1981). A review of research on Schachter's theory of emotion and the misattribution of arousal. *European Journal of Social Psychology, 11,* 365–397.

Crook, J. H. (1990). Mind in western Zen. In J. Crook & D. Fontana (Eds.), *Space in mind* (pp. 92–109). Longmead, Shaftesbury, Dorset, Great Britain: Element Books.

Crook, J., & Fontana, D. (Eds.). (1990). *Space in mind: East-West psychology and contemporary Buddhism.* Longmead, Shaftesbury, Dorset, Great Britain: Element Books.

Crook, J., & Rabgyas, T. (1988). The essential insight: A central theme in the philosophical training of Mahayanist monks. In A. C. Paranjpe, D. Y. F. Ho, & R. W. Rieber (Eds.), *Asian contributions to psychology* (pp. 149–183). New York: Praeger.

Cushman, P. (1990). Why the self is empty: Toward a historically situated psychology. *American Psychologist, 45,* 599–611.

Daly, M. (1973). *Beyond god the father: Toward a philosophy of women's liberation.* Boston: Beacon Press.

Daly, M. (1978). *Gyn/ecology: The metaethics of radical feminism.* Boston: Beacon Press.

Daly, M. (1984). *Pure lust: Elemental feminist philosophy.* Boston: Beacon Press.

Danziger, K. (1990a). *Constructing the subject: Historical origins of psychological research.* Cambridge: Cambridge University Press.

Danziger, K. (1990b). Generative metaphor and the history of psychological discourse. In D. E. Leary (Ed.), *Metaphors in the history of psychology* (pp. 331–356). Cambridge: Cambridge University Press.

Dass, R. (1974). *The only dance there is.* Garden City, NY: Anchor Press/Doubleday.

Dass, R., & Gorman, P. (1985). *How can I help?* New York: Knopf.

Dass, R., with Levine, S. (1977). *Grist for the mill.* Santa Cruz, CA: Unity Press.

Davidson, M. (1983). *Uncommon sense: The life and thought of Ludwig von Bertalanffy (1901–1972), father of general systems theory.* Los Angeles: J. P. Tarcher.

Davies, P. (1984). *Superforce.* New York: Simon & Schuster/Touchstone.

Davies, P. C. W., & Brown, J. (Eds.). (1988). *Superstrings: A theory of everything?* Cambridge: Cambridge University Press.

Day, R. S. (1980). Teaching from notes: Some cognitive consequences. In W. J. McKeachie (Ed.), *New directions for teaching and learning: Learning, cognition, and college teaching* (pp. 95–112). San Francisco: Jossey-Bass.

Deikman, A. J. (1973). Bimodal consciousness. In R. E. Ornstein (Ed.), *The nature of human consciousness: A book of readings* (pp. 67–86). San Francisco: Freeman.

Deikman, A. J. (1982). *The observing self.* Boston: Beacon Press.

Delaney, H. D. (1978). Interaction of individual differences with visual and verbal elaboration instructions. *Journal of Educational Psychology, 70,* 306–318.

Dement, W. C. (1976). *Some must watch while some must sleep.* New York: Norton.

Dennett, D. C. (1982, December). The imagination extenders. *Psychology Today, 16,* pp. 32–39.

Dent, C., & Rosenberg, L. (1990). Visual and verbal metaphors: Developmental interactions. *Child Development, 61,* 983–994.

Devall, B., & Sessions, G. (1985). *Deep ecology.* Salt Lake City, UT: Gibbs M. Smith/Peregrine Smith Books.

Diamond, I., & Orenstein, G. F. (Eds.). (1990). *Reweaving the world: The emergence of ecofeminism.* San Francisco: Sierra Club Books.

Dilts, R., Grinder, J., Bandler, R., Bandler, L. C., & DeLozier, J. (1980). *Neuro-linguistic programming, Vol. 1: The study of the structure of subjective experience.* Cupertino, CA: Meta Publications.

Dinnerstein, D. (1976). *The mermaid and the minotaur: Sexual arrangements and human malaise.* New York: Harper & Row.

Doczi, G. (1981). *The power of limits: Proportional harmonies in nature, art and architecture.* Boulder, CO: Shambhala.

Doi, T. (1990). The cultural assumptions of psychoanalysis. In J. W. Stigler, R. A. Shweder, & G. Herdt (Eds.), *Cultural psychology* (pp. 446–453). Cambridge: Cambridge University Press.

Domhoff, G. W. (1973). But why did they sit on the king's right in the first place? In R. E. Ornstein (Ed.), *The nature of human consciousness: A book of readings* (pp. 143–147). San Francisco: Freeman.

Dunlap, R. E. (1980). Paradigmatic change in social science. *American Behavioral Scientist, 24*(1), 5–14.

Eacker, J. N. (1972). On some elementary philosophical problems of psychology. *American Psychologist, 27*, 553–565.

Edinger, E. F. (1972). *Ego and archetype: Individuation and the religious function of the psyche.* Baltimore, MD: Penguin.

Eiseley, L. (1957). *The immense journey.* New York: Vintage Books/Randon House.

Eiseley, L. (1969). *The unexpected universe.* New York: Harcourt Brace Jovanovich/Harvest.

Eiseley, L. (1971). *The night country*. New York: Charles Scribner's Sons.

Eisler, R. (1987). *The chalice and the blade.* San Francisco: Harper & Row.

Eldredge, N., & Gould, S. J. (1972). Punctuated equilibria: An alternative to phyletic gradualism. In T. J. M. Schopf (Ed.), *Models in paleobiology* (pp. 82–115). San Francisco: Freeman, Cooper.

Eliade, M. (1958). *Patterns in comparative religion.* New York: New American Library.

Eliade, M. (1959). *The sacred and the profane: The nature of religion.* New York: Harcourt, Brace & World.

Eliade, M. (1963). *Myth and reality.* New York: Harper & Row.

Epstein, G. (Ed.), with Fosshage, J. L., Frank, K. A., Grayson, H., Loew, C. A., & Lowenheim, H. (1980). *Studies in non-deterministic psychology.* New York: Human Sciences Press.

Erikson, E. H. (1963). *Childhood and society* (2d rev. ed.). New York: Norton.

Farrell, E. (1986). Metaphor and psychology: A reply to Gholson and Barker. *American Psychologist, 41*, 719–720.

Feinstein, D., & Krippner, S. (1988). *Personal mythology: The psychology of your evolving self.* Los Angeles: J. P. Tarcher.

Feldenkrais, M. (1972). *Awareness through movement.* New York: Harper & Row.

Ferguson, E. S. (1977). The mind's eye: Nonverbal thought in technology. *Science, 197*, 827–836.

Ferguson, M. (1978, May). Karl Pribram's changing reality. *Human Behavior*, pp. 28–33.

Ferré, F. (1968). Mapping the logic of models in science and theology. In J. H. Gill (Ed.), *Philosophy and religion: Some contemporary perspectives* (pp. 265–294). Minneapolis: Burgess.

Feyerabend, P. (1978). *Against method.* London: Verso.

Feyerabend, P. (1987). *Farewell to reason.* London: Verso.

Forisha, B. L. (1983). Relationship between creativity and mental imagery: A question of cognitive styles? In A. A. Sheikh (Ed.), *Imagery: Current theory, research, and application* (pp. 310–339). New York: Wiley.

Foster, J. (1987). An appeal for objectivism in psychological metatheory. In H. J. Stam, T. B. Rogers, & K. J. Gergen (Eds.), *The analysis of psychological theory: Metapsychological perspectives* (pp. 93–111). Washington, DC: Hemisphere.

Fox, M. (1985). *Illuminations of Hildegard of Bingen* (Commentaries by Fox; text by Hildegard of Bingen). Santa Fe, NM: Bear & Company.

Fox, W. (1990). *Toward a transpersonal ecology: Developing new foundations for environmentalism.* Boston: Shambhala.

Frank, L. K. (1970). Organized complexities. In J. R. Royce (Ed.), *Toward unification in psychology* (pp. 225–233). Toronto: University of Toronto Press.

Franz, C. W., & White, K. M. (1985). Individuation and attachment in personality development: Extending Erikson's theory. *Journal of Personality, 53,* 224–256.

Freud, S. (1965). *New introductory lectures on psychanalysis* (J. Strachey, Trans. and Ed.). New York: Norton.

Fromm, E. (1951). *The forgotten language: An introduction to the understanding of dreams, fairy tales and myths.* New York: Grove Press.

Fuller, R. B. (1969). *Operating manual for spaceship earth.* Carbondale and Edwardsville, IL: Southern Illinois University Press.

Fuller, R. B. (1972). *Buckminster Fuller to children of earth.* (C. Smith, Comp.). Garden City, NY: Doubleday.

Fuller, R. B. (1979). Ever rethinking the Lord's prayer. Unpublished paper, September 17.

Gamow, G. (1961). *One two three . . . infinity.* New York: Bantam Books.

Gamow, G. (1965). *Mr. Tompkins in paperback.* London: Cambridge University Press.

Gardiner, J. K. (1987). Kohut's self psychology as feminist theory. In P. Young-Eisendrath & J. A. Hall (Eds.), *The book of the self: Person, pretext, and process* (pp. 225–248). New York: New York University Press.

Gardner, H., & Winner, E. (1978). The development of metaphoric competence: Implications for humanistic disciplines. *Critical Inquiry, 5*, 123–141.

Gardner, H., with Winner, E. (1982). The child is father to the metaphor. In H. Gardner, *Art, mind, and brain: A cognitive approach to creativity* (pp. 158–167). New York: Basic Books.

Gawain, S. (1978). *Creative visualization.* New York: Bantam Books.

Gazzaniga, M. S. (1983a). Right hemisphere language following brain bisection: A 20-year perspective. *American Psychologist, 38*, 525–537.

Gazzaniga, M. S. (1983b). Reply to Levy and to Zaidel. *American Psychologist, 38*, 547–549.

Gebser, J. (1985). *The ever-present origin.* Athens, OH: Ohio University Press.

Geertz, C. (1973). Religion as a cultural system. In C. Geertz, *The interpretation of cultures: Selected essays* (Ch. 4, pp. 87–125). New York: Basic Books.

Gelso, C. J. (1991). Galileo, Aristotle, and science in counseling psychology: To theorize or not to theorize. *Journal of Counseling Psychology, 38*, 211–213.

Gentner, D. (1988). Metaphor as structure mapping: The relational shift. *Child Development, 59*, 47–59.

Gentner, D., & Grudin, J. (1985). The evolution of mental metaphors in psychology: A 90-year retrospective. *American Psychologist, 40*, 181–192.

Gergen, K. J. (1971). *The concept of self.* New York: Holt, Rinehart and Winston.

Gergen, K. J. (1973). Social psychology as history. *Journal of Personality and Social Psychology, 26*, 309–320.

Gergen, K. J. (1978). Toward generative theory. *Journal of Personality and Social Psychology, 36*, 1344–1360.

Gergen, K. J. (1980). Exchange theory: The transient and the enduring. In K. J. Gergen, M. S. Greenberg, & R. H. Willis (Eds.), *Social exchange: Advances in theory and research* (pp. 261–280). New York: Plenum Press.

Gergen, K. J. (1981). The functions and foibles of negotiating self-conception. In M. D. Lynch, A. A. Norem-Hebeisen, & K. J. Gergen (Eds.), *Self-concept: Advances in theory and research* (pp. 59–73). Cambridge, MA: Ballinger.

Gergen, K. J. (1982). *Toward transformation in social knowledge.* New York: Springer-Verlag.

Gergen, K. J. (1985). The social constructionist movement in modern psychology. *American Psychologist, 40*, 266–275.

Gergen, K. J. (1987a). Introduction: Toward metapsychology. In H. J. Stam, T. B. Rogers, & K. J. Gergen (Eds.), *The analysis of psychological theory: Metapsychological perspectives* (pp. 1–21). Washington, DC: Hemisphere.

Gergen, K. J. (1987b). The language of psychological understanding. In H. J. Stam, T. B. Rogers, & K. J. Gergen (Eds.), *The analysis of psychological theory: Metapsychological perspectives* (pp. 1115–129). Washington, DC: Hemisphere.

Gergen, K. J. (1988). If persons are texts. In S. B. Messer, L. A. Sass, & R. L. Woolfolk (Eds.), *Hermeneutics and psychological theory: Interpretive perspectives on personality, psychotherapy, and psychopathology* (pp. 28–51). New Brunswick, NJ: Rutgers University Press.

Gergen, K. J. (1990a). Metaphor, metatheory, and the social world. In D. E. Leary (Ed.), *Metaphors in the history of psychology* (pp. 267–299). Cambridge: Cambridge University Press.

Gergen, K. J. (1990b). Social understanding and the inscription of self. In J. W. Stigler, R. A. Shweder, & G. Herdt (Eds.), *Cultural psychology: Essays on comparative human development* (pp. 569–606). Cambridge: Cambridge University Press.

Gergen, K. J. (1991). *The saturated self.* New York: Basic Books.

Gergen, K. J., & Davis, K. E. (Eds.). (1985). *The social construction of the person.* New York: Springer-Verlag.

Gergen, K. J., & Gergen, M. M. (Eds.). (1984). *Historical social psychology*. Hillsdale, NJ: Lawrence Erlbaum.

Gergen, K. J., & Gergen, M. M. (1986). Narrative form and the construction of psychological science. In T. R. Sarbin (Ed.), *Narrative psychology* (pp. 22–44). New York: Praeger.

Gergen, M. M. (1987). Toward a diachronic social psychology: Pointing with more than one finger. In H. J. Stam, T. B. Rogers, & K. J. Gergen (Eds.), *The analysis of psychological theory: Metapsychological perspectives* (pp. 267–279). Washington, DC: Hemisphere.

Gerhart, M., & Russell, A. M. (1984). *Metaphoric Process: The creation of scientific and religious understanding*. Fort Worth: Texas Christian University Press.

Gholson, B., & Barker, P. (1985). Kuhn, Lakatos, and Laudan: Applications in the history of physics and psychology. *American Psychologist*, *40*, 755–769.

Gholson, B., & Barker, P. (1986). On metaphor in psychology and physics: A reply to Farrell. *American Psychologist*, *41*, 720–721.

Giambra, L. M. (1974). Daydreaming across the lifespan: Late adolescent to senior citizen. *International Journal of Aging and Human Development*, *5*(2), 115–140.

Gilkey, L. (1969). *Naming the whirlwind: The renewal of God-language.* Indianapolis, IN: Bobbs-Merrill.

Gill, J. H. (1982). Winch, science and embodiment. *Soundings, 65*, 417–429.

Gilligan, C. (1982). *In a different voice.* Cambridge: Harvard University Press.

Giorgi, A. (1970). *Psychology as a human science: A phenomenologically based approach.* New York: Harper & Row.

Girardot, N. J. (1983). *Myth and meaning in early Taoism: The theme of chaos (hun-tun).* Berkeley: University of California Press.

Gleick, J. (1987). *Chaos: Making a new science.* New York: Penguin.

Gluck, S. B., & Patai, D. (Eds.). (1991). *Women's words: The feminist practice of oral history.* New York: Routledge.

Glucksberg, S., & Keysar, B. (1990). Understanding metaphorical comparisons: Beyond similarity. *Psychological Review, 97,* 3–18.

Goldenberg, N. R. (1979). *Changing of the gods: Feminism and the end of traditional religions.* Boston: Beacon Press.

Goldstein, K. (1939). *The organism.* New York: American Book Company.

Goldstein, K. (1963). *Human nature in the light of psychopathology.* New York: Schocken Books.

Goleman, D. (1974). Perspectives on psychology, reality, and the study of consciousness. *The Journal of Transpersonal Psychology, 6,* 73–91.

Goleman, D. (1979, February). Holographic memory: Karl Pribram interviewed. *Psychology Today,* pp. 70–72, 74, 76, 79–80, 83–84.

Gordon, D. (1978). *Therapeutic metaphors: Helping others through the looking glass.* Cupertino, CA: Meta Publications.

Gould, S. J. (1977). *Ever since Darwin: Reflections in natural history.* New York: Norton.

Gould, S. J. (1980). *The panda's thumb: More reflections in natural history.* New York: Norton.

Greeley, A. M. (1972). *Unsecular man: The persistence of religion.* New York: Dell/Delta.

Green, E. E., & Green, A. M. (1971). On the meaning of transpersonal: Some metaphysical perspectives. *The Journal of Transpersonal Psychology, 3,* 27–46.

Green, T. F. (1979). Learning without metaphor. In A. Ortony (Ed.), *Metaphor and thought,* pp. 462–473. Cambridge: Cambridge University Press.

Gregory, B. (1990). *Inventing reality: Physics as language.* New York: Wiley/Wiley Science.

Gregory, R. L. (1981). *Mind in science: A history of explanations in psychology and physics.* Cambridge: Cambridge University Press.

Gregson, R. A. M. (1983). Some criticisms of *Mind and Nature.* In W. Maxwell (Ed.), *Thinking: The expanding frontier* (pp. 275–279). Philadelphia: Franklin Institute Press.

Grene, M. (1987). Hierarchies in biology. *American Scientist, 75,* 504–510.

Griffin, D. R. (Ed.). (1988). *The reenchantment of science: Postmodern proposals.* Albany: State University of New York Press.

Griffin, D. R. (1989). *God and religion in the postmodern world.* Albany: State University of New York Press.

Griffin, D. R. (Ed.). (1990). *Sacred interconnections.* Albany: State University of New York Press.

Griffin, D. R., & Smith, H. (1989). *Primordial truth and postmodern theology.* Albany: State University of New York Press.

Grinker, R. R. (Ed.). (1967). *Toward a unified theory of human behavior: An introduction to general systems theory* (2d ed.). New York: Basic Books.

Grof, S. (1988). *The adventure of self-discovery.* Albany: State University of New York Press.

Grover, S. C. (1981). *Toward a psychology of the scientist.* Washington, DC: University Press of America.

Gurdjieff, G. I. (1975). *Views from the real world.* New York: E. P. Dutton.

Haber, R. N. (1979). Twenty years of haunting eidetic imagery: Where's the ghost? *The Behavioral and Brain Sciences, 2,* 583–629.

Haley, J. (Ed.). (1971). *Changing families: A family therapy reader.* New York: Grune & Stratton.

Haley, J. (1976). *Problem-solving therapy: New strategies for effective family therapy.* New York: Harper Colophon.

Hall, C. S., & Lindzey, G. (1978). *Theories of personality.* New York: Wiley.

Hall, D. L., & Ames, R. T. (1987). *Thinking through Confucius.* Albany: State University of New York Press.

Hampden-Turner, C. (1981). *Maps of the mind.* New York: Macmillan.

Harding, D. E. (1979). *The hierarchy of heaven and earth: A new diagram of man in the universe.* Gainesville, FL: University Presses of Florida.

Harding, D. E. (1986). *On having no head: Zen and the re-discovery of the obvious.* London: Penguin/Arkana.

Harris, M. J., & Rosenthal, R. (1985). Mediation of interpersonal expectancy effects: 31 meta-analyses. *Psychological Bulletin, 97,* 363–386.

Hartmann, H. (1958). *Ego psychology and the problem of adaptation.* New York: International Universities Press.

Hartshorne, C. (1948). *The divine relativity.* New Haven: Yale University Press.

Hartshorne, C. (1967). *A natural theology for our time.* La Salle, IL: Open Court.

Hartshorne, C. (1984). *Omnipotence and other theological mistakes.* Albany: State University of New York Press.

Havens, J. (Ed.), with the collaboration of Bakan, D., Clark, W. H., Curran, C. A., Dittes, J. E., Irwin, K., Kimball, R. C., MacLeod, R. B., Pruyser, P. W., Rogers, W. B., Royce, J. R., & Rubenstein, R. (1968). *Psychology and religion: A contemporary dialogue.* Princeton, NJ: Van Nostrand.

Hawking, S. (1988). *A brief history of time.* New York: Bantam Books.

Hayward, J. W. (1987). *Shifting worlds, changing minds: Where the sciences and Buddhism meet.* Boston: Shambhala/New Science.

Heelas, P., & Lock, A. (Eds.). (1981). *Indigenous psychologies: The anthropology of the self.* New York: Academic Press.

Heisenberg, W. (1958). *Physics and philosophy.* New York: Harper & Row.

Heisenberg, W. (1974). *Across the frontiers.* New York: Harper & Row.

Henshel, R. L. (1982). The boundary of the self-fulfilling prophecy and the dilemma of social prediction. *The British Journal of Sociology, 33,* 511–528.

Herbert, N. (1987). *Quantum reality: Beyond the new physics.* Garden City, NY: Anchor Press/Doubleday.

Hesse, M. B. (1966). *Models and analogies in science.* Notre Dame, IN: University of Notre Dame Press.

Hewitt, J. P. (1989). *Dilemmas of the American self.* Philadelphia: Temple University Press.

Hilgard, E. R. (1977). *Divided consciousness: Multiple controls in human thought and action.* New York: Wiley/Wiley-Interscience.

Hilgard, E. R. (1983, August). Return of consciousness to psychology. Distinguished lecture at the American Psychological Association Annual Convention, Anaheim, CA.

Hillman, J. (1975). *Re-visioning psychology.* New York: Harper & Row.

Hjelle, L. A., & Ziegler, D. J. (1981). *Personality theories: Basic assumptions, research, and applications.* New York: McGraw-Hill.

Hoffman, L. (1971). Deviation-amplifying processes in natural groups. In J. Haley (Ed.), *Changing families: A family therapy reader* (pp. 285–311). New York: Grune & Stratton.

Hoffman, R. R., Cochran, E. L., & Nead, J. M. (1990). Cognitive metaphors in experimental psychology. In D. E. Leary (Ed.), *Metaphors in the history of psychology* (pp. 173–229). Cambridge: Cambridge University Press.

Hofstadter, D. R. (1979). *Gödel, Escher, Bach: An eternal golden braid.* New York: Vintage/Random House.

Hofstadter, D. R., & Dennett, D. C. (Eds.). (1981). *The mind's I: Fantasies and reflections on self and soul.* New York: Basic Books.

Holbrook, B. (1981). *The stone monkey: An alternative, Chinese-scientific, reality.* New York: William Morrow.

Holmes, D. S. (1984). Meditation and somatic arousal reduction: A review of the experimental evidence. *American Psychologist, 39,* 1–10.

Holt, R. R. (1964). Imagery: The return of the ostracised. *American Psychologist, 19,* 254–264.

Hoshmand, L. L. S. T. (1989). Alternate research paradigms: A review and teaching proposal. *The Counseling Psychologist, 17,* 3–79.

Houston, J. (1982). *The possible human*. Los Angeles: J. P. Tarcher.

Howard, G. S. (1991). Culture tales: A narrative approach to thinking, cross-cultural psychology, and psychotherapy. *American Psychologist, 46,* 187–197.

Hsu, F. L. K. (1985). The self in cross-cultural perspective. In A. J. Marsella, G. DeVos, & F. L. K. Hsu, *Culture and self: Asian and Western perspectives* (pp. 24–55). New York: Tavistock.

Huff, M. C. (1989, November). Self-in-relation psychology: Its implications for agency and justice. Paper presented at American Academy of Religion Annual Meeting, Anaheim, CA.

Ingram, P. O. (1990). Nature's jeweled net: Kūkai's ecological Buddhism. *The Pacific World,* n.s. 6, 50–64.

Jaffé A. (1971). *The myth of meaning.* New York: Penguin.

James, W. (1963). *Pragmatism and other essays.* New York: Washington Square Press.

Jaynes, J. (1976). *The origin of consciousness in the breakdown of the bicameral mind.* Boston: Houghton Mifflin.

Jeans, J., Sir. (1937). *The mysterious universe.* New York: Macmillan.

Jeans, J., Sir. (1943). *Physics and philosophy.* Cambridge: Cambridge University Press and New York: Macmillan.

Johnson, M. (1987). *The body in the mind: The bodily basis of meaning, imagination, and reason.* Chicago: University of Chicago Press.

Jones, R. S. (1982). *Physics as metaphor.* New York: New American Library.

Judson, H. F. (1980). *The search for solutions.* New York: Holt, Rinehart and Winston.

Jung, C. G. (1933). *Modern man in search of a soul.* New York: Harvest/Harcourt Brace Jovanovich.

Jung, C. G. (1963). Septem Sermones ad mortuos. In C. G. Jung, *Memories, dreams, reflections* (A. Jaffé, Ed.; Appendix V, pp. 378–390). New York: Random House/Vintage.

Jung, C. G. (1966). *Two essays on analytical psychology* (rev. ed.). In H. Read, M. Fordham, & G. Adler (Eds.), *The collected works of C. G. Jung* (Vol. 7, 2d ed.). Princeton: Princeton University Press.

Jung, C. G. (1968a). *The archetypes and the collective unconscious.* In H. Read, M. Fordham, & G. Adler (Eds.), *The collected works of C. G. Jung* (Vol. 9, Part I, 2d ed.). Princeton: Princeton University Press.

Jung, C. G. (1968b). *Aion: Researches into the phenomenology of the self.* In H. Read, M. Fordham, & G. Adler (Eds.), *The collected works of C. G. Jung* (Vol. 9, Part II, 2d ed.). Princeton: Princeton University Press.

Jung, C. G. (1969a). *Answer to Job.* In C. G. Jung, *Psychology and religion: West and east.* In H. Read, M. Fordham, & G. Adler (Eds.), *The collected works of C. G. Jung* (Vol. 11, 2d ed., pp. 355-470). Princeton: Princeton University Press.

Jung, C. G. (1969b). *Psychology and religion: West and east.* In H. Read, M. Fordham, & G. Adler (Eds.), *The collected works of C. G. Jung* (Vol. 11, 2d ed.). Princeton: Princeton University Press.

Jung, C. G. (1969c). *The structure and dynamics of the psyche.* In H. Read, M. Fordham, & G. Adler (Eds.), *The collected works of C. G. Jung* (Vol. 8, 2d ed.). Princeton: Princeton University Press.

Jung, C. G. (1971). *Psychological types.* In H. Read, M. Fordham, & G. Adler (Eds.), *The collected works of C. G. Jung* (Vol. 6). Princeton: Princeton University Press.

Jussim, L. (1989). Teacher expectations: Self-fulfilling prophecies, perceptual biases, and accuracy. *Journal of Personality and Social Psychology, 57*, 469–480.

Kakar, S. (1990). Stories from Indian psychoanalysis: Context and text. In J. W. Stigler, R. A. Shweder, & G. Herdt (Eds.), *Cultural psychology* (pp. 427–445). Cambridge: Cambridge University Press.

Kalupahana, D. J. (1987). *The principles of Buddhist psychology.* Albany: State University of New York Press.

Kant, I. (1949). *Critique of practical reason, and other writings in moral philosophy* (L. W. Beck, Trans. and Ed.). Chicago: University of Chicago Press.

Katz, N. (Ed.). (1983). *Buddhist and Western psychology.* Boulder, CO: Prajñā Press.

Kaufmann, G. (1979). *Visual imagery and its relation to problem solving: A theoretical and experimental inquiry.* Bergen, Norway: Universitetsforlaget; New York: Irvington-on-Hudson (Distributed by Columbia University Press).

Keen, E. (1970). *Three faces of being: Toward an existential clinical psychology.* New York: Appleton-Century-Crofts.

Keller, C. (1986). *From a broken web: Separation, sexism, and self.* Boston: Beacon Press.

Keller, C. (1990). Warriors, women and the nuclear complex: Toward a postnuclear postmodernity. In D. R. Griffin (Ed.), *Sacred interconnections* (pp. 63–82). Albany: State University of New York Press.

Keller, E. F. (1982). Feminism and science. *Signs: Journal of Women in Culture and Society, 7,* 589–602.

Keller, E. F., & Grontkowski, C. R. (1983). The mind's eye. In S. Harding & M. B. Hintikka (Eds.), *Discovering reality: Feminist perspectives on epistemology, metaphysics, methodology, and philosophy of science* (pp. 207–224). Dordrecht, Holland: D. Reidel.

Kelly, G. A. (1963). *A theory of personality: The psychology of personal constructs.* New York: Norton.

Kerényi, C. (1963). Kore. In C. G. Jung and C. Kerényi (Eds.), *Essays on a science of mythology: The myth of the divine child and the mysteries of Eleusis* (pp. 101–155). Princeton: Princeton University Press.

Keutzer, C. S. (1983a). Toward a unified theory of personality: A plausible paradigm. Unpublished paper.

Keutzer, C. S. (1983b, August). Transpersonal psychology workshop as part of the Oregon Psychological Association Continuing Workshop Series, Portland, OR.

Kimble, G. A. (1984). Psychology's two cultures. *American Psychologist, 39,* 833–850.

Kinsbourne, M. (1982). Hemispheric specialization and the growth of human understanding. *American Psychologist, 37,* 411–420.

Kirschenbaum, H., & Henderson, V. L. (Eds). (1989). *The Carl Rogers reader.* Boston: Houghton Mifflin.

Kittay, E. F., & Meyers, D. T. (Eds.). (1987). *Women and moral theory.* Totowa, NJ: Rowman & Littlefield.

Klein, A. C. (1987). Finding a self: Buddhist and feminist perspectives. In C. W. Atkinson, C. H. Buchanan, & M. R. Miles (Eds.), *Shaping new vision: Gender and values in American culture* (pp. 191–218). Ann Arbor: UMI Research Press.

Klein, M. (1957). *Envy and gratitude: A study of unconscious sources.* New York: Basic Books.

Kluckhohn, C. (1972). Myths and rituals: A general theory. In W. A. Lessa & E. Z. Vogt, *Reader in comparative religion: An anthropological approach* (pp. 93–105). New York: Harper & Row.

Kobayashi, V. N. (1983). The symposium on *Mind and Nature:* A brief summary. In W. Maxwell (Ed.), *Thinking: The expanding frontier* (pp. 281–283). Philadelphia: Franklin Institute Press.

Koch, S. (1981). The nature and limits of psychological knowledge. *American Psychologist, 36,* 257–269.

Koestler, A. (1967). *The ghost in the machine*. New York: Macmillan.

Koestler, A. (1978). *Janus.* New York: Vintage Books/Random House.

Kohak, E. (1984). *The embers and the stars: A philosophical inquiry into the moral sense of nature.* Chicago: University of Chicago Press.

Kohut, H. (1977). *The restoration of the self.* New York: International Universities Press.

Koplowitz, H. (1984). A projection beyond Piaget's formal-operations stage: A general system stage and a unitary stage. In M. L. Commons, F. A. Richards, & C. Armon (Eds.), *Beyond formal operations: Late adolescent and adult cognitive development* (pp. 272–295). New York: Praeger.

Kornfield, J. (1979). Intensive insight meditation: A phenomenological study. *The Journal of Transpersonal Psychology, 11,* 41–58.

Korzybski, A. (1958). *Science and sanity: An introduction to non-Aristotelian systems and general semantics* (4th ed.). Lakeville, CT: International Non-Aristotelian Library.

Kosslyn, S. (1975). Information representation in visual images. *Cognitive Psychology, 7,* 341–370.

Kosslyn, S. M. (1980). *Image and mind.* New York: Macmillan.

Kosslyn, S. M. (1983). *Ghosts in the mind's machine: Creating and using images in the brain.* New York: Norton.

Kreisler, A. F. (1982). Understanding understanding: The psychology of sentence comprehension. *Casements, 3*(1), 32–40.

Kugler, P. K. (1987). Jacques Lacan: Postmodern depth psychology and the birth of the self-reflexive subject. In P. Young-Eisendrath & J. A. Hall (Eds.), *The book of the self: Person, pretext, and process* (pp. 173–184). New York: New York University Press.

Kuhn, T. S. (1970). *The structure of scientific revolutions* (2d ed.). Chicago: University of Chicago Press.

Laing, R. D. (1967). *The politics of experience*. New York: Pantheon.

Lakoff, G., & Johnson, M. (1980). *Metaphors we live by.* Chicago: University of Chicago Press.

Lakoff, G., & Turner, M. (1989). *More than cool reason: A field guide to poetic metaphor.* Chicago: University of Chicago Press.

Langer, S. K. (1957). *Philosophy in a new key: A study in the symbolism of reason, rite, and art.* Cambridge: Harvard University Press.

Lashley, K. S. (1950). In search of the engram. In *Symposia of the society for experimental biology, No. 4: Physiological mechanisms in animal behavior* (pp. 454–482). New York: Academic Press.

Laszlo, E. (1972). *The systems view of the world.* New York: George Braziller.

Laszlo, E. (1973). *Introduction to systems philosophy: Toward a new paradigm of contemporary thought.* New York: Harper Torchbooks.

Laszlo, E. (1977). Framework for a general systems theory of world order. In N. A. Nyiri & R. Preece (Eds.), *Unity in diversity: Proceedings of the Interdisciplinary Research Seminar at Wilfred Laurier University* (Vol. 1, pp. 1–13). Waterloo, Ontario: Wilfred Laurier University Press.

Laszlo, E. (1981). Biperspectivism: An evolutionary systems approach to the mind-body problem. *Zygon: Journal of Religion and Science, 16,* 151–164.

Laszlo, E. (1987). *Evolution: The grand synthesis.* Boston: Shambhala/New Science.

Lawlor, R. (1982). *Sacred geometry: Philosophy and practice.* New York: Crossroad.

Lazarus, R. S. (1982). Thoughts on the relations between emotion and cognition. *American Psychologist, 37,* 1019–1024.

Lazarus, R. S. (1984). On the primacy of cognition. *American Psychologist, 39,* 124–129.

Lazarus, R. S. (1991). Cognition and motivation in emotion. *American Psychologist, 46,* 352–367.

Leary, D. E. (Ed.). (1990a). *Metaphors in the history of psychology.* Cambridge: Cambridge University Press.

Leary, D. E. (1990b). Psyche's muse: The role of metaphor in the history of psychology. In D. E. Leary (Ed.), *Metaphors in the history of psychology* (pp. 1–78). Cambridge: Cambridge University Press.

L'Ecuyer, R. (1981). The development of the self-concept through the life span. In M. D. Lynch, A. A. Norem-Hebeisen, & K. J. Gergen (Eds.), *Self-concept: Advances in theory and research* (pp. 203–218). Cambridge, MA: Ballinger.

Leder, D. (1990). *The absent body.* Chicago: University of Chicago Press.

Lee, D. (1973). Codifications of reality: Lineal and nonlineal. In R. E. Ornstein (Ed.), *The nature of human consciousness: A book of readings* (pp. 128–142). San Francisco: Freeman.

LeGare, M. (1987). The use of general systems theory as metatheory for developing and evaluating theories in the neurosciences. *Behavioral Science, 32*, 106–120.

Lessa, W. A., & Vogt, E. Z. (1972). *Reader in comparative religion: An anthropological approach.* New York: Harper & Row.

Lévi-Strauss, C. (1963). The structural study of myth. In C. Lévi-Strauss, *Structural anthropology* (chap. 11, pp. 206–231). New York: Basic Books.

Lévi-Strauss, C. (1966). *The savage mind.* Chicago: University of Chicago Press.

Lévi-Strauss, C. (1969). *Introduction to a science of mythology: Vol. 1. The raw and the cooked.* New York: Harper & Row.

Lévi-Strauss, C. (1978). *Myth and meaning.* New York: Schocken Books.

Levy, J. (1983). Language, cognition, and the right hemisphere: A response to Gazzaniga. *American Psychologist, 38*, 538–541.

Lewin, K. (1931). The conflict between Aristotelian and Galileian modes of thought in contemporary psychology. *Journal of General Psychology, 5*, 141–176.

Lewin, K. (1935). *A dynamic theory of personality.* New York: McGraw-Hill.

Lewin, K. (1936). *Principles of topological psychology.* New York: McGraw-Hill.

Lewin, K. (1951). *Field theory in social science.* (D. Cartwright, Ed.). New York: Harper & Brothers.

Lipset, D. (1980). *Gregory Bateson: The legacy of a scientist.* Englewood Cliffs, NJ: Prentice-Hall.

Lovelock, J. E. (1979). *Gaia: A new look at life on Earth.* Oxford: Oxford University Press.

Lowen, W. (1982). *Dichotomies of the mind: A systems science model of the mind and personality.* New York: Wiley.

Loy, D. (1988). *Nonduality: A study in comparative philosophy.* New Haven: Yale University Press.

Lykes, M. B. (1985). Gender and individualistic vs. collectivist bases for notions about the self. *Journal of Personality, 53*, 356–383.

Maas, J. P. (1983). The pattern that connects. In W. Maxwell (Ed.), *Thinking: The expanding frontier* (pp. 271–274). Philadelphia: Franklin Institute Press.

MacCormac, E. R. (1976). *Metaphor and myth in science and religion.* Durham, NC: Duke University Press.

MacCormac, E. R. (1985). *A cognitive theory of metaphor.* Cambridge: MIT Press.

Macy, J. R. (1976). Systems philosophy as a hermeneutic for Buddhist teachings. *Philosophy East and West, 26,* 21–32.

Macy, J. R. (1983). *Despair and personal power in the nuclear age.* Philadelphia: New Society Publishers.

Macy, J. (1990). The ecological self: Postmodern ground for right action. In D. R. Griffin (Ed.), *Sacred interconnections* (pp. 35-48). Albany: State University of New York Press.

Macy, J. (1991). *Mutual causality in Buddhism and general systems theory: The dharma of natural systems.* Albany: State University of New York Press.

Mahrer, A. R. (1988). Discovery-oriented psychotherapy research: Rationale, aims, and methods. *American Psychologist, 43,* 694–702.

Mair, M. (1989). *Between psychology and psychotherapy: A poetics of experience.* London: Routledge.

Malinowski, B. (1948). *Magic, science and religion, and other essays.* Garden City, NY: Anchor/Doubleday.

Malville, J. McK. (1981). *The fermenting universe.* New York: Seabury Press.

Manicas, P. T., & Secord, P. F. (1983). Implications for psychology of the new philosophy of science. *American Psychologist, 38,* 399–413.

March, R. H. (1978). *Physics for poets.* Chicago: Contemporary Books.

Margolis, J. (1987). Eliminating selves in the psychological sciences. In P. Young-Eisendrath & J. A. Hall (Eds.), *The book of the self: Person, pretext, and process* (pp. 42–66). New York: New York University Press.

Marks, D. F. (1983). Mental imagery and consciousness: A theoretical review. In A. A. Sheikh (Ed.), *Imagery: Current theory, research, and application* (pp. 96–130). New York: Wiley.

Marks, L. E., Hammeal, R. J., & Bornstein, M. H. (1987). Perceiving similarity and comprehending metaphor. *Monographs of the Society for Research in Child Development, 52*(1), Serial No. 215.

Marsella, A. J., DeVos, G., & Hsu, F. L. K. (Eds.). (1985). *Culture and self: Asian and Western perspectives.* New York: Tavistock.

Marshall, G. D., & Zimbardo, P. G. (1979). Affective consequences of inadequately explained physiological arousal. *Journal of Personality and Social Psychology, 37,* 970–988.

Maruyama, M. (1963). The second cybernetics: Deviation-amplifying mutual causal processes. *American Scientist, 51,* 164–179.

Maslow, A. H. (1966). *The psychology of science.* South Bend, IN: Gateway Editions.

Matson, K. (1977). *The psychology today omnibook of personal development.* New York: William Morrow.

Maturana, H. R., & Varela, F. J. (1987). *The tree of knowledge: The biological roots of human understanding.* Boston: Shambhala/New Science.

Maxwell, W. (Ed.). (1983). *Thinking: The expanding frontier.* Philadelphia: Franklin Institute Press.

May, J., & Groder, M. (1989). Jungian thought and dynamical systems. *Psychological Perspectives, 20*(1), 142–155.

May, R. (1976). Gregory Bateson and humanistic psychology. *Journal of Humanistic Psychology, 16*(4), 33–51.

Mayr, E. (1954). Change of genetic environment and evolution. In J. S. Huxley, A. C. Hardy, & E. B. Ford (Eds.), *Evolution as a process* (pp. 157–180). London: Allen & Unwin.

Mayr, E. (1988). *Toward a new philosophy of biology.* Cambridge: The Belknap Press of Harvard University Press.

McFague, S. (1982). *Metaphorical theology.* Philadelphia: Fortress Press.

McFague, S. (1987). *Models of God: Theology for an ecological, nuclear age.* Philadelphia: Fortress Press.

McGlashan, A. (1967). *Savage and beautiful country: The secret life of the mind.* New York: Hillstone/Stonehill.

McGuire, W. J. (1973). The yin and yang of progress in social psychology: Seven koan. *Journal of Personality and Social Psychology, 26,* 446–456.

McKim, R. H. (1980). *Experiences in visual thinking.* Monterey, CA: Brooks/Cole.

McReynolds, P. (1990). Motives and metaphors: A study in scientific creativity. In D. E. Leary (Ed.), *Metaphors in the history of psychology* (pp. 133–172). Cambridge: Cambridge University Press.

Mead, G. H. (1934). *Mind, self and society from the standpoint of a social behaviorist.* (C. W. Morris, Ed.). Chicago: University of Chicago Press.

Meichenbaum, D. (1988). What happens when the "brute data" of psychological inquiry are meanings: Nurturing the dialogue between hermeneutics and empiricism. In S. B. Messer, L. A. Sass, & R. L. Woolfolk (Eds.), *Hermeneutics and psychological theory* (pp. 116–130). New Brunswick, NJ: Rutgers University Press.

Merchant, C. (1980). *The death of nature: Women, ecology and the scientific revolution.* San Francisco: Harper & Row.

Merten, D., & Schwartz, G. (1982). Metaphor and self: Symbolic process in everyday life. *American Anthropologist, 84,* 796–810.

Merton, R. K. (1948). The self-fulfilling prophecy. *The Antioch Review, 8,* 193–210.

Messer, S. B., Sass, L. A., & Woolfolk, R. L. (Eds.). (1988). *Hermeneutics and psychological theory: Interpretive perspectives on personality, psychotherapy, and psychopathology.* New Brunswick, NJ: Rutgers University Press.

Metzner, R. (1987). Resonance as metaphor and metaphor as resonance. *ReVision, 10*(1), 37–44.

Milgram, S., Greenwald, J., Kessler, S., McKenna, W., & Waters, J. (1977). A psychological map of New York City. In I. L. Janis (Ed.), *Current trends in psychology* (pp. 362–368). Los Altos, CA: William Kaufmann.

Miller, D. L. (1981). *The new polytheism: Rebirth of the gods and goddesses.* Dallas, TX: Spring.

Miller, G. A., Galanter, E., & Pribram, K. H. (1960). *Plans and the structure of behavior.* New York: Holt, Rinehart and Winston.

Miller, James G. (1978). *Living Systems.* New York: McGraw-Hill.

Miller, Joan G. (1984). Culture and the development of everyday social explanation. *Journal of Personality and Social Psychology, 46*, 961–978.

Miller, Joan G. (1988). Bridging the content-structure dichotomy: Culture and the self. In M. H. Bond (Ed.), *The cross-cultural challenge to social psychology* (pp. 266–281). Newbury Park, CA: Sage.

Mischel, W. (1968). *Personality and assessment.* New York: Wiley.

Mischel, W. (1973). Toward a cognitive social learning reconceptualization of personality. *Psychological Review, 80*, 252–283.

Mollencott, V. R. (1983, October). Power: A liberation perspective. Lecture at Linfield College, McMinnville, OR.

Morawski, J. G. (1984). Historiography as a metatheoretical text for social psychology. In K. J. Gergen & M. M. Gergen (Eds.), *Historical social psychology* (pp. 37–60). Hillsdale, NJ: Lawrence Erlbaum.

Morowitz, H. J. (1972). Biology as a cosmological science. *Main Currents in Modern Thought, 28*, 151–157.

Morrison, P., Morrison, P., & the Office of Eames, C., & Eames, R. (1982). *Powers of ten.* New York: Scientific American Library.

Murchie, G. (1967). *Music of the spheres: The material universe—from atom to quasar, simply explained.* New York: Dover.

Napier, A. Y., with Whitaker, C. A. (1978). *The family crucible.* New York: Bantam Books.

Natsoulas, T. (1981). Basic problems of consciousness. *Journal of Personality and Social Psychology, 41*, 132–178.

Needham, J., with Wang Ling. (1956). *Science and civilization in China* (Vol. 2). Cambridge: Cambridge University Press.

Needleman, J. (1965). *A sense of the cosmos: The encounter of modern science and ancient truth.* New York: E. P. Dutton.

Needleman, J. (1980). *Lost Christianity.* Garden City, NY: Doubleday.

Neumann, E. (1954). *The origins and history of consciousness.* Princeton: Princeton University Press.

Neumann, E. (1973). On the moon and matriarchal consciousness. In J. Hillman, E. Neumann, M. Stein, A. Vitale, & V. von der Heydt, *Fathers and mothers* (pp. 40–63). Zürich, Switzerland: Spring.

Norman, D. A. (1980). What goes on in the mind of the learner. In W. J. McKeachie (Ed.), *New directions for teaching and learning: Learning, cognition, and college teaching* (pp. 37–49). San Francisco: Jossey-Bass.

Northrop, F. S. C. (1946). *The meeting of east and west.* New York: Macmillan.

Ochs, C. (1977). *Behind the sex of god.* Boston: Beacon Press.

Odin, S. (1982). *Process metaphysics and Hua-yen Buddhism.* Albany: State University of New York Press.

O'Donohue, W. (1989). The (even) Bolder model: The clinical psychologist as metaphysician-scientist-practitioner. *American Psychologist*, *44*, 1460–1468.

O'Flaherty, W. D. (1980). *Women, androgynes, and other mythical beasts.* Chicago: University of Chicago Press.

Ogilvy, J. (1977). *Many dimensional man: Decentralizing self, society, and the sacred.* New York: Harper Colophon.

Olds, L. E. (1981). *Fully human.* Englewood Cliffs, NJ: Prentice-Hall.

Olds, L. E. (1985). Cognitive imagery and diagrams in teaching personality theory. Paper presented at Western Psychological Association, San Jose, CA, April 18. Bloomington, IN: Educational Resources Information Center (ERIC) Clearinghouse Database and Microfiche Collection, Document No. ED 263 036.

Olds, L. E. (1986). The neglected feminine: Promises and perils. *Soundings: A Journal of Interdisciplinary Studies, 69*, 226–240.

Olds, L. E. (1989). Metaphors of hierarchy and interrelatedness in Hildegard of Bingen and Mary Daly. *Listening: A Journal of Religion and Culture*, *24*(1), 54–66.

Olds, L. E. (1990). Integrating ontological metaphors: Hierarchy and interrelatedness. Unpublished paper.

Olds, L. E. (1991). Chinese metaphors of interrelatedness: Re-imaging body, nature, and the feminine. *Contemporary Philosophy*, *13*(8), 16–22.

Oliver, H. H. (1981). *A relational metaphysic.* The Hague: Martinus Nijhoff.

Olsen, T. (1979, February). The mother tongue. Lecture at a Reed College symposium on The First Word: Women, Language, Writing, Portland, OR.

Ornstein, R. E. (1972). *The psychology of consciousness.* San Francisco: Freeman.

Ornstein, R. E. (Ed.). (1973). *The nature of human consciousness: A book of readings.* San Francisco: Freeman.

Ortony, A. (Ed.). (1979). *Metaphor and thought.* Cambridge: Cambridge University Press.

Ortony, A., Reynolds, R. E., & Arter, J. A. (1978). Metaphor: Theoretical and empirical research. *Psychological Bulletin, 85,* 919–943.

Osborne, J. (1981). Approaches to consciousness in North American academic psychology. *The Journal of Mind and Behavior, 2,* 271–291.

Oyle, I. (1975). *The healing mind.* New York: Pocket Books.

Pagels, H. R. (1982). *The cosmic code: Quantum physics as the language of nature.* New York: Bantam Books.

Pagels, H. R. (1988). *The dreams of reason.* New York: Simon and Schuster.

Paivio, A. (1970). On the functional significance of imagery. *Psychological Bulletin, 3,* 385–392.

Paivio, A. (1971). *Imagery and verbal processes.* New York: Holt, Rinehart and Winston.

Paranjpe, A. C. (1988). A personality theory according to Vedanta. In A. C. Paranjpe, D. Y. F. Ho, & R. W. Rieber (Eds.), *Asian contributions to psychology* (pp. 185–213). New York: Praeger.

Paranjpe, A. C., Ho, D. Y. F., & Rieber, R. W. (1988). *Asian contributions to psychology.* New York: Praeger.

Parker, I., & Shotter, J. (1990). *Deconstructing social psychology.* London: Routledge.

Patton, M. J., & Jackson, A. P. (1991). Theory and meaning in counseling research: Comment on Strong (1991). *Journal of Counseling Psychology, 38,* 214–216.

Pederson, P. B. (1977). Asian personality theories. In R. J. Corsini (Ed.), *Current personality theories* (chap. 13, pp. 367–397). Itasca, IL: F. E. Peacock.

Pellegrino, J. W. (1985, October). Anatomy of analogy. *Psychology Today,* pp. 49–54.

Penrose, R. (1989). *The emperor's new mind.* New York: Penguin.

Pepper, S. C. (1942). *World hypotheses.* Berkeley and Los Angeles: University of California Press.

Peterson, I. (1988). *The mathematical tourist.* New York: Freeman.

Petrie, H. G. (1979). Metaphor and learning. In A. Ortony (Ed.), *Metaphor and thought*, pp. 438–461. Cambridge: Cambridge University Press.

Phillips, D. C. (1976). *Holistic thought in social science.* Stanford, CA: Stanford University Press.

Pirsig, R. M. (1974). *Zen and the art of motorcycle maintenance.* New York: Bantam Books.

Platt, J. R. (1961). Beauty: Pattern and change. In D. W. Fiske & S. R. Maddi (Eds.), *Functions of varied experience* (pp. 402–430). Homewood, IL: Dorsey Press.

Polanyi, M. (1946). *Science, faith and society*. Chicago: University of Chicago Press.

Polanyi, M. (1959). *The study of man.* Chicago: University of Chicago Press.

Polanyi, M. (1962). *Personal knowledge: Towards a post-critical philosophy.* Chicago: University of Chicago Press.

Polanyi, M. (1966). *The tacit dimension.* Garden City, NY: Anchor Books/Doubleday.

Polanyi, M., & Prosch, H. (1975). *Meaning.* Chicago: University of Chicago Press.

Popper, K. R., Sir. (1985). *Popper selections* (D. Miller, Ed.). Princeton: Princeton University Press.

Porkert, M. (1974). *The theoretical foundations of Chinese medicine: Systems of correspondence.* Cambridge: MIT Press.

Post, J. F. (1987). *The faces of existence: An essay in nonreductive metaphysics.* Ithaca, NY: Cornell University Press.

Postle, D. (1976). *Fabric of the universe.* New York: Crown Publishers.

Potter, K. H. (1988). Metaphor as key to understanding the thought of other speech communities. In G. J. Larson & E. Deutsch (Eds.), *Interpreting across boundaries: New essays in comparative philosophy* (pp. 19–35). Princeton: Princeton University Press.

Pribram, K. H. (1971). *Languages of the brain.* Englewood Cliffs, NJ: Prentice-Hall.

Pribram, K. H. (1980). The role of analogy in transcending limits in the brain sciences. *Daedalus, 109*(2), 19–38.

Pribram, K. H. (1986). The cognitive revolution and mind/brain issues. *American Psychologist, 41*, 507–520.

Pribram, K. H. (1990). From metaphors to models: The use of analogy in neuropsychology. In D. E. Leary (Ed.), *Metaphors in the history of psychology* (pp. 79–103). Cambridge: Cambridge University Press.

Pulaski, M. A. S. (1974, January). The rich rewards of make believe. *Psychology Today*, pp. 68–72, 74.

Quine, W. V. (1960). *Word and object.* New York: Wiley and the Technology Press of MIT.

Quine, W. V. (1969). *Ontological relativity and other essays.* New York: Columbia University Press.

Rao, K. R. (1988). Psychology of transcendence: A study in early Buddhistic psychology. In A. C. Paranjpe, D. Y. F. Ho, & R. W. Rieber (Eds.), *Asian contributions to psychology* (pp. 123–148). New York: Praeger.

Rapoport, A., & Horvath, W. J. (1959). Thoughts on organization theory and a review of two conferences. *General Systems* (Yearbook of the Society for General Systems Research), *4*, 87–93.

Reisenzein, R. (1983). The Schachter theory of emotion: Two decades later. *Psychological Bulletin, 94*, 239–264.

Reynolds, D. K. (1976). *Morita therapy.* Berkeley: University of California Press.

Reynolds, D. K. (1980). *The quiet therapies.* Honolulu: University of Hawaii Press.

Reynolds, D. K. (1983). *Naikan psychotherapy*. Chicago: University of Chicago Press.

Reynolds, D. K. (1984a). *Constructive living.* Honolulu: University of Hawaii Press.

Reynolds, D. K. (1984b). *Playing ball on running water.* New York: Quill.

Reynolds, D. K. (1986). *Even in summer the ice doesn't melt.* New York: William Morrow/Quill.

Reynolds, D. K. (1987). *Water bears no scars.* New York: William Morrow/Quill.

Reynolds, D. K. (1989a). *Flowing bridges, quiet waters.* Albany: State University of New York Press.

Reynolds, D. K. (1989b). *Pools of lodging for the moon.* New York: William Morrow.

Reynolds, D. K. (1990). *A thousand waves.* New York: William Morrow/Quill.

Richardson, G. E., & Wylie, W. E. (1984). The effects of educational imagery on university students' creativity levels and locus of control. *Health Education, 15*(1), 42–47.

Ricoeur, P. (1970). *Freud and philosophy: An essay on interpretation.* New Haven: Yale University Press.

Ricoeur, P. (1977). *The rule of metaphor* (R. Czerny, Trans.). Toronto: University of Toronto Press.

Ricoeur, P. (1979). The metaphorical process as cognition, imagination, and feeling. In S. Sacks (Ed.), *On metaphor* (pp. 141–157). Chicago: University of Chicago Press.

Rieff, P. (1961). *Freud: The mind of the moralist.* Garden City, NY: Anchor/Doubleday.

Rifkin, J. (1983). *Algeny.* New York: Penguin.

Rifkin, J., with Howard, T. (1980). *Entropy.* New York: Bantam Books.

Rigney, J. W., & Lutz, K. A. (1976). Effect of graphic analogies of concepts in chemistry on learning and attitudes. *Journal of Educational Psychology, 68*, 305–311.

Rinzler, C., & Gordon, B. (1980). Buddhism and psychotherapy. In G. Epstein (Ed.), *Studies in non-deterministic psychology* (pp. 52–69). New York: Human Sciences Press.

Rizzuto, A-M. (1979). *The birth of the living god: A psychoanalytic study.* Chicago: University of Chicago Press.

Robbins, S. S., & Oliva, T. A. (1982). The empirical identification of fifty-one core general systems theory vocabulary components. *Behavioral Science, 27*, 377–386.

Robbins, S. S., & Oliva, T. A. (1984). Usage of general systems theory core concepts by discipline type, time period, and publication category. *Behavioral Science, 29*, 28–39.

Robinson, D. N. (1979). *Systems of modern psychology.* New York: Columbia University Press.

Rogers, C. R. (1951). *Client-centered therapy: Its current practice, implications, and theory.* Boston: Houghton Mifflin.

Rogers, C. R. (1959). A theory of therapy, personality, and interpersonal relationships, as developed in the client-centered framework. In S. Koch (Ed.), *Psychology: A study of a science* (Vol. 3, pp. 184–256). New York: McGraw-Hill.

Rogers, C. R. (1961). *On becoming a person.* Boston: Houghton Mifflin.

Rogers, C. R. (1980). *A way of being.* Boston: Houghton Mifflin.

Rogerson, J. W. (1984). Slippery words: Myth. In A. Dundes (Ed.), *Sacred narrative: Readings in the theory of myth* (pp. 62–71). Berkeley: University of California Press.

Roland, A. (1988). *In search of self in India and Japan: Toward a cross-cultural psychology.* Princeton: Princeton University Press.

Roloff, L. (1980, July). Literate and post-literate society. Lecture at C. G. Jung and Education Seminar, Küsnacht (Zürich), Switzerland.

Romanyshyn, R. D. (1982). *Psychological life: From science to metaphor.* Austin: University of Texas Press.

Rorty, R. (1979). *Philosophy and the mirror of nature.* Princeton: Princeton University Press.

Rosemont, H., Jr. (1988). Against relativism. In G. J. Larson & E. Deutsch (Eds.), *Interpreting across boundaries: New essays in comparative philosophy* (pp. 36–70). Princeton: Princeton University Press.

Rosenthal, R. (1966). *Experimenter effects in behavioral research.* New York: Appleton-Century-Crofts.

Rosenthal, R. (1987). Pygmalion effects: Existence, magnitude, and social importance/A reply to Wineburg. *Educational Researcher, 16*(9), 37–41.

Rosenthal, R., & Fode, K. L. (1963). The effect of experimenter bias on the performance of the albino rat. *Behavioral Science, 8,* 183–189.

Rosenthal, R., & Jacobson, L. (1968). *Pygmalion in the classroom: Teacher expectation and pupils' intellectual development.* New York: Holt, Rinehart and Winston.

Ross, N. W. (1966). *Three ways of Asian wisdom: Hinduism, Buddhism, Zen and their significance for the West.* New York: Simon and Schuster.

Ross, N. W. (1980). *Buddhism: A way of life and thought.* New York: Vintage/Random House.

Rothberg, D. (1990). Contemporary epistemology and the study of mysticism. In R. K. C. Forman (Ed.), *The problem of pure consciousness: Mysticism and philosophy* (pp. 163–210). New York: Oxford University Press.

Rothenberg, A. (1979). *The emerging goddess: The creative process in art, science, and other fields.* Chicago: University of Chicago Press.

Royce, J. R. (1959). The search for meaning. *American Scientist, 47,* 515–535.

Royce, J. R. (1964). *The encapsulated man.* Princeton, NJ: D. Van Nostrand.

Royce, J. R. (1965a). Pebble picking versus boulder building. *Psychological Reports, 16,* 447–450.

Royce, J. R. (1965b). Psychology at the crossroads between the sciences and the humanities. In J. R. Royce (Ed.), *Psychology and the symbol: An interdisciplinary symposium* (pp. 3–25). New York: Random House.

Royce, J. R. (1970a). The present situation in theoretical psychology. In J. R. Royce (Ed.), *Toward unification in psychology.* Toronto: University of Toronto Press.

Royce, J. R. (Ed.). (1970b). *Toward unification in psychology.* Toronto: University of Toronto Press.

Royce, J. R. (1982). Philosophic issues, Division 24, and the future. *American Psychologist, 37*, 258–266.

Ruether, R. R. (1972). *Liberation theology.* New York: Paulist Press.

Ruether, R. R. (1979). Motherearth and the megamachine: A theology of liberation in a feminine, somatic and ecological perspective. In C. P. Christ & J. Plaskow (Eds.), *Womanspirit rising: A feminist reader in religion* (pp. 43–52). San Francisco: Harper & Row.

Ruether, R. R. (1983). *Sexism and God-talk.* Boston: Beacon Press.

Russell, P. (1983). *The global brain.* Los Angeles: J. P. Tarcher.

Rychlak, J. F. (1968). *A philosophy of science for personality theory.* Boston: Houghton Mifflin.

Rychlak, J. F. (1977). *The psychology of rigorous humanism.* New York: Wiley/Wiley-Interscience.

Sagan, C. (1980). *Cosmos.* New York: Random House.

Salthe, S. N. (1985). *Evolving hierarchical systems.* New York: Columbia University Press.

Sampson, E. E. (1987). A critical constructionist view of psychology and personhood. In H. J. Stam, T. B. Rogers, & K. J. Gergen (Eds.), *The analysis of psychological theory: Metapsychological perspectives* (pp. 41–59). Washington, DC: Hemisphere.

Sampson, E. E. (1989). The deconstruction of the self. In J. Shotter & K. J. Gergen (Eds.), *Texts of identity* (pp. 1–19). Newbury Park, CA: Sage.

Sampson, E. E. (1990). Social psychology and social control. In I. Parker & J. Shotter (Eds.), *Deconstructing social psychology* (pp. 117–126). London: Routledge.

Samuels, M., & Samuels, N. (1975). *Seeing with the mind's eye: The history, techniques and uses of visualization.* New York: Random House and Berkeley, CA: The Bookworks.

Sanders, A. F. (1986). Religion and science as cultural systems: Polanyi's view on the problem of meaning. In H. G. Hubbeling & H. G. Kippenberg (Eds.), *On symbolic representation of religion* (pp. 9–23). Berlin and New York: Walter de Gruyter.

Sarbin, T. R. (1986a). The narrative as a root metaphor for psychology. In T. R. Sarbin (Ed.), *Narrative psychology* (pp. 3–21). New York: Praeger.

Sarbin, T. R. (Ed.). (1986b). *Narrative psychology: The storied nature of human conduct.* New York: Praeger.

Sarbin, T. R. (1990). Metaphors of unwanted conduct: A historical sketch. In D. E. Leary (Ed.), *Metaphors in the history of psychology* (pp. 300–330). Cambridge: Cambridge University Press.

Sass, L. A. (1988). Humanism, hermeneutics, and the concept of the human subject. In S. B. Messer, L. A. Sass, & R. L. Woolfolk (Eds.), *Hermeneutics and psychological theory* (pp. 222–271). New Brunswick, NJ: Rutgers University Press.

Satir, V. (1983). *Conjoint family therapy* (3d rev. ed.). Palo Alto, CA: Science and Behavior Books.

Schachter, S., & Singer, J. E. (1962). Cognitive, social, and physiological determinants of emotional state. *Psychological Review, 69*, 379–399.

Schrödinger, E. (1969). *What is life? & Mind and matter.* London: Cambridge University Press.

Schultz, S. J. (1984). *Family systems therapy: An integration.* New York: Jason Aronson.

Schumacher, J. A. (1981). Prolegomena to any future inquiry: The paradigm of undivided wholeness. *International Philosophical Quarterly, 21*, 439–459.

Seidler, M. J. (1979). Problems of systems epistemology. *International Philosophical Quarterly, 19*, 29–60.

Shah, I. (1972). *The exploits of the incomparable Mulla Nasrudin.* New York: E. P. Dutton.

Shainberg, D. (1980). Non-deterministic supervision. In G. Epstein (Ed.), *Studies in non-deterministic psychology* (pp. 135–154). New York: Human Sciences Press.

Shainberg, D. (1983). Teaching therapists how to be with their clients. In J. Welwood (Ed.), *Awakening the heart* (pp. 163–175). Boulder, CO: Shambhala/New Science.

Shaw, G. A. (1987). Creativity and hypermnesia for words and pictures. *The Journal of General Psychology, 114*, 167–178.

Shaw, M. C. (1988). *The paradox of intention* (American Academy of Religion Studies in Religion, No. 48). Atlanta, GA: Scholars Press.

Sheikh, A. A. (Ed.). (1983). *Imagery: Current theory, research, and application.* New York: Wiley.

Sheikh, A. A., & Jordan, C. S. (1983). Clinical uses of mental imagery. In A. A. Sheikh (Ed.), *Imagery: Current theory, research, and application* (pp. 391–435). New York: Wiley.

Sheldrake, R. (1981). *A new science of life.* Los Angeles: J. P. Tarcher.

Shorr, J. E., Sobel, G. E., Robin, P., & Connella, J. A. (1980). *Imagery: Its many dimensions and applications.* New York: Plenum Press.

Shotter, J., & Gergen, K. J. (Eds.). (1989). *Texts of identity*. Newbury Park, CA: Sage.

Sibicky, M., & Dovidio, J. F. (1986). Stigma of psychological therapy: Stereotypes, interpersonal reactions, and the self-fulfilling prophecy. *Journal of Counseling Psychology*, *33*, 148–154.

Simonton, O. C., Matthews-Simonton, S., & Creighton, J. (1978). *Getting well again: A step-by-step, self-help guide to overcoming cancer for patients and their families.* Los Angeles: J. P. Tarcher.

Singer, Jerome L. (1973). *The child's world of make-believe: Experimental studies of imaginative play.* New York: Academic Press.

Singer, J. L. (1974). *Imagery and daydream methods in psychotherapy and behavior modification.* New York: Academic Press.

Singer, J. L. (1975). *The inner world of daydreaming.* New York: Harper & Row.

Singer, Jerome, & Singer, Dorothy. (1979). The values of the imagination. In B. Sutton-Smith (Ed.), *Play and learning* (pp. 195–218). New York: Gardner Press.

Singer, June. (1973). *Boundaries of the soul: The practice of Jung's psychology.* Garden City, NY: Anchor Press/Doubleday.

Singer, June. (1990). *Seeing through the visible world: Jung, gnosis, and chaos.* San Francisco: Harper & Row.

Sirgy, M. J. (1988). Strategies for developing general systems theories. *Behavioral Science*, *33*, 25–37.

Siu, R. G. H. (1957). *The tao of science.* New York: Wiley and the Technology Press of MIT.

Skinner, B. F. (1971). *Beyond freedom and dignity.* New York: Bantam/Vintage Books.

Skinner, B. F. (1983, September). Origins of a behaviorist. *Psychology Today*, pp. 22–33.

Skinner, B. F. (1990). Can psychology be a science of mind? *American Psychologist*, *45*, 1206–1210.

Skinner, Q. (Ed.). (1985). *The return of grand theory in the human sciences.* Cambridge: Cambridge University Press.

Slater, P. (1974). *Earthwalk.* Garden City, NY: Anchor Press/Doubleday.

Smith, H. (1958). *The religions of man.* New York: Harper Colophon.

Smith, H. (1976). *Forgotten truth: The primordial tradition.* New York: Harper & Row.

Smith, H. (1989). *Beyond the post-modern mind* (rev. ed.). Wheaton, IL: Theosophical Publishing House/Quest.

Smith, J. C. (1976). Psychotherapeutic effects of transcendental meditation with control for expectation of relief and daily sitting. *Journal of Consulting and Clinical Psychology, 44*, 630–637.

Smith, J. M. (1958). *The theory of evolution.* Baltimore: Penguin.

Smith, L. D. (1990). Metaphors of knowledge and behavior in the behaviorist tradition. In D. E. Leary (Ed.), *Metaphors in the history of psychology* (pp. 239–266). Cambridge: Cambridge University Press.

Smith, M. B. (1985). The metaphorical basis of selfhood. In A. J. Marsella, G. DeVos, & F. L. K. Hsu (Eds.), *Culture and self: Asian and Western perspectives* (pp. 56–88). New York: Tavistock.

Smuts, J. C. (1926). *Holism and evolution.* New York: Viking Press/Macmillan.

Soskice, J. M. (1985). *Metaphor and religious language.* Oxford: Clarendon Press.

Spence, D. P. (1987). *The Freudian metaphor: Toward paradigm change in psychoanalysis.* New York: Norton.

Sperry, R. W. (1988). Psychology's mentalist paradigm and the religion/science tension. *American Psychologist, 43*, 607–613.

Springer, S. P., & Deutsch, G. (1981). *Left brain, right brain.* San Francisco: Freeman.

Stam, H. J., Rogers, T. B., & Gergen, K. J. (Eds.). (1987). *The analysis of psychological theory: Metaphysical perspectives.* Washington, D C: Hemisphere.

Stampfl, T. G., & Levis, D. J. (1967). Essentials of implosive therapy: A learning-theory-based psychodynamic behavioral therapy. *Journal of Abnormal Psychology, 72*, 496–503.

Stanley, S. M. (1981). *The new evolutionary timetable.* New York: Basic Books.

Steiner, C. M. (1974). *Scripts people live: Transactional analysis of life scripts.* New York: Grove Press.

Sternberg, R. J. (1990). *Metaphors of mind: Conceptions of nature of intelligence.* Cambridge: Cambridge University Press.

Stevens, P. S. (1974). *Patterns in nature.* Boston: Little, Brown.

Sticht, T. G. (1979). Educational uses of metaphor. In A. Ortony (Ed.), *Metaphor and thought* (pp. 474–485). Cambridge: Cambridge University Press.

Stone, H. & Winkelman, S. (1989). *Embracing our selves.* San Rafael, CA: New World Library.

Strong, S. R. (1991). Theory-driven science and naive empiricism in counseling psychology. *Journal of Counseling Psychology, 38*, 204–210.

Stulman, J. (Publisher). (1972). *Fields within fields . . . within fields: The methodology of pattern, 5*(1). New York: World Institute Council.

Suinn, R. M. (1983). Imagery and sports. In A. A. Sheikh (Ed.), *Imagery: Current theory, research, and application* (pp. 507–534). New York: Wiley.

Suit, J. L., & Paradise, L. Y. (1985). Effects of metaphors and cognitive complexity on perceived counselor characteristics. *Journal of Counseling Psychology, 32*, 23–28.

Sullivan, B. S. (1989). *Psychotherapy grounded in the feminine principle.* Wilmette, IL: Chiron.

Sullivan, H. S. (1953). *The interpersonal theory of psychiatry.* New York: Norton.

Sutherland, J. W. (1973). *A general systems philosophy for the social and behavioral sciences.* New York: George Braziller.

Sutton-Smith, B. (1971, December). Children at play. *Natural History*, pp. 54–59.

Sutton-Smith, B. (1979). Epilogue: Play as performance. In B. Sutton-Smith (Ed.), *Play and learning* (pp. 295–322). New York: Gardner Press.

Sutton-Smith, B. (1985, October). The child at play. *Psychology Today*, pp. 64–65.

Sutton-Smith, B. (1986). *Toys as culture.* New York: Gardner Press.

Suzuki, S. (1970). *Zen mind, beginner's mind.* New York: Weatherhill.

Szasz, T. (1961). *The myth of mental illness.* New York: Harper & Row.

Tart, C. T. (1975a). *States of consciousness.* New York: E. P. Dutton.

Tart, C. T. (Ed.). (1975b). *Transpersonal psychologies.* New York: Harper Colophon.

Tart, C. T. (Ed.). (1990). *Altered states of consciousness* (3d rev. ed.). San Francisco: Harper.

Taylor, A. M. (1977). General systems and their value for academic research and teaching. In N. A. Nyiri & R. Preece (Eds.), *Unity in diversity: Proceedings of the Interdisciplinary Research Seminar at Wilfred Laurier University* (Vol. 1, pp. 15–43). Waterloo, Ontario: Wilfred Laurier University Press.

Taylor, C. (1988). The moral topography of the self. In S. B. Messer, L. A. Sass, & R. L. Woolfolk (Eds.), *Hermeneutics and psychological theory* (pp. 298–320). New Brunswick, NJ: Rutgers University Press.

Taylor, C. (1989). *Sources of the self.* Cambridge: Harvard University Press.

Teilhard de Chardin, P. (1959). *The phenomenon of man.* New York: Harper & Row.

Thomas, L. (1974). *The lives of a cell: Notes of a biology watcher.* New York: Bantam Books.

Thomas, L. (1979). *The medusa and the snail.* New York: Viking Press.

Thomas, L. (1983). *Late night thoughts on listening to Mahler's ninth symphony.* New York: Bantam Books.

Thompson, K. O. (1988). Li and yi as immanent: Chu Hsi's thought in practical perspective. *Philosophy East and West*, *38*, 30–46.

Tillich, P. (1952). *The courage to be.* New Haven: Yale University Press.

Tillich, P. (1957). *Dynamics of faith.* New York: Harper & Row.

Tobias, M. (Ed.). (1984). *Deep ecology.* San Diego: Avant Books.

Tolman, E. C. (1948). Cognitive maps in rats and men. *Psychological Review*, *55*, 189–208.

Tolman, E. C. (1967). *Purposive behavior in animals and men.* New York: Irvington.

Tomm, W. A. (1987). Autonomy and interrelatedness: Spinoza, Hume, and Vasubandhu. *Zygon: Journal of Religion and Science 22*, 459–478.

Toth, M. A. (1980). Figures of thought: The use of diagrams in teaching sociology. *Teaching Sociology*, *7*(4), 409–424.

Tower, R. B. (1983). Imagery: Its role in development. In A. A. Sheikh (Ed.), *Imagery: Current theory, research, and application* (pp. 222–251). New York: Wiley.

Tracy, D. (1981). *The analogical imagination.* New York: Crossroad.

Trungpa, C. (1984). *Shambhala: The sacred path of the warrior.* (C. R. Gimian, Ed.). Boulder, CO: Shambhala.

Turner, V. W. (1974). *Dramas, fields, and metaphors: Symbolic action in human society.* Ithaca, NY: Cornell University Press.

Tyson, P. D. (1982). A general systems theory approach to consciousness, attention, and meditation. *The Psychological Record*, *32*, 491–500.

Vaihinger, H. (1924). *The philosophy of 'as if': A system of the theoretical, practical and religious fictions of mankind.* London: Routledge & Kegan Paul.

Valle, R. S., & von Eckartsberg, R. (1981). *The metaphors of consciousness.* New York: Plenum.

Van Herik, J. (1984). "Thick description" and psychology of religion. In R. L. Moore & F. E. Reynolds (Eds.), *Anthropology and the study of religion* (pp. 56–74). Chicago: Center for the Scientific Study of Religion.

Vaughan, F. (1986). *The inward arc: Healing and wholeness in psychotherapy and spirituality.* Boston: Shambhala/New Science.

Vaught, C. G. (1987). Metaphor, analogy, and the nature of truth. In R. C. Neville (Ed.), *New essays in metaphysics* (pp. 217–236). Albany: State University of New York Press.

Verhave, T., & van Hoorn, W. (1984). The temporalization of the self. In K. J. Gergen & M. M. Gergen (Eds.), *Historical social psychology* (pp. 325–345). Hillsdale, NJ: Lawrence Erlbaum.

Vosniadou, S. (1987). Children and metaphors. *Child Development, 58*, 870–885.

Vosniadou, S., & Ortony, A. (1983). The emergence of the literal—metaphorical—anomalous distinction in young children. *Child Development*, 54, 154–161.

Vosniadou, S., Ortony, A., Reynolds, R. E., & Wilson, P. T. (1984). Sources of difficulty in the young child's understanding of metaphorical language. *Child Development, 55*, 1588–1606.

Waddington, C. H. (1942). Canalization of development and the inheritance of acquired characters. *Nature, 150*, 563–565.

Waddington, C. H. (1957). *The strategy of the genes.* London: Allen & Unwin.

Waggoner, J. E., Messe, M. J., & Palermo, D. S. (1985). Grasping the meaning of metaphor: Story recall and comprehension. *Child Development, 56*, 1156–1166.

Waggoner, J. E., & Palermo, D. S. (1989). Betty is a bouncing bubble: Children's comprehension of emotion-descriptive metaphors. *Developmental Psychology, 25*, 152–163.

Wallach, M. A., & Wallach, L. (1983). *Psychology's sanction for selfishness.* San Francisco: Freeman.

Walsh, R. N. (1979). Meditation research: An introduction and review. *The Journal of Transpersonal Psychology, 11*, 161–174.

Walsh, R., & Vaughan, F. (Eds.). (1980). *Beyond ego: Transpersonal dimensions in psychology.* Los Angeles: J. P. Tarcher.

Watson, J. B. (1928). *The ways of behaviorism.* New York: Harper & Brothers.

Watson, L. (1979). *Lifetide: The biology of the unconscious.* New York: Bantam Books.

Watts, A. W. (1951). *The wisdom of insecurity.* New York: Vintage/Random House.

Watts, A. W. (1957). *The way of Zen.* New York: New American Library.

Watts, A. W. (1961). *Psychotherapy east and west.* New York: New American Library.

Watts, A. W. (1963). *The two hands of god: The myths of polarity.* New York: Collier Books.

Watts, A. W. (1966). *The book: On the taboo against knowing who you are.* New York: Collier Books.

Watzlawick, P. (1978). *The language of change: Elements of therapeutic communication.* New York: Basic Books.

Watzlawick, P., Beavin, J. H., & Jackson, D. D. (1967). *Pragmatics of human communication*. New York: Norton.

Weaver, W. (1948). Science and complexity. *American Scientist, 36,* 536–544.

Weber, R. (1986). *Dialogues with scientists and sages: The search for unity.* London: Routledge & Kegan Paul.

Weisz, J. R., Rothbaum, F. M., & Blackburn, T. C. (1984). Standing out and standing in: The psychology of control in America and Japan. *American Psychologist, 39,* 955–969.

Welwood, J. (Ed.). (1983). *Awakening the heart: East/west approaches to psychotherapy and the healing relationship.* Boulder, CO: Shambhala/New Science.

Weyl, H. (1980). *Symmetry.* Princeton: Princeton University Press.

Wharton, W. P. (1980). Higher-imagery words and the readability of college history texts. *Journal of Mental Imagery, 4*(2), 129–147.

Wheelwright, P. (1954). *The burning fountain: A study in the language of symbolism.* Bloomington, IN: Indiana University Press.

Wheelwright, P. (1962). *Metaphor and Reality.* Bloomington, IN: Indiana University Press.

Wheelwright, P. (1982). *The burning fountain* (rev. ed.). Gloucester, MA: Peter Smith.

Whitehead, A. N. (1925). *Science and the modern world.* New York: Mentor.

Whitehead, A. N. (1954). *Religion in the making.* Cleveland, OH: Meridian Books/World.

Whitehead, A. N. (1978). *Process and reality* (corrected ed.). (D. R. Griffin & D. W. Sherburne, Eds.). New York: Free Press.

Wiener, N. (1948). *Cybernetics, or control and communication in the animal and the machine.* New York: Wiley and the Technology Press.

Wiener, N. (1950). *The human use of human beings: Cybernetics and society.* Boston: Houghton Mifflin/Cambridge, MA: Riverside Press.

Wilber, K. (1977). *The spectrum of consciousness.* Wheaton, IL: Theosophical Publishing House.

Wilber, K. (1980a). *The atman project: A transpersonal view of human development.* Wheaton, IL: Theosophical Publishing House.

Wilber, K. (1980b). Development and transcendence. In G. Epstein (Ed.), *Studies in non-deterministic psychology* (pp. 254–275). New York: Human Sciences Press.

Wilber, K. (1981). *No boundary: Eastern and Western approaches to personal growth.* Boulder, CO: Shambhala.

Wilber, K. (Ed.). (1982). *The holographic paradigm and other paradoxes.* Boulder, CO: Shambhala.

Wilber, K. (1983). *Eye to eye: The quest for a new paradigm.* Garden City, NY: Anchor Press/Doubleday.

Wilber, K. (1984a). *A sociable god: Toward a new understanding of religion.* Boulder, CO: Shambhala/New Science.

Wilber, K. (Ed.). (1984b). *Quantum questions: Mystical writings of the world's great physicists.* Boulder, CO: Shambhala/New Science.

Wilson, E. O. (1978). *On human nature.* New York: Bantam Books.

Wilson, E. O. (1980). *Sociobiology: The abridged edition.* Cambridge: The Belknap Press of Harvard University Press.

Wineburg, S. S. (1987a). The self-fulfillment of the self-fulfilling prophecy/A critical appraisal. *Educational Researcher, 16*(9), 28–37.

Wineburg, S. S. (1987b). Does research count in the lives of behavioral scientists?/ A rejoinder. *Educational Researcher, 16*(9), 42–44.

Winnecott, D. W. (1971). *Playing and reality.* New York: Penguin.

Winner, E., Wapner, W., Cicone, M., & Gardner, H. (1979). Measures of metaphor. In E. Winner & H. Gardner (Eds.), *Fact, fiction, and fantasy in childhood, New directions for child development*, Number 6 (pp. 67–75). San Francisco: Jossey-Bass.

Winter, G. (1981). *Liberating creation.* New York: Crossroad.

Wolf, F. A. (1981). *Taking the quantum leap: The new physics for nonscientists.* San Francisco: Harper & Row.

Woolfolk, R. L., Sass, L. A., & Messer, S.B. (1988). Introduction to hermeneutics. In S. B. Messer, L. A. Sass, & R. L. Woolfolk (Eds.), *Hermeneutics and psychological theory* (pp. 2–26). New Brunswick, NJ: Rutgers University Press.

Wynne, L. C., McDaniel, S. H., & Weber, T. T. (1986). *Systems consultation: A new perspective for family therapy.* New York: Guilford Press.

Young-Eisendrath, P., & Hall, J. A. (Eds.). (1987). *The book of the self: Person, pretext, and process.* New York: New York University Press.

Yuille, J. C., & Catchpole, M. J. (1977). The role of imagery in models of cognition. *Journal of Mental Imagery, 1*(1), 171–180.

Zaidel, E. (1983). A response to Gazzaniga: Language in the right hemisphere, convergent perspectives. *American Psychologist, 38*, 542–546.

Zajonc, R. B. (1980). Feeling and thinking: Preferences need no inferences. *American Psychologist, 35*, 151–175.

Zajonc, R. B. (1984). On the primacy of affect. *American Psychologist, 39,* 117–123.

Zukav, G. (1979). *The dancing wu li masters: An overview of the new physics.* New York: Bantam Books.

Zurcher, L. A., Jr. (1977). *The mutable self.* Beverly Hills, CA: Sage.